CIVIL VENGEANCE

CIVIL VENGEANCE

LITERATURE, CULTURE, AND EARLY MODERN REVENGE

EMILY L. KING

CORNELL UNIVERSITY PRESS
Ithaca and London

First published 2019 by Cornell University Press

Library of Congress Cataloging-in-Publication Data

Names: King, Emily L., 1982–author.
Title: Civil vengeance : literature, culture, and early modern revenge / Emily L. King.
Description: Ithaca : Cornell University Press, 2019. | Includes bibliographical references and index.
Identifiers: LCCN 2019008043 (print) | LCCN 2019009150 (ebook) | ISBN 9781501739668 (pdf) | ISBN 9781501739675 (epub/mobi) | ISBN 9781501739651 | ISBN 9781501739651 (cloth)
Subjects: LCSH: English drama—Early modern and Elizabethan, 1500–1600—History and criticism. | English literature—Early modern, 1500–1700—History and criticism. | Revenge in literature. | Civil society in literature. | Revenge—Social aspects—England—History.
Classification: LCC PR658.R45 (ebook) | LCC PR658.R45 K56 2019 (print) | DDC 822/.309353—dc23
LC record available at https://lccn.loc.gov/2019008043

For my big love, Diego Alonso Millan Muñoz

If a Jew wrong a Christian, what is his humility? Revenge. If a Christian wrong a Jew, what should his sufferance be by Christian example? Why, revenge. The villainy you teach me I will execute, and it shall go hard but I will better the instruction.
   —Shakespeare, *Merchant of Venice*

The purpose of polite behavior is never virtuous. Deceit, surrender, and concealment: these are not virtues. The goal of the mannerly is comfort . . . If you make and keep my life horrible then, when I can tell the truth, it will be a horrible truth; it will not sound good or look good or, God willing, feel good for you either.
   —June Jordan, *Civil Wars*

CONTENTS

ACKNOWLEDGMENTS

For a book that insists on the correspondence between vengeance and civility, it is perhaps odd to take such delight in acknowledging the many whose intellects and beings have sustained me. But contradictions are, of course, the stuff of life. Glimmers of this book first emerged when I had the pleasure of working closely with Lee Edelman and Judith Haber at Tufts University. I thank them for their many lessons—several of which I have only learned belatedly yet appreciate all the more. Anyone familiar with their scholarship knows they are two astonishingly careful readers, and it's my hope that their collective influence remains visible on the following pages and all future ones. Kevin Dunn—a model of empathy and wit—improves everything around him, and I'm always delighted when our paths cross. I thank my peers at Tufts as well as Noah Barrientos, Chantal Hardy, Joseph Litvak, Wendy Medeiros, Douglas Riggs, Modhumita Roy, and Christina Sharpe.

The book evolved considerably during the two years I spent at Vanderbilt University as an Andrew W. Mellon Assistant Professor. I regard that period with great fondness and remain most appreciative to the English department faculty and staff for their intellectual support, opportunities for professional development, myriad kindnesses, and continued friendships. At Louisiana State University, I want to recognize the support and companionship of my colleagues, including Chris Barrett, Michael Bibler, Lauren Coats, Rebecca Crump, Bill Demastes, Philip Geheber, Angeletta Gourdine, Joseph Kronick, Isiah Lavender III, Elsie Michie, Rick Moreland, Laura Mullen, LeRoy Percy, Malcolm Richardson, Jean Rohloff, Irina Shport, Sue Weinstein, Jim Wilcox, Katie Will, Sunny Yang, and Michelle Zerba. Our administrative staff—Robin Collor, Nancy Fontenot, Valerie Hudson, Richard Landry, and Ashley Thibodeaux—assists with matters both catastrophic and ordinary. Finally, I wish to thank my ever-enlivening students, past and present; they, too, are a part of this project.

During the 2017–18 academic year, I was a Visiting Scholar at Brown University's Pembroke Center, and I thank Suzanne Stewart-Steinberg as well as

Leela Gandhi, Donna Goodnow, Bonnie Honig, and Drew Walker for making possible this splendid opportunity. Anjuli Gunaratne and Ron Wilson were (and remain) a most unexpected blessing from that year, and I am grateful for their friendship. Thanks to my proximity to Cambridge, I was able to participate in and present at the Shakespearean Seminar, led by the inimitable Bill Carroll and Coppélia Kahn, at Harvard University's Mahindra Humanities Center.

I have benefited enormously from the opportunity to share this work with audiences at meetings of the Shakespeare Association of America, the International Congress on Medieval Studies at Kalamazoo, the Renaissance Society of America, and the Modern Language Association. In particular, I give thanks for a community of scholars who have supported this project at various stages; they include Joseph Campana, Jay Clayton, Jennifer Clement, Barbara Correll, Elizabeth Covington, Katie Crawford, Holly Crocker, Lynn Enterline, Natalie Eschenbaum, Carla Freccero, Rick Hilles, Bradley Irish, Amanda Kellogg, Donika Kelly, Sarah Kersh, Marcela Kostihova, James Knapp, Nancy Reisman, Mark Schoenfield, Kathryn Schwarz, and Katie Will.

My research has been supported by the generosity of the Andrew W. Mellon Foundation as well as the Louisiana Board of Regents, which gave me an Award to Louisiana Artists & Scholars (ATLAS) grant. At Louisiana State University, the Office of Research and Economic Development has provided me with a Council on Research Fellowship, a Manship Summer Research Fellowship, a Regent Research award, and multiple travel grants—all of which contributed to the development of this book. I thank, too, the College of Humanities and Social Sciences and Dean Stacia Haynie for a fourth-year teaching release. Finally, I thank Assistant Dean Ann Whitmer for her expertise and unflappably good nature regarding all things related to funding.

An excerpt of the introduction was published in "Spirited Flesh: The Animation and Hybridization of Flesh in the Early Modern Imaginary," *Postmedieval: A Journal of Medieval Culture* 4, no. 4 (2013): 479–90. I thank Palgrave Macmillan for permission to include this work here. A portion of chapter 2 originally appeared in "Affect Contagion in John Donne's *Deaths Duell*," *Studies in English Literature 1500–1900* 56, no. 1 (2016): 111–30. I appreciate Rice University for its permission to include this work here.

I am profoundly grateful to my editor at Cornell University Press, Mahinder Kingra, for his original interest in the project and for the care with which he has shepherded the book through each stage of the publication process. My thanks to all the splendid members of my editorial and production team including Bethany Wasik, Susan Specter, Kate Gibson, David Prout, Martyn Beeny, and Carmen Torrado Gonzalez. Marcela Kostihova and the anonymous reader offered astute suggestions for revision, and their incisive feedback has improved the book all the more. Thank you.

In my personal life, which so often suffuses the professional realm, I remain inspired by and grateful for the enduring friendship of Kathryn Schwarz and Katie Crawford. I marvel at their exquisite kindness and intellectual generosity. Being in the presence of Katie Will is a privilege and a pleasure, and I am heartily glad for her excellent company on the bayou. Bill Demastes and Jean Rohloff are invaluable colleagues who have become family over the years—a simple yet extraordinary metamorphosis. As my faculty mentor, Bill helped me navigate the pre-tenure years with his seasoned guidance, characteristic levity, and abiding care. I thank Edward Dornblaser—literary saboteur, fellow correspondent, and kin who is kind—for so very much and indeed much more than I can put words to.

My partner in crime and for life, Diego Millan, is particularly eager to read what I have written about him (such are the residual pathologies of a middle child). Yet it remains a nearly impossible task to summarize how his presence nourishes this project and me. A trusted reader and confidante, he has been actively involved in this book since its inception, and his intelligence has improved every page. Thank you, D, for impressing upon me that the best revenge—civil or otherwise—is the embrace of a happy life, and thank you, dear one, for making that possible.

List of Abbreviations

EBBA   English Broadside Ballad Archive
OED   Oxford English Dictionary

Note on Citation

In citing early modern texts, I have preserved their original spellings but modernize typography in the following fashion. Consonantal *u* and *i* are revised to *v* and *j*; vocalic *v* is revised to *u*; long *s* is revised to *s*; *vv* is revised to *w*; *&* is altered to *and*; where a macron indicates the suspension of *m* or *n*, I supply the letter. Unless otherwise noted, all emphases appear in the originals.

CIVIL VENGEANCE

Introduction

Playing the Long Game

> Here we see force in its grossest and most summary form—the force that kills. How much more varied in its processes, how much more surprising in its effects is the other force, the force that does *not* kill, i.e., that does not kill just yet. It will surely kill, it will possibly kill, or perhaps it merely hangs, poised and ready, over the head of the creature it *can* kill, at any moment, which is to say at every moment. In whatever aspect, its effect is the same: it turns a man into a stone.
>
> —Simone Weil, from "The Illiad, or, The Poem of Force"

It is a familiar story. A melancholic prince haunts the halls of his Denmark castle only to chance upon his unguarded uncle and king. When the king departs precipitately from an evening performance, he confirms his nephew's worst suspicions. Confident that he now knows the identity of his father's murderer, the prince anticipates his duty of filial vengeance, and this convergence seems most opportune. Yet what inhibits him from taking action is the unwelcome realization that his murderous uncle is in prayer; if the prince were to strike now, he would permit his uncle to evade eternal—and deserved—punishment for his sins:

Now might I do it pat, now a is praying,
And now I'll do't,
   [*He draws his sword*]
        and so a goes to heaven,
And so am I revenged. That would be scanned.
A villain kills my father, and for that
I, his sole son, do this same villain send

To heaven.

O, this is hire and salary, not revenge!

$(3.3.73–79)^1$

As a quintessential early modern revenge play, *Hamlet* drives toward the self-destructive embrace of vengeance, even as it foregrounds its avenger's indecision. Yet embedded within Hamlet's oft-discussed hesitation, his preoccupation with appropriate timing, is a definition of revenge already in flux. As he shifts the verb tense from present conditional to present continuous in the first line and then to simple future in the second, he confuses each instance with the anaphoric insistence on "now" such that the repetitious present intrudes on possibility (that is, "might I do it") and certain future (that is, "I'll do't"). In this articulation of hesitation, the conditional present and the future collapse into the present moment, for the future—what could be and will be—is *now*.[2] What the passage's confused relationship to time reveals is a tension between two competing desires: a longing for the revenge act as a temporally bound event and the wish to keep that act in potentiality or even extend it indefinitely into the future. The final line makes explicit this distinction as it isolates lesser forms of vengeance—that is, the mercenary retribution of "hire and salary"—from the more desirable revenge that would propel Claudius into the unceasing torments of hell. Even the metrical irregularity of the penultimate line, compounded by the reference to "scanning," registers the error of killing his uncle in this moment.

Like Hamlet, the titular character of John Marston's *Antonio's Revenge* is also spurred to vengeance by his father's phantom. When Antonio initially restrains himself from slaughtering his father's murderer, Piero, he justifies his inaction by pointing to the pleasures of protracted retaliation: "I'll force him feed on life / Till he shall loathe it. This shall be the close / Of vengeance' strain" (3.1.140–42).[3] For Antonio, compulsory life transforms into a retributive substitute for death when he revises revenge as a punctual event and "strain[s]" its boundaries to include an indeterminate period of forced feeding. In generating a lively surplus that enlarges the scope of and sadistic possibilities for vengeance, he also disrupts the fundamental expectations for revenge. His desire

---

1. William Shakespeare, *Hamlet*, in *The Norton Shakespeare*, ed. Stephen Greenblatt et al. (New York: W. W. Norton, 1997), 1659–759. This is based on the Folio. Q2 (1604) substitutes "a" for "he" in the cited lines.

2. See also Carolyn Dinshaw's gorgeous reading of the temporality of "now" in *How Soon Is Now? Medieval Texts, Amateur Readers, and the Queerness of Time* (Durham, NC: Duke University Press, 2012), 1–4.

3. Subsequent references are to John Marston, *Antonio's Revenge: The Second Part of Antonio and Mellida*, ed. G. K. Hunter (London: Edward Arnold, 1966).

for prolonged retribution is realized more fully later in the play at the time of Piero's death. During the final scene, one of the avengers cries: "Sa, sa; no, let him die and die, and still be dying. [*They offer to run all at Piero, and on a sudden stop.*] And yet not die, till he hath died and died / Ten thousand deaths in agony of heart" (5.3.105–7). Thanks to the conflation of verb tenses as well as the start-and-stop movement of the avengers themselves, we glimpse the tension between their embrace of the punctual act (that is, the climactic execution of Piero) and the competing desire to extend the present moment—that delicious *now* of revenge—indefinitely.

Of course, the most effective moments of dramatic literature are achieved by the presence of competing and often contradictory aims. Yet these instances from *Hamlet* and *Antonio's Revenge* also make available a more capacious definition of retribution than is acknowledged by the critical discourse. For example, revenge has been traditionally understood as a discrete event, a finite episode that has a discernible beginning and end, yet the above examples herald the prospect of unending or infinitely repeatable acts of vengeance. When Antonio and Hamlet articulate their desire for interminable revenge, they simultaneously direct our attention to the inadequacy of episodic forms while enlarging retributive options. And even as they most certainly wish their targets dead, they also depend upon the promise of perverse liveliness, a guarantee of life after death through which they might execute the full scope of their vengeful ambitions. Antonio, for instance, instrumentalizes life as the weapon with which he will destroy Piero, while Hamlet depends on divine judgment and everlasting punishment. All of this complicates how we recognize retribution even in canonical revenge plays. Therefore, in presupposing specific parameters of revenge, filtered through the concept of time as I have shown here only in brief, we foreclose its potential for mutation, adaptation, and assimilation, which are present in traditional revenge literature and early modern culture more broadly. Mesmerized by the spectacular theatricality of onstage revenge acts, we fall inattentive to vengeance's uncanny permutations as well as the modes by which they slip into civil discourse and structure social interactions.

This book is founded on the premise that both the genre and the definition of vengeance are far from settled. To make this case, I not only excavate an archive of early modern revenge literature but also revisit familiar plays that have been historically categorized as revenge tragedy. Yet my primary objective is to effect a fundamental change in the discourse of retribution by attending to texts outside the traditional genre. When we examine alternatives—religious sermons, conduct books, and elegies—what might we learn about vengeance? How does the concept of revenge transform beyond the high-pressure cooker of the early modern stage? Although this study challenges the revenge tragedy genre, this is no wholesale revolt against it. Rather, when we return to canonical plays—those engaged here include the works of Kyd, Marston, Middleton, and Shakespeare—what might this revised revenge optic yield? Such are the questions that occupy the following chapters.

To identify the phenomena of recurring retaliations and vengeful orientations, I employ the phrase "civil vengeance" as a designation for revenge's integration into the social fabric, by which I mean government, law, and religion as well as noninstitutional discourse. Put simply, civil vengeance is retribution in the guise of civility. As such, it thrives within and is sanctioned by the realms of court and law—an idea running counter to, it seems, our usual expectations for revenge. Relentlessly social, civil vengeance structures interactions and cements connections between community members, but despite its systematic integration and normalization within the social body, civil vengeance is never politically neutral—even as or especially when it may give the appearance as such.[4] Indeed, the expectation that revenge deliver grotesque spectacle and fatality obscures, inadvertently or otherwise, the modes by which civil vengeance formulates, animates, and polices the social body—both its members and its outliers.

What we currently regard as the genre of early modern revenge tragedy is, in fact, a twentieth-century phenomenon, and I wish to trace its formation precisely because it shapes much of contemporary scholarship. A. H. Thorndike established the genre in 1902 and defined it as a subset of dramatic tragedy "whose leading motive is revenge and whose main action deals with the progress of this revenge, leading to the death of the murderers and often the death of the avenger himself."[5] Attending to the veritable explosion of such plays on the early modern stage between 1599 and 1604, Thorndike charts the evolution of revenge tragedy as it culminates in Shakespeare's *Hamlet*, the revenge play par excellence.[6] Fredson Thayer Bowers, who builds on

---

4. Étienne Balibar's discussion of embedded violence might be extended to the matter of vengeance. He writes: "There is also extreme violence in the indefinite repetition of certain forms of habitual domination that are, at the limit, invisible or unidentifiable as violence because they would appear to be part of the very foundations of society and culture," *Violence and Civility: On the Limits of Political Philosophy*, trans. G. M. Goshgarian (New York: Columbia University Press, 2015), 129–30.

5. A. H. Thorndike, "The Relations of *Hamlet* to the Contemporary Revenge Play," *PMLA* 17 (1902): 125–220, quote from 125.

6. For Thorndike, *Hamlet* was indebted to prior revenge tragedies but elevates itself in its efforts to successfully address the central themes with which the genre grapples, which include questions of "insanity, philosophical meditations, bewilderment under a burden of responsibility . . . and a passionate sense of fate" ("Contemporary Revenge Play," 218).

the foundation laid by Thorndike, embarks on the first book-length study of the genre, *Elizabethan Revenge Tragedy*.[7] Although Bowers relies heavily on Thorndike's definition of the genre, he offers further explanation as well as a labyrinthine system of categorization. He writes: "Revenge tragedy customarily (but by no means necessarily) portrays the ghosts of the murdered urging revenge, a hesitation on the part of the avenger, a delay in proceeding to his vengeance, and his feigned or actual madness."[8] Despite an exhaustive study that appears to account for the genre's many permutations, this parenthetical caveat insinuates the expansive nature of revenge tragedy, for even as one can identify traditional characteristics, the genre exceeds those markers.

The legacy of *Elizabethan Revenge Tragedy* extends to subsequent critical conversations when, for instance, scholars debate the ethics of vengeance. Thanks to Bowers's insistence that early modern English culture denounced private revenge on religious grounds,[9] successive studies embark from that premise.[10] For those investigating the relation among gender, agency, and retribution, they position their valuable insights as a corrective of Bowers's exclusive focus on male avengers.[11] Whether identifying the subversive elements inherent in the genre or cataloguing female avengers and their modi operandi, feminist scholars decenter the often unconscious but nevertheless pervasive

---

7. Providing a historical context for revenge, *Elizabethan Revenge Tragedy, 1587–1642* (Princeton, NJ: Princeton University Press, 1940), moves from discussions of the Anglo-Saxon *wergild* to early modern receptions of the stage-revenger. As Bowers assembles a catalogue of revenge plays, he details their literary influences, which range from Seneca to Machiavelli, subsets of the genre, and the general evolution of the dramatic form. The Elizabethan and Jacobean plays that fall under the scope of revenge tragedy include *The Spanish Tragedy*, *The Jew of Malta*, *Titus Andronicus*, *The Tragedy of Hoffman*, *The Revenger's Tragedy*, *The Maid's Tragedy*, and *The Atheist's Tragedy*.

8. Fredson Thayer Bowers, *Elizabethan Revenge Tragedy, 1587–1642*, 2nd ed. (Gloucester, MA: Peter Smith, 1959), 63–64.

9. For instance, Bowers writes: "There is no question that the Elizabethans firmly believed the law of God to forbid private vengeance" (ibid., 40).

10. Moral condemnations of vengeance abound in scholarship. See Charles A. Hallett and Elaine S. Hallett, *The Revenger's Madness: A Study of Revenge Tragedy Motifs* (Lincoln: University of Nebraska Press, 1981), 11; Harry Keyishian, *The Shapes of Revenge: Victimization, Vengeance, and Vindictiveness in Shakespeare* (Atlantic Highlands, NJ: Humanities Press International, 1995), 156; and Michael Neill, "English Revenge Tragedy," in *A Companion to Tragedy*, ed. Rebecca Bushnell (Malden, MA: Blackwell, 2005), 328–50, 345. By contrast, Catherine Belsey refuses the binary logic of prohibition, leading her to conclude that vengeance "deconstructs the antithesis which fixes the meanings of good and evil, right and wrong" (*The Subject of Tragedy* [London: Methuen, 1985], 115).

11. Examples of feminist scholarship that challenge phallocentric notions of honor and retribution and take seriously women's vengeance include Alison Findlay, *A Feminist Perspective on Renaissance Drama* (Oxford: Blackwell, 1999), 49–86, 51; Kirilka Stavreva, *Words Like Daggers: Violent Female Speech in Early Modern England* (Lincoln: University of Nebraska Press, 2015), 103–28; Allyna E. Ward, *Women and Tudor Tragedy: Feminizing Counsel and Representing Gender* (Teaneck, NJ: Fairleigh Dickinson University Press, 2013), 75–108; and Judith Weil, "Visible Hecubas," in *The Female Tragic Hero in English Renaissance Drama*, ed. Naomi Conn Liebler (London: Palgrave Macmillan, 2002), 51–69.

associations of masculinity with revenge in contemporary conversations.[12] Still others aim to situate the genre within particular aspects of early modern culture[13] or in relation to its Greek and Roman predecessors.[14] As a result, this varied scholarship provides valuable historical-cultural context for the genre and its evolution on the early modern stage.

Yet even these diverse approaches to revenge tragedy consolidate and reinforce specific characteristics; among the most notable are the genre's associations with grotesque spectacle and fatality. "When we think of the genre now," Tanya Pollard opines, "we think especially of blood, poison and melodrama, of crowd-pleasers teeming with corpses and dismembered body parts, steeped in occasionally raucous black humor."[15] On the avengers' "ethos of excess," Michael Neill prophecies that "it is the destiny of every revenge-hero to produce a holocaust—one in which the ends of justice are swamped in a savage mini-apocalypse of blood."[16] Likewise, Stevie Simkin cites violence that is "more explicit and extreme than the norm" as a primary attribute of the

---

12. "The very coupling of the concepts of *woman* and *revenge*," Marguerite A. Tassi explains, "activates . . . long-standing gender norms of feminine nurturance, domesticity, and subordination that form the basis of Western constructions of femininity" (*Women and Revenge in Shakespeare: Gender, Genre, and Ethics* [Selinsgrove, PA: Susquehanna University Press, 2012], 20).

13. On the connection between theology and revenge tragedy, see Michael Neill, *Issues of Death: Mortality and Identity in English Renaissance Tragedy* (Oxford: Oxford University Press, 1997), 46; and Thomas Rist, *Revenge Tragedy and the Drama of Commemoration in Reforming England* (Farnham, UK: Ashgate, 2008). Neill understands the genre's development as a consequence of the Protestant Reformation, while Rist insists that revenge tragedy harbors remnants of distinctly Catholic modes of memorialization. For a discussion of how the genre engages questions of monarchical authority, see Eileen Allman, *Jacobean Revenge Tragedy and the Politics of Virtue* (Newark: University of Delaware Press, 1999). Linda Woodbridge's comprehensive study examines the genre alongside campaigns for equity in economic, political, and social spheres (*English Revenge Drama: Money, Resistance, Equality* [Cambridge: Cambridge University Press, 2010]); Chris McMahon examines the centrality of the family unit in *Family and the State of Early Modern Revenge Drama* (London: Routledge, 2011); and Derek Dunne demonstrates the genre's relationship to early modern law in *Shakespeare, Revenge Tragedy, and Early Modern Law: Vindictive Justice* (London: Palgrave Macmillan, 2016). For an examination of legal injustice and grievance, see *Taking Exception to the Law: Materializing Injustice in Early Modern Literature*, ed. Donald Beecher, Travis DeCook, Andrew Wallace, and Grant Williams (Toronto: University of Toronto Press, 2015). Christopher Crosbie uncovers how the genre engages with and extends classical philosophies in *Revenge Tragedy and Classical Philosophy on the Early Modern Stage* (Edinburgh: Edinburgh University Press, 2018).

14. See Gordon Braden, *Renaissance Tragedy and the Senecan Tradition: Anger's Privilege* (New Haven, CT: Yale University Press, 1985); John Kerrigan, *Revenge Tragedy: Aeschylus to Armageddon* (Oxford: Clarendon Press, 1996); and Anne Burnett Pippin, *Revenge in Attic and Later Tragedy* (Berkeley: University of California Press, 1998). For a careful examination of the 1560s translation of Seneca's tragedies into English, see Jessica Winston, "Seneca and Early Elizabethan England," *Renaissance Quarterly* 59, no. 1 (2006): 29–59.

15. Tanya Pollard, "Tragedy and Revenge," in *Cambridge Companion to English Renaissance Tragedy*, ed. Emma Smith and Garrett A. Sullivan Jr. (Cambridge: Cambridge University Press, 2010), 58–72, quote from 58.

16. Neill, "English Revenge Tragedy," 342.

genre.[17] But the scholarly descriptions of revenge tragedy evolve into our definition of vengeance itself, a definition predicated on arresting spectacle and readily identifiable in traditional revenge plays. That is, the basis on which we organize the genre becomes conflated with how we understand revenge as a concept.

From the scholarship on retribution, antisociality appears as the second major characteristic of revenge tragedy and, by extension, of vengeance. Here, I refer not only to the avengers' proximity to or expulsion from the social body but also to the law that, in part, organizes that body. Identifying the liminality and consequent precariousness of the avenger, Katharine Eisaman Maus describes the figure as "simultaneously an avatar and enemy of the social order."[18] Even as theatrical avengers regularly insist on and enforce normative values, the specific modes by which they achieve their objectives upend the bedrock of social expectation as avengers flout religious proscriptions, legal mandates, and social expectations. For this reason, they are nearly always purged by the play's conclusion. A glib Vindice reminds his audience of this convention at the conclusion to *The Revenger's Tragedy*: "'Tis time to die, when we are ourselves our foes" (5.3.130). Insisting on antisociality as consonant with revenge, Neill puts the matter in stark terms: "The man with revenge in his heart, like Malvolio or Shylock, however cruelly wronged, must be expelled from the reordered community."[19] In his focus on matters of the "heart," Neill specifies an inward orientation toward vengefulness as itself deserving of expulsion from the social body; thus, misanthropic attitudes become sufficient grounds for exclusion and symbolic death. Such are the ways scholars crystallize the opposition between civility and vengeance.[20] But make no mistake: there are political consequences for clinging to this opposition. By promulgating the heroic mythos of a lone avenger, the social body—government, law, or custom—washes its hands of its covert associations with and deployment of vengeance, directing our attention to more obvious displays that are necessarily located *elsewhere*. Moreover, an insistence on the dichotomy between civility and vengeance enables the exportation of the social body's barbarism (i.e., surveillance, repression, torture, execution) to an outside group. As for strictly literary consequences, if we take these two qualities—spectacular fatality and antisociality—to be the requisite

---

17. Stevie Simkin, Introduction to *Revenge Tragedy: A New Casebook* (London: Palgrave Macmillan, 2001), 1–23, quotes from 9, 6.

18. Katharine Eisaman Maus, Introduction to *Four Revenge Tragedies: The Spanish Tragedy; The Revenger's Tragedy; The Revenge of Bussy d'Ambois; and The Atheist's Tragedy*, ed. Katharine Eisaman Maus (New York: Oxford University Press, 2008), ix–xxxi, quote from xiii.

19. Neill, "English Revenge Tragedy," 328.

20. On this note, Derek Dunne puts forth a contradictory argument. Stressing that "communal justice [is] at the heart of revenge tragedy," Dunne understands the genre to simultaneously engage with and revise early modern law (*Shakespeare, Revenge Tragedy, and Early Modern Law*, 47–49).

criteria for retribution, we cordon off revenge plays from a broader set of possibilities for vengeance already present in early modern culture.

When it comes to understanding more fully the mechanisms of and possibilities for vengeance, the reliance on revenge plays remains the major limiting factor, for at the foundation of these generative studies, one finds the very plays that Bowers identified in *Elizabethan Revenge Tragedy*, a study published in 1940.[21] In their selection of early modern plays, scholars confirm a predetermined definition of spectacular vengeance, which is envisioned to be at odds with the social body; as a result, the modes of revenge that inhere within civil society get overlooked entirely. Thus, *Civil Vengeance* both benefits from and productively shifts this robust body of scholarship through its examination of materials beyond the revenge tragedy canon. Even as my study must tacitly enforce its own boundaries—this is not an exhaustive catalogue of revenge in the period—it investigates the cultural work that revenge performs by incorporating an extensive array of artifacts and texts.

When I use the term "civil vengeance," I refer to retributive acts ensconced within extensive social networks that are not only comparatively mundane to examples of spectacular revenge but are also perceived and relayed as undeniably "good." A moment from George Puttenham's *The Arte of English Poesie* proves illustrative here. Advising the cautious deployment of revenge against equals rather than subordinates, he makes use of an anecdote from the coronation of Elizabeth I in which a knight who had offended her prior to her ascension to the throne sought pardon to avoid imprisonment. In Puttenham's account of the exchange, Elizabeth assured the knight "most mildly" that he need not fear further consequences for his past infraction: "Do you not know that we are descended of the Lion, whose nature is not to harme or pray upon the mouse, or any other such small vermin?"[22] Even as Puttenham makes use of this example as a disavowal of revenge, it persists as a rhetorical act of vengeance, one that skillfully emasculates the knight for his poor behavior within a public arena. Thanks to Elizabeth's sovereignty, her words accumulate a weight commensurate to her exceptional standing, and by posing the insult as a rhetorical question, she extracts a verbal assent from the knight, an assent that admits his inferiority before Her Majesty. Of course, there are clear distinctions to be made between the public shaming of a cutting remark and

21. Although a few scholars admit the limits of Bowers's classification, these admissions have not generated a reconsideration of the revenge tragedy genre itself. "Much is to be gained by transgressing such boundaries," Linda Woodbridge argues, even as her excellent study focuses exclusively on early modern drama and, in particular, the very plays featured in *Elizabethan Revenge Tragedy* (Woodbridge, *English Revenge Drama*, 5).

22. George Puttenham, *The Arte of English Poesie* (London: Richard Field, 1589), 249.

cutting off someone's head; there is no doubt that Elizabeth exercised clemency in this instance. But it is precisely the appearance of mercy valorized by Puttenham's account that I wish to pursue further. The social phenomenon that I call civil vengeance makes legible interactions of covert aggression and animosity, especially ones that substitute for death or, in this example, imprisonment. Something beyond clemency rears its head in the exchange, and the hostile surplus beckons us to expand the definition of revenge to include both the deliciously malicious and the tyrannically good that underpin otherwise civil interactions.

But how might we distinguish civil vengeance from mercy, especially given that the two often appear similar, as in the above example from Puttenham? Though we might differentiate the two on the basis of intention, it remains the case that neither subjects nor sovereigns fully apprehend their motives, much less those of others. Thus, it is for good reason that civil vengeance is confused with mercy—it may constitute mercy in some material sense, and those who employ civil vengeance may also cloak their acts in clemency or believe themselves to be merciful. An affective edge makes visible civil vengeance, however, as does a hierarchy that reaffirms the power structure and permits the extension of clemency in the first place. The *Oxford English Dictionary* emphasizes this power differential when it defines mercy as compassion extended to one who is in a powerless position or to one "with no right or claim to receive kindness."[23] Yet genuine mercy, should such a virtue exist in this fallen world, would not be a reiteration of the subject's abject status. By contrast, civil vengeance in its mercy-like incarnations retreats to and reaffirms the power differential such that the pardon functions to aggrandize the pardoner's superiority.

Like mercy, punishment is another term that seems related to vengeance, civil or otherwise. The *OED* defines punishment, a term that enters English in 1402, as an "infliction of a penalty or sanction in retribution for an offense or transgression" and is something inflicted "to ensure the application and enforcement of law."[24] Here, punishment exists as a legal transaction, a consequence specified under law for a prior offense. The transactional nature of punishment also presumes a commensurability between offense and consequence and, in this way, resembles traditional vengeance as an iteration of talionic law—a point tacitly registered by Tudor England in its interchangeable usage of the terms in government documents and decrees.[25] And, much

---

23. *OED*, s.v. "mercy, *n.*," def. 1a.

24. *OED*, s.v. "punishment, *n.*," def. 1.

25. For a broad history of *lex talionis*, see William Ian Miller, *Eye for an Eye* (Cambridge: Cambridge University Press, 2006). For a brief discussion of terms related to revenge and their circulation in Tudor England, see Woodbridge, *English Revenge Drama*, 20–21.

like mercy, punishment typically necessitates a hierarchical distinction between parties, as in the relationship between magistrates and criminal subjects, for instance. Even if the hierarchy is less formal—say, that of parents and children or instructors and their pupils—the structure is sufficiently secure and presumed self-evident such that the prerogatives of the punisher are unquestioned. Here, then, is where traditional revenge diverges from punishment insofar as individuals who would not be permitted to punish another then appropriate retribution. Consider Vindice's chaotic purge of the corrupt Duke and his disastrous family or Hieronimo's covert campaign against Lorenzo and Balthazar. In these literary examples of spectacular vengeance, the avengers squarely occupy the realm of the extralegal. Civil vengeance, by contrast, wraps itself in courtesy and flourishes under law. And though civil vengeance benefits from its association with punishment, precisely because the dynamic of penalty flattens otherwise complex narratives, it is imprecise to conflate the two.

Of course one might object to this study's expansion of vengeance on the basis that nearly any act of aggression might fall under its purview. That is, one might argue that the very broadness of civil vengeance overwhelms whatever use value it might hold for the genre of early modern revenge tragedy and, in particular, for the theorization of revenge. Indeed, it may be the fear of revenge's capaciousness that drives so many scholars to seek refuge in drama as a way to negotiate this unwieldiness. Even as vengeance and violence are close cousins insofar as one often seems to subsume the other, I distinguish the terms in a couple of ways. To begin, narrative converts violence into vengeance because it designates and makes legible positions of power (e.g., victim and perpetrator). Although this designation of roles may be disingenuous or even fundamentally false—a prospect I will consider more fully in my third chapter—narrative affords vengeance meaning from which otherwise "senseless" violence is barred. And although both vengeance and violence are directional—that is, whether I strike another without cause or pursue "justifiable" retribution, both acts move toward another—vengeance is indebted to causality. Presumed to be a temporal response to grievance, revenge emerges as a teleological outcome for an initial act of injustice. Thus, in subscribing to the logic of repayment, we position vengeance as an attempt at rectification or balance, even as such attempts generally spiral beyond the avenger's control—a phenomenon visible in traditional revenge plays with their cathartic baths of blood.

How, then, does the application of "civil" contribute to the book's elaboration of vengeance? The term enters English through Anglo-Norman law as the name for cases that were neither criminal nor canonical but rather those pertaining to the "relations between ordinary citizens."[26] In later centuries, "civil" names modes of belonging that include the "community, state, or body politic as a whole" as well as the relation between or designation of individuals who live together.[27] Yet when the *OED* glosses civil as a "condition of advanced social development such as is considered typical of an organized community of citizens," it tacitly links belonging to behavior such that one's proper conduct evolves into the guarantor of one's membership in a social group.[28] In the late sixteenth century and the seventeenth century, the definitional force of civil as behavioral intensifies to specify attributes that include "educated; cultured; cultivated; well-bred" as well as "courteous" or "obliging . . . behavior to others."[29] To conduct oneself with civility secures membership in a community as well as the legal privileges concomitant with that membership insofar as civil also defines one's "legal rights or status."[30] Thus, when I use civil as a modifier, I link issues of belonging—community and national identity, for example—with behavior.

As *Civil Vengeance* ventures beyond the revenge tragedy genre, it differs from previous studies in its attention to comparatively mundane instances of retribution, even though the cumulative effects of quotidian revenge may be more extensive, more permanent, and potentially more violent. Insofar as civil vengeance is legalized and legitimized by specific institutional frameworks—identifiable in, for example, royal proclamations and religious sermons—it is distinguished from spectacular or traditional revenge.[31] And it is the tidy integration of civil vengeance into the social fabric that masks its diffuse presence and effects. To expand the archive of revenge literature and to demonstrate the connection to civil institutions, I engage other cultural and literary artifacts that enable us to theorize vengeance and its guises in the early modern period. Spectacular episodes of revenge, then, might be more productively reframed as the cover story, so to speak, that obscures the modes by which ordinary vengeance structures the social body and interpersonal relationships therein. If, as my study proposes, vengeance and vengeful affects structure early modern sociality, they produce—and reward—particular orientations and

---

26. *OED*, s.v. "civil, *adj.*," def. 12b.

27. Ibid., def. 2.

28. Ibid., def. 5.

29. Ibid., def. 6a.

30. Ibid., def. 14a.

31. When I refer to institutions, I have in mind Sara Ahmed's definition as a "persistent structure or mechanism of social order governing the behavior of a set of individuals within a given community" (*Living a Feminist Life* [Durham, NC: Duke University Press, 2017], 152–53).

behaviors over time, and it is the exclusive focus on a specific event that hinders us from visualizing fully that phenomenon. No doubt, though, the temporal unwieldiness of civil vengeance poses methodological challenges and invites questions. In particular, how might we identify, analyze, and write about civil vengeance in early modern texts, especially given the fact that it is obscured and often disguised? Answering this question represents another stake of this study, and individual chapters will model various approaches.

Given my innovative selection of primary materials, more than a few words are necessary to address those decisions. As *Civil Vengeance* recovers a sixteenth- and seventeenth-century discourse on vengeance, sociality, and emotional management, it engages a diverse set of artifacts that include conduct manuals, scientific writing, elegiac poetry, religious sermons, imaginative letters, and parliamentary acts. With these texts, we may track how theorizations of vengeance shift when we adjust our optic as well as our objects of study. We may also visualize the permeation of and preoccupation with vengeance in early modern culture, and this assemblage makes clear that revenge was not relegated to the stage but rather was a phenomenon that was rhetorically employed, incentivized, and disguised, and that remains sufficiently complicated to merit further study. Even as my arguments rely on a wide and sometimes obscure archive, my engagement with major writers in the period—Margaret Cavendish, John Donne, Thomas Kyd, Thomas Nashe, and William Shakespeare—forms the book's backbone. And while *Civil Vengeance* incorporates traditional literature, that is, familiar revenge plays, it systematically decenters the exclusive focus on drama that has characterized the study of early modern vengeance.

Just as Hamlet and Antonio yearn to try the limits of traditional revenge—"I'll force him feed on life"—my pursuit of an eclectic archive of artifacts and literary strategies aims to enlarge our understanding of retribution. As such, this archive brings forward conceptualizations of vengeance that might otherwise be jettisoned from the established framework. In looking to examples that evade categorization, the individual chapters of *Civil Vengeance* investigate vindictive possibilities: anticipatory revenge that circumvents causality; diffuse vengeance that circulates through a social body; retributive fantasies that shore up national identity; and social mobility predicated on retaliation against oneself. Thus, *Civil Vengeance* foregrounds the peculiar and often contradictory modes of vengeance that have become embedded into the social sphere. As in the revenge archive this study assembles, the outlined characteristics of civil vengeance gesture toward revenge's capacious potential; indeed, this study does not shore up and consolidate generic borders but remains open to and invested in alternatives.

To establish how the period understood the physiological and emotional consequences of revenge, I read medical tracts that include Robert Burton's *The
Anatomy of Melancholy* and Thomas Wright's *The Passions of the Minde in Generall* in the following pages. Echoing my earlier readings of *Hamlet* and *Antonio's
Revenge*, this framework also expands the temporal possibilities for civil vengeance as a kind of revenge that persists beyond traditional episodic structures.
In fact, the early modern medical texts we will examine promise a retributive
strain that may be revived perpetually and even multiplied—a feature that affects subjects as well. Much like the fevered cry of the avengers who demand
the impossible in their call for Piero to "die and die, and still be dying," expansive acts of revenge require correspondingly enduring targets. The final pages
of this introduction, then, will return to *Antonio's Revenge* as a model for how
characters are specifically transformed to withstand the superlative demands
of civil vengeance. That is, how might this retributive phenomenon alter its
objects? And, more broadly, what is the relationship between civil vengeance
and subjectivity?

In a familiar passage from *The Anatomy of Melancholy*, Robert Burton discusses how vengeful emotions disrupt the body's delicate equilibrium, potentially conspiring to destroy the vulnerable subject altogether: "Ajax had no
other cause [than anger] of his madnesse; and *Charles the 6*, that Lunaticke
French King, fell into this misery, out of the extremity of his passion, and desire of revenge and malice, incensed against the Duke of Britaine, he could
neither eate, drinke, nor sleepe for some dayes together."[32] For Burton, an excess of anger predisposes individuals to vengeance and consequent insanity,
even as, in the case of Charles VI, insanity functions as simultaneously the origin and end point of vengeance. Likewise, Timothie Bright gives voice to a
perspective that places revenge and reason in opposition, writing in *A Treatise
of Melancholie* that "if choller have yeelded matter to this sharpe kind of melnn-
cholie, then rage, revenge, and furie, possesse both hart and head, and the
whole bodie is caried with that storme, contrarie to persuasion of reason."[33]
For Bright, the physiological origins of vengeance are located in a choleric excess that propels negative passions (i.e., "rage, revenge, and furie") to over-
take the major organs of the melancholic subject.

But not all presumed vengeance to spring forth from pathology or to cause
deleterious physiological effects. In *The Passions of the Minde in Generall*, the
English Jesuit Thomas Wright understands revenge as a corollary of the

---

32. Robert Burton, *The anatomy of melancholy* (London: John Lichfield and James Short, 1621),
142.

33. Timothie Bright, *A treatise of melancholie* (London: Thomas Vautrollier, 1586), 111–12.

humoral body and its particular constitutions: "Others are all fiery, and in a moment, at every trifle they are inflamed, and, till their heartes be consumed (almost) with choller, they never cease, except they be revenged. By this we may confirme that olde saying to be true . . . the manners of the soule followe the temperature of the body."[34] Yet unlike Burton, Wright does not linger on the ill effects of revenge as a means to dissuade but rather presumes vengeance to be a purgative for those plagued by an abundance of choler. In fact, as Wright identifies the adverse consequences of restraining oneself from retribution, his discourse veers into sympathy for the fractious and testy: "For as a River abounding with water, must make an inundation, and runne over the bankes; even so, when the heart is overflowen with affections, it must find some passage by the mouth, minde, or actions. And for this cause, I have divers time heard some persons very passionate affirme, that they thought their hearts would have broken if they had not vented them in some sort, either with spitefull words, or revenging deeds: and that they could do no otherwise than their Passions inforced them."[35] Given that early modern passions are anchored to a humoral body perpetually in flux, it seems fitting that "spitefull words" and "revenging deeds" are the result of "Passions inforced" in ire-filled subjects. By making his argument through the analogy of flooded rivers that overflow their banks, he naturalizes the emotional phenomenon such that subjects have no choice but to locate alternative spaces for their surplus affections. Moreover, in proposing that these ephemeral but nevertheless naturalized affections effect physiological harm by dint of their excess (i.e., "hearts would have broken"), Wright underscores the substance of passions and their material consequences within and beyond the subject's body. Though *The Passions of the Minde in Generall* does not endorse revenge per se, the logical extension of his claims—one must speak "spitefull words" or engage in "revenging deeds" or else one's heart will break—suggests how moderate indulgence in vengeance preserves the integrity of one's physical body and identity.

But even as Wright aims to contextualize revenge and move beyond simple prohibition, he also restricts greatly the agency of vengeful subjects through his subscription to humoral theory.[36] Specifying the causal relation between

---

34. Thomas Wright, *The passions of the minde in generall* (London: Valentine Simmes and Adam Islip, 1604), D3r–D3v.

35. Ibid., F8r.

36. For scholarship that decenters the humoral model to pursue "more active and willful experiences of emotion," see Richard Meek and Erin Sullivan, eds., Introduction to *The Renaissance of Emotion: Understanding Affect in Shakespeare and His Contemporaries* (Manchester, UK: Manchester University Press, 2015), 1–24, quote from 5.

anger, injury, and retribution, he explains: "Ire proceedeth from some injurie offered, and therefore hateth the inflictor, and by all meanes possible seeketh revenge."[37] While the first clause preserves the traditional causality between emotion and injury insofar as violation breeds anger, subsequent clauses obscure the active subject of the sentence. Grammatically speaking, "ire," not the injured party, emerges as that which "hateth the inflictor," even as this makes little logical sense. The effect of the inconsistency acts by imparting sovereignty to the emotions and by occluding the angry subject's active decisions and resultant behavior. As Wright clarifies his definition in later pages, he articulates latent aspects of revenge: "Ire includeth in it a certaine hatred of enmitie, and thereunto super-addeth a desier of revenge: the first part hath the same motives as hatred: and the desier of revenge may be revived, quickned and increased by the exaggeration of the injury receyved."[38] Because anger necessarily includes a hatred of one's enemy, this affective component augments ("super-addeth") one's desire for revenge. And if vengeful desire cannot be extinguished unless it is enacted, as Wright has established elsewhere in his text, there are no emergency brakes—only accelerators—in this vehicle.

Wright paves the way for an entombed form of revenge that remains a perpetual, though sleeping, threat. Thanks to his usage of "may be," retribution is held in the thrall of the future conditional in which vengeful reanimation, resurrection, and multiplication all remain possible. That these potentialities hinge on the "exaggeration" of an injury suggests the crucial role of imagination in fanning the embers of the revenge-wish. Finally, as Wright theorizes revenge, he moves beyond the temporal restriction of an episode or discrete event and into a kind of unfolding situation. Distinguishing the situation from the Deleuzian "becoming" and from Alain Badiou's event, Lauren Berlant defines it as "a state of things in which something that will perhaps matter is unfolding amidst the usual activity of life."[39] For Berlant, a situation arises in "the ongoing present out of which are refracted near pasts and near futures."[40] How might the situation instantiated by civil vengeance—that is, persistent, ongoing revenge—shape early modern subjects? More precisely, if a desire for revenge may be indefinitely revived and increased, how might this affect the targets of avengers?

To engage these questions, let us return to *Antonio's Revenge* and examine the scene in which Antonio, after delaying his murder of Piero, turns his wild

---

37. Wright, *The passions of the minde*, S4r.
38. Here, "enmitie" is a corruption of "enemy." Ibid., T3v.
39. Lauren Berlant, "Thinking about Feeling Historical," *Emotion, Space and Society* 1 (2008): 4–9, quote from 5.
40. Ibid., 5n9.

eye to Piero's young son, Julio. To torture Piero and yet prolong his life, Antonio butchers Julio in a church and sprinkles his innocent blood upon the altar, crying: "Lo, thus I heave my blood-dyed hands to heaven, / Even like insatiate hell, still crying; 'More! / My heart hath thirsting dropsies after gore'" (3.2.211–13). Given that Antonio has just murdered a child, one who considered him a "dear friend," his revenge lust is difficult to fathom and even harder to swallow. That this grotesquerie fails to quell his retributive fury is presumably due to the fact that Julio is not the primary but the ancillary target, and insofar as the revenge plot is unfolding and extensive, one particular moment could not—and indeed does not—satisfy Antonio. In light of this peculiar rapaciousness, one more question springs to mind: What kind of subject is demanded by unpunctual, indefatigable vengeance?

The infinite vengeance that Antonio and other avengers pursue—think only, for instance, of the ominous lines issued by Revenge at the conclusion to *The Spanish Tragedy*—necessitates the production of a subject who can be punished unceasingly.[41] It is not that certain subjects are more enduring or that they are able to withstand greater amounts of violence, but that civil vengeance produces the very subjects it needs. Repurposing Antonio's frantic exclamation, we might say that the targets of civil vengeance are themselves compelled to endure "More!" We catch a glimpse of the process in which ordinary subjects metamorphose into hyperanimate ones who can be punished unceasingly when we return to the grisly scene of Julio's death. Before Antonio slaughters Piero's son, he attempts to mitigate his actions with the assurance that "it is not thee I hate, not thee I kill. / Thy father's blood that flows within thy veins / Is it I loathe, is that revenge must suck" (3.2.177–79). In spite of his dizzying cognitive dissonance, the operating logic demands that Julio, the subject who is to be killed in service of a tangled revenge plot, transforms into his "father's blood." Of course, Antonio's fantasy makes good sense within the play's diegesis: his genuine affection for Julio compels him to pretend that his actions are different from what they are in order to accomplish the awful deed. Once he has executed the child, Antonio refers affectionately to his lingering spirit as the "sprite of Julio" while regarding the mutilated corpse in his hands as "all Piero, father, all; this blood, / This breast, this heart, Piero all, / Whom thus I mangle" (3.2.200–202). To some extent, it fails to matter whether this is Antonio's fantasy or his deft rhetorical maneuvering precisely because either option turns the mutilated trunk of Julio into "Piero all," for this transformed Piero is the labile subject of vengeance. And the very idea that Antonio could partition and preserve Julio from his paternal components depends on a be-

---

41. Revenge proclaims: "I'll there begin their endless tragedy" (4.5.48).

lief in an enduring liveliness. As Antonio insists that the child's essence continues its existence in another sphere (despite all evidence to the contrary), he conversely obliges Piero to persist, which is indicated through the present tense of "mangle."[42] That is, Piero remains necessarily alive, even as the receptacle of his blood (i.e., Julio) most certainly is not. Such is the way Antonio enforces perpetual liveliness in the midst of these charnel house moments.[43]

If the metamorphosis of the retributive object seems too extraordinary, consider the shift expected of the targeted corpse. Here, revenge animates the deceased target even—or especially—to withstand the inexhaustible affective surplus; that is, the treatment of the corpse realizes most fully the modes by which civil vengeance instantiates its necessarily radical subject. To the shroud of his entombed nemesis and father of Antonio, Andrugio, Piero apostrophizes:

> Rot there, thou cerecloth that enfolds the flesh
> Of my loath'd foe; molder to crumbling dust . . .
> Let naught of him, but what was vicious, live.
> Though thou art dead, think not my hate is dead;
> I have but newly twone my arm in the curl'd locks
> Of snaky vengeance. Pale beetle-brow'd hate
> But newly bustles up.
>
> *(2.1.1–9)*

Piero commences his peculiar apostrophe with an imperative to the shroud itself, exhorting it along the natural process of decay. In issuing directives for decomposition as if he exerts control over biological inevitability, his words function to appropriate power that he manifestly does not possess and to incorporate the seemingly punctual vengeance (i.e., murder of his enemy) into the ongoing process of putrefaction. Like Antonio, Piero aims to selectively kill parts of his target and extend the liveliness of others. In this case, he attempts to prolong his opponent's former "vicious[ness]" such that it becomes Andrugio's only legacy, thereby carrying forward the past into an indefinite future. By the third sentence, Piero addresses the corpse directly to assure him

---

42. For their part, the stage directions that immediately follow puncture this convenient narrative, as they direct Antonio to sprinkle "Julio's blood" on the altar. However, these directions are absent in John Marston, *Antonio's Revenge*, in *Tragedies and comedies collected into one volume* (London: A. M[atthewes], 1633), E7r–I7v, H1r–H1v.

43. Admittedly, Antonio's cognitive dissonance does not persist for long, given what he crows to his spectral father in the following scene: "O, my soul's enthron'd / In the triumphant chariot of revenge. / Methinks I am all air and feel no weight / Of human dirt clog. This is Julio's blood; / Rich music, father! This is Julio's blood" (3.2.80–84).

that his hate remains as robust as ever. This affective surplus serves to prop up and otherwise animate the obviously inanimate—after all, the act is premised upon the notion that the lively corpse is present and could register the perverse address. Thanks to the hyperbolic threat that concludes his speech—"hate but newly bustles up"—Piero suggests that he is merely in the initial stages of his revenge project. Yet his prior actions—the surreptitious poisoning of Andrugio in order to marry his widow—would seem to contradict that claim. What would otherwise constitute conclusive action—that is, the successful elimination of one's rival and conquest of his "goods"—is merely the opening salvo of his far-reaching vengeance.

Given that *Antonio's Revenge* fits neatly within the revenge tragedy genre, it offers no shortage of spectacular fatal episodes of vengeance. But insofar as both Piero and Antonio insist on modes of retribution that persist beyond their perceived expiration dates, they move toward civil vengeance—that is, unpunctual, ongoing revenge. Or, to put it in slightly different terms, they demand a kind of vengeance that might supply ample, even unlimited venting, and as such, they stand in as voices of civil vengeance. As a consequence, then, infinitely enduring targets are needed, even if what is demanded of those targets would, as in the example of Piero's apostrophe to Andrugio's corpse, contradict reality within the play itself. Avengers require targets sufficiently labile to withstand their interminable revenge, yet because such endurance is not innate, the avengers' fantasies refashion their targets into superhuman vessels capaciously matched to their affective surplus. At the heart of this fantasy is the seduction that one could experience again and again the strange pleasures of unceasing retribution. Civil vengeance—the partygoer who arrives unfashionably late and insists on staying long after the hosts have gone to bed—revises the very subjectivity of its targets. With its cries for "more" and its insistence on "yet again," civil vengeance remains distinct from traditional revenge, which demands a tidy economical exchange, the proverbial eye for an eye as talionic law demands. What, then, is to distinguish early modern subjects who are constructed to withstand unceasing punishment from modern subjects whose worth might best be measured via their capacity to withstand the ever-increasing expectations of our contemporary world?

The first half of this book identifies revenge discourse in medical texts, religious sermons, and conduct manuals to define more precisely the phenomenon of civil vengeance in relation to the early modern subject. While those chapters engage briefly with institutional legacies (e.g., the Church of England), their focus remains on subjects themselves, literary and historical. What is the effect of civil vengeance on subjectivity? How are individuals made literate in this new style of revenge? "Teaching Revenge," the first chapter, explores the triangulated relationship among education, civil vengeance, and social mobility through an examination of early modern conduct literature. The opening portion connects the veritable explosion of conduct manuals to the Tudor dynasty's consolidation of power through its prohibition of private vengeance. These texts, I propose, perform valuable cultural work for the Crown as they dissuade their young readers from exacting personal revenge and instead initiate them into the subtleties of civil vengeance. The remainder of the chapter investigates the effect of conduct formation on identity. Insofar as behavioral training instantiates a requisite split within the subject—there is a distinction between that which one is and that which one ought to be (or wishes to be)—I read the self-estrangement demanded by conduct formation as civil vengeance. Much like Lacanian psychoanalysis, the legacy of conduct manuals is a subject constituted through lack. Because conduct literature relies on and employs the aversive specter of vulgar laboring classes, it trains aspirational individuals to demonstrate their civility by repudiating incivilities as well as those who have historically displayed them, even if that includes aspirational subjects themselves. Thomas Kyd's *The Spanish Tragedy* visualizes the violence of this psychic split in the vengeful collisions between middling sorts and their social superiors.

If aspirational subjects are trained in but also punished by civil vengeance, my second chapter, "Feeling Revenge," complicates further the relationship between the aggressor and the injured party in the traditional revenge schema. What happens if revenge is not—or cannot be—directed or controlled? What if it is diffused through a social collective? For these questions, I turn to a selection of religious materials that includes the writings of Thomas Beard, William Perkins, and John Donne. Commencing with a corrective regarding early modern religious prohibitions of revenge, the chapter demonstrates that vengeance was not antithetical to early modern Protestant Christianity. Rather, it honed vengeful impulses and redirected them through displays of orthodox behavior. With this premise established, I examine Donne's final sermon, *Deaths Duell*, wherein he devotes much space to aversive meditations on decomposition as an extension of God's punishment for humanity's original sin. Present too in this strange text is an underlying frustration with God for this grotesque inevitability. Making use of the concept of affect contagion, I hypothesize that the sermon's delivery introduced and circulated negative emotion in the Whitehall congregation through its reliance on content (i.e., rhetoric of the sermon itself) and atmosphere (i.e., the unperceived smells or signals of emotional distress). To visualize this possibility, the chapter combines contemporary studies on the circulation of emotion with an analysis of early modern medicine. While Donne may not be able to retaliate against God for the undeserved punishment of decomposition, conceiving of civil vengeance as affect contagion enables us to understand the phenomenon as a disease that might be contracted by and disseminated through the social body rather than directed along an intended trajectory.

In the introduction and the first two chapters, the book privileges the individual subject in relation to civil vengeance—specifically, how the excesses of protracted revenge necessitate radically enduring targets, how subjects are trained in the principles of civil vengeance as well as the consequences of conduct formation, and how enraged subjects might transmit their negative emotions through a social body without specific intention or even direction. *Civil Vengeance* then pivots from the individual to the social in the final two chapters to identify how revenge's peculiar sociability shapes community and national identities. Serving as a transitional figure for the book as a whole, the early modern vagrant is one constituted by movement and promiscuous contact with community members in, for instance, the act of begging or migration for seasonal agricultural work.

My penultimate chapter, "Fantasizing about Revenge," takes up the significance of fantasy in relation to vengeance by focusing on the vagrant, an outlier aligned with biological disease and social death in the early modern imaginary, who foments social cohesion and even the project of nation-building. As English civil society organizes itself against these so-called parasites, it also keeps them in close proximity as effective scapegoats. And insofar as vagrants are presumed responsible for major social issues—scarcity, crime, and terrorism—civil society justifies its poor treatment as retribution. Reading Jack Cade's rebellion in Shakespeare's *2 Henry VI*, the chapter proposes that normative society's fantasy of its own victimhood produces vagrant bodies that are constructed to withstand extreme forms of labor and punishment, and the resulting bodies then sustain an expanding nation-state. Thomas Nashe's *The Unfortunate Traveller, or The Life of Jack Wilton* reveals the dynamic at work on the international stage in its attempts to define early modern Englishness against not only the Continent but also cosmopolitanism, which the novel classifies as a form of vagrancy. While the impoverished vagrant offers social cohesion to normative subjects within the domestic project of nationalism, the affluent cosmopolitan vagrant and his eventual recoil from other cultures offer the fiction of a secure English identity.

The final chapter, "Commemorating Revenge," examines the relationship between civil vengeance and national memory during the English Interregnum, which begins with the 1649 execution of Charles I and concludes with the return of his son and heir to London in 1660. As government authorities aim to establish and inculcate a new national memory, I connect their attempts—discernible in Parliament's declarations of fasting and thanksgiving, for instance—to the phenomenon of civil vengeance. But such indoctrination was not without considerable resistance, as royalists focused their challenges to the new government, I argue, through their insistence on remembering differently and circulating countermemories in ballads, drama, and elegiac verse. Often these texts demonstrate familiarity with the popular revenge tragedies of past decades, espousing an affinity for spectacular and divine vengeance, as they craft a more suitably royalist history and articulate their hopes for the future. Although the cultivation of countermemory might constitute resistance—and thereby offer an antidote to civil vengeance—it substitutes terms without revising the structural system. To pursue an escape from the ideological intractability between parliamentarians and royalists, I read Margaret Cavendish's *Sociable Letters*, a collection of epistles to an imaginary interlocutor that foregrounds other possibilities for memory, history, and community. While the latter half of my book considers how civil vengeance energizes the formation of the nation-state in terms of social bonds, identity, and memory, the concluding section of the fourth chapter marks a significant departure from what precedes it by investigating possibilities for a sustainable method of circumventing the saturated network of civil vengeance.

Thanks to its communal nature, civil vengeance is never in service simply to the individual but also to the social body. And insofar as the phenomenon permeates institutional relationships as well as those between subjects, it moves in both hierarchical and lateral directions. Finally, because civil vengeance remains available to individuals, it grants them some measure of agency while incentivizing their participation: if acts of civil vengeance are also on behalf of the greater good, the subjects who undertake them may bolster their worth before the social body. What early modern literary and cultural artifacts demonstrate is that civil vengeance is neither an interruption of nor a departure from civility but rather that which actively constitutes it. Indeed, because this study strips away civility's polish by revealing the restrictions that lie beneath, its intervention holds steady in our contemporary moment. Given the term's recent apotheosis—namely, its use as a political weapon to distract from substantive issues, to restrict dissension, to enshrine hate-based ideologies and their venomous adherents, and to enforce a toleration of the unconscionable— calls for greater civility might be better met with incredulity, if not outright contempt.

CHAPTER 1

Teaching Revenge

Social Aspirations and the Fragmented Subject of Early Modern Conduct Books

How were early modern subjects trained in civil vengeance, and what were the consequences of that training? These are the central questions that organize my first chapter. To propose an answer, I read popular conduct manuals, which include the works of Desiderius Erasmus, Baldassare Castiglione, and Roger Ascham, to chart how they refashioned their readers' retributive impulses. Situating the genre of conduct literature within the context of another major cultural movement—the Tudor ban on private vengeance—I argue that these manuals provided valuable service in the cultural shift from private vengeance to the punishments meted out by the Crown. The second half of the chapter examines the process of conduct formation alongside the period's entrenched class divisions and expanded opportunities for social mobility. As I theorize the relation between social grooming and civil vengeance, I demonstrate how conduct literature mobilizes disgust to elicit shame and direct its readers' behaviors. Disgust fractures individual subjects and estranges them from their laboring-class origins; such consequences I read as examples of civil vengeance against aspirational sorts. Thus, this first chapter offers both a historical account of the turn to civil vengeance and an examination of its class-based permutations.

Thomas Kyd's *The Spanish Tragedy*, a play that inaugurates the genre of early modern revenge tragedy and whose central conflicts are distinctly class-based, emerges as the ideal text through which to frame this chapter's concerns.

There, romantic trysts temporarily bridge the chasm between the nobility and the middle class yet culminate predictably in disaster; spoiled brats compete against the lower classes and resort to deception to secure victory; and dutiful civil servants learn only too late how little their loyalty is regarded, retaliating in spectacular fashion against their social superiors. Indeed, what presents in *The Spanish Tragedy* is an implicit relationship between vengeance and social status, and scholarship bears out the play's preoccupation with social division. James Siemon identifies Kyd's tragedy as a "fantasy of a middling social stratum [that] meets an impasse inherent in its position,"[1] while C. L. Barber insists that Hieronimo's liminal status marks him as the character with whom early modern London middle classes identify.[2] In the play, Brian Sheerin recognizes an analogue to and warning about the Elizabethan court's precarious system of patronage and gift bestowal, which exacerbates existing class tensions.[3] Extending the class analysis to Kyd himself, a few scholars have even identified him as a political radical who intimates his political leanings in *The Spanish Tragedy* and makes explicit those views in, for instance, his translation of Torquato Tasso's *Il Padre de Famiglia*.[4]

With this critical history in mind, I proceed to two moments from the play to tease out the matter of early modern class tensions as they relate to vengeance, social mobility, and performance—issues that will concern the remainder of the chapter. Let us first begin with Hieronimo in his capacity as Knight Marshal and as he meets with the aggrieved subjects of Spain—all in the wake of his beloved son's murder. Of Hieronimo's unimpeachable reputation, First Citizen insists, "There's not any advocate in Spain / That can prevail, or will take half the pain, / That he will in pursuit of equity" (3.13.52–54).[5] But

---

1. James Siemon, "Sporting Kyd," *English Literary Renaissance* 24, no. 3 (1994): 553–82, quote from 556.

2. As C. L. Barber famously observed, "Hieronimo had a very clearly defined social position that makes him an appropriate figure for a middle-class London audience to identify with. He is not a member of the high nobility but a high civil servant, a former advocate who has the confidence and affection of the king in performing the office of knight marshal." *Creating Elizabethan Tragedy: The Theater of Marlowe and Kyd* (Chicago: University of Chicago Press, 1988), 135. See also Kevin Dunn, "'Action, Passion, Motion': The Gestural Politics of Counsel in *The Spanish Tragedy*," *Renaissance Drama* 31 (2002): 27–60. In a later article, Christopher Crosbie clarifies that the play's class conflict is less between aristocratic and laboring classes and rather "between the aristocracy and a middling household." "*Oeconomia* and the Vegetative Soul: Rethinking Revenge in *The Spanish Tragedy*," *English Literary Renaissance* 38, no. 1 (2008): 3–33, quote from 5.

3. Brian Sheerin, "Patronage and Perverse Bestowal in *The Spanish Tragedy* and *Antonio's Revenge*," *English Literary Renaissance* 41, no. 2 (2011): 247–79, quote from 264.

4. See Crosbie, "*Oeconomia* and the Vegetative Soul," 6; Arthur Freeman, *Thomas Kyd: Facts and Problems* (Oxford: Clarendon Press, 1967), 39; and Katharine Eisaman Maus, *Inwardness and Theater in the English Renaissance* (Chicago: University of Chicago Press, 1995), 58.

5. Unless otherwise noted, all quotations from *The Spanish Tragedy* are based on the 1592 Q1 edition and from *English Renaissance Drama*, ed. David Bevington et al. (New York: W. W. Norton, 2002), 8–73.

neither characters nor audience members are obliged to rely on secondhand assessment, for they soon witness how Hieronimo's commitment to equity directs his professional dealings. When Don Bazulto, a fellow father of a murdered son, approaches the Knight Marshal with his supplication for justice, Hieronimo's grief overwhelms him, and he conflates Bazulto's loss with his own. This conflation is staged expressly through an exchange of belongings in which Hieronimo impulsively offers his possessions to Bazulto: "But here, take this, and this—what, my purse?— / Ay, this and that, and all of them are thine, / For all as one are our extremities" (3.13.90–92).[6] Because "extremities" catalyze a remarkable democratization, metamorphosing "all" into "one," Hieronimo also imagines his position as structurally interchangeable with the very subjects he serves, and we can chart this through his transfer of property. For instance, his use of singular demonstrative pronouns strips him of prior ownership, and his solitary reference to a personal possession is complicated by the fact that it prompts confusion (i.e., "what, my purse?"). That is, Hieronimo's use of the interrogative puts into question the very subject of ownership and its attendant privileges, and this challenge to the logic of property remains a central conundrum of the play: property, propriety, and *what is proper*.

Interpreting Hieronimo's behavior as an affecting display of empathy rather than disconcerting mania, Second Citizen concludes, "This gentleness shows him a gentleman" (3.13.94). Insofar as he acts in his assigned capacity as Knight Marshal, he cannot be mistaken for nobility, of course; therefore, the compliment divorces aristocratic behavior or "gentleness" from social status, subscribing to broader definitions of nobility. Even still, the passage's meaning hinges on and is complicated by the multivalence of "show." Because the term refers to proof, Hieronimo's kindness functions as the guarantor of his aristocratic status. But "show" also gestures toward the realm of spectacle or playacting, and *The Spanish Tragedy* in particular leans heavily on this second definition.[7] Thus, the overlapping definitions of "show" tap into the triangulation of nobility, proof, and performance only to raise additional questions: Who may claim nobility? How does nobility appear? And might the ephemeral performance itself count as material proof?

Whereas the first example from *The Spanish Tragedy* suggests how the text expands definitions of nobility and gentility, the second example that I will ex-

---

6. Although the stage directions inform readers that Hieronimo "draws out more objects" from his purse, these objects remain unnamed. But because he refers specifically to his purse, one might reasonably assume that he offers Bazulto various possessions and money.

7. Consider, for instance, when Hieronimo reveals the hidden corpse of his beloved son Horatio. To a stunned court, he proclaims: "See here my show! Look on this spectacle" (4.4.89). As he deploys stage language to describe a "real" event in the diegesis of the play, he effects a dizzying conflation of reality and theatricality.

amine gestures toward the consequences reserved for those who would over-step their stations. For this, let us turn to the scene of Horatio's death. Following the demise of his beloved friend Don Andrea at the outset of the play, Hora-tio finds himself wooed by Bel-imperia and an unwitting participant in her project of revenge. When the two meet in Hieronimo's garden one evening, they exchange tokens of love and playful words of war. Yet Lorenzo's machi-nations soon disrupt their consummation, while Bel-imperia is "rescued" from the disastrous consequences of a dalliance with a social inferior. Lorenzo's pri-mary objective here is the disposal of Horatio, who is both hanged and stabbed to death in his father's arbor. The gratuitous hanging creates a per-verse spectacle, and Lorenzo offers a vicious eulogy for his victim: "Although his life were still ambitious proud, / Yet is he at the highest now he is dead" (2.4.60–61). His contemptuous words, in conjunction with the humiliation of the hanging, function as an ironized punishment for the threat Horatio posed to Lorenzo, to his kin, and to his kind. Although the origins of Lorenzo's ag-gression are not especially transparent in the play—much like Iago's, his is a motiveless malignity—his words intimate that part of his animus derives from class-based competition. "Once Horatio begins to seem a rival to people like Lorenzo and Balthazar," as Katharine Eisaman Maus observes, "his very excellences make him vulnerable."[8] Because Horatio is left hanging in his father's arbor, his lynching also functions as an episode of terrorism intended for other "middling sorts" who might overstep their positions as well as for their too-proud parents. In fact, Hieronimo signals his receipt of the message when he laments his lack of recourse and naturalizes this class-based oppres-sion: "Nor aught avails it me to menace them, / Who, as a wintry storm upon a plain, / Will bear me down with their nobility" (3.13.36–38).[9] Despite the fact that both the play and its historical period rely on an expanded definition of gentility, Horatio's death highlights how middling sorts remain vulnerable to the retribution of their social superiors for their perceived encroachment on the privileges reserved for higher classes. With the issues raised by *The Span-ish Tragedy* in mind, issues that will be developed further in our examination of conduct literature, we now contextualize a privilege long reserved for the aristocracy: the execution of private vengeance.

The cultural transition away from private vengeance was a shift centuries in the making. Because one's honor was bound up in the ability to avenge wrongs,

---

8. Maus, *Inwardness*, 59.

9. In the lines that follow, it is here that Hieronimo realizes that dissembling obsequiousness ("Thy cap to courtesy, and thy knee to bow") will serve him in his revenge project.

the tradition of private vengeance proved especially difficult to criminalize. Anglo-Saxon freemen viewed their right to feud (*faehthe*) in order to resolve conflict and pursue justice as "inalienable," and the privilege distinguished them from lower classes.[10] Rulers who remained vulnerable in their need for loyalty and support did not challenge the right to engage in private warfare, but enterprising ones—recognizing the siren call of opportunity—could exploit private vengeance to consolidate their power and augment their coffers. By making public an otherwise private concern, sovereigns could demand a share of the *wergild*, or payment reserved for the injured family.[11] Further, when they were paid in criminal cases, the transaction established that offenses were never just between subjects but also against the sovereign and state.[12]

Such mercenary impulses, rather than a genuine investment in justice, impelled Tudor rulers to pursue a program of state justice in England. Ronald Broude explains that by expanding the felony category (i.e., offenses against the king) to include traditionally lesser offenses (i.e., "torts"), the Crown received fees for cases tried in its courts and also seized the possessions of convicted felons.[13] Though legal reform held great financial appeal for Tudor rulers, other motives prompted the shift as well. With the memory of the Wars of the Roses too close for comfort, Henry VII consolidated his power against forces that could challenge his rule or even hurl it into the path of destruction.[14] Specifically, he remained wary of the vengeful feuds between aristocratic families and their enduring effect on sovereigns and their kingdoms. To criminalize the tenacious tradition, the Tudor government promulgated a vision of revenge "as an antisocial act, a threat to which society as a whole responds through the appropriate agents."[15] Writing decades later, Francis Bacon gave voice to private vengeance's threat to the social fabric: "Noe man can foresee the danders [dangers] and inconveniences that may arise and multiply thereupon. It may cause soddaine stormes in Court, to the disturbance of his Majestie, and unsaftie of his person. It may grow from quarrells, to banding, and from banding to trooping, and so to tumulte and commotion, from perticuler persons to dissention of families and aliances, yea to nationall quarrells . . . so that the State by this meanes shal be like to a distempered, and unperfect body,

10. Bowers, *Elizabethan Revenge Tragedy*, 2nd ed., 5.

11. For an exhaustive study of personal injury tariffs throughout western Europe, see Lisi Oliver, *The Body Legal in Barbarian Law* (Toronto: University of Toronto Press, 2011).

12. Bowers, *Elizabethan Revenge Tragedy*, 2nd ed., 5.

13. Ronald Broude, "Revenge and Revenge Tragedy in Renaissance England," *Renaissance Quarterly* 28, no. 1 (1975): 38–58, quote from 46.

14. Ibid., 7–8.

15. Ibid., 43.

continually subject to inflamations and convulsions."[16] When Elizabeth I ascended the throne in 1558, she maintained that vengeance was a crime against God and sovereign, and insofar as her courts were sufficient to the task of prosecuting murderers, avengers were punished as severely as the original murderers.[17] For instance, she exercised her sovereign prerogative to curb the pernicious habit of dueling among her courtiers, the means by which aristocratic men could handle matters of honor (i.e., offenses that went unpunished by civil authorities) or in cases of bodily injury for which justice might not be obtained.[18] Elizabeth negotiated civil resolutions between opposing parties or, in the event that they disobeyed her commands, enforced legal consequences that included imprisonment.[19] Because revenge "puts the law out of office," as Bacon memorably remarked, her prohibition consolidated and displayed her power over so-called private matters of honor and offense.[20] And given Elizabeth's extraordinary vulnerability prior to and throughout her rule, the ban on private vengeance became all the more necessary to exert control over conflicts that could disrupt it or even signal the impotence of her laws.

James I lacked Elizabeth's inimitable control, and a sudden and significant increase in dueling followed his ascension.[21] Witnessing the distressing trend, he wrote: "The slaughters which We find to have bene strangely multiplied and increased in these later times, by the boldnesse which many of Our subjects take, to challenge any man into the field, towards, whom they cary either grudge or malice in their minds, under the pretext of satisfaction to pretended wrongs, without imploring aide either of the Lawes, or Civil Magistrates: have mooved Us."[22] In an attempt to stem the tide, James plied his subjects with myriad edicts and tracts against private vengeance. Even for those who would merely report on real-life duels but nevertheless glamorize them before a curious public, James assured those writers that they would be "punished at the discretion and censure of that Court for their high contempt against Us; to be hereafter banished . . . for the space of seven yeeres."[23] But his threats did little

---

16. Francis Bacon, *The charge of Sir Francis Bacon* (London: George Eld, 1614), B1r.

17. Bowers, *Elizabethan Revenge Tragedy*, 2nd ed., 11.

18. Broude, "Revenge and Revenge Tragedy," 44.

19. Bowers, *Elizabethan Revenge Tragedy*, 2nd ed., 31 and n103.

20. Francis Bacon, "Of Revenge," in *Essays*, ed. John Pitcher (London: Penguin, 1986), 72–73, quote from 72.

21. Bowers, *Elizabethan Revenge Tragedy*, 31–32.

22. James I, "A Proclamation against private Challenges and Combats: With Articles annexed for the better directions to be used therein, and for the more judiciall proceeding against Offenders," in *Stuart Royal Proclamations*, vol. 1, *Royal Proclamations of King James I, 1603–1625*, ed. James F. Larkin and Paul L. Hughes (Oxford: Oxford University Press, 1973), 302–8.

23. James I, "A Proclamation prohibiting the publishing of any reports or writings of Duels," in *Stuart Royal Proclamations*, 295–97, quote from 297.

to quell the cultural investment in private vengeance, an investment that was, according to Bacon, who served as both attorney general and Lord Chancellor under the king, "grounded upon a false conceipt of honour."[24] Though James's failure in this regard could be read as symptomatic of greater political weakness, subsequent leaders—among them Cromwell and Charles II—would also face the intractable problem of revenge; like James I, they too would be compelled to threaten harsher penalties in the face of an obdurate populace.

Yet the period's popular literary and cultural texts indicate a more complex relationship to vengeance within the early modern world, raising skepticism regarding the claim that vengeance threatened sovereignty. In the highly influential *The Book of the Courtier*, Baldassare Castiglione deters his aristocratic readers from skirmishes with a measured reminder that "quarelles and controversies . . . may happen," instead admonishing them to exhibit "alwaies in everye pointe bothe courage and wisedome," for, in the matter of dueling, one ought to maintain a cautious balance between impulsiveness and "prudent" daring.[25] "Beside the greate daunger that is in the doubtfull lotte," he opines, "hee that goeth headlonge to these thynges and without urgent cause, deserveth verye great blame, although his chaunce bee good."[26] But Castiglione reserves his greatest disdain for the litigious and those preoccupied with personal safety. One must "not as some dooe, passe the matter in arguing and pointes, and having the choise of weapon, take suche as have neyther poynte nor edge. And arme themselves as thoughe they shoulde goe against the shotte of a Cannon. And weening it sufficyt not to be vanquished, stande alwaies at their defence and geve grounde, in so muche that they declare an extreme faint hert, and are a mocking stocke to the verye chyldren."[27] In their too scrupulous care of self, duelers reveal their rightful place as objects of scorn in Castiglione's universe, and the inclusion of this lampoon functions to dissuade others who might be motivated by the sensational appeal of duels rather than by a genuine commitment to the defense of one's honor. However, no mention is made of dueling's corrosive effect on sovereign power. As *The Book of the Courtier* negotiates the judicious defense of one's honor, vengeance remains a private matter with little or no observable effect on the workings of a nation.

In *The Civil Conversation*, Stefano Guazzo elaborates on the restraint valued by Castiglione and ties it to the qualities of an ideal ruler: "A prince must not

---

24. Bacon, *The charge of Sir Francis Bacon*, C1r.
25. Baldassare Castiglione, *The Courtier*, trans. Thomas Hoby (London: Wyllyam Seres, 1561), D3r.
26. Ibid.
27. Ibid., D3r–D3v.

only shew himself curteous, affable, and gratious, in conversing with his subjects, but besides, must use his autority modestly, especially in offenses comit-
ted against himselfe: wherin it ought to suffice him that he might have taken
vengeance: and to imitate those mighty and strong beasts, which never turne
againe against little curres which run barking after them."[28] For Guazzo, it is
the counterfactual that ought to satisfy, the vengeance that one "might have
taken" as would-be avengers revel in their superior power. In urging his readers to reduce their opponents to nothing more than tedious "curres," Guazzo
permits a mode of revenge held in the thrall of the potential yet never put
into action. This, taken with the initial counterfactual, speaks to the pleasures
reserved for the vengeance-not-taken yet always to remain in reserve. Thus,
in *The Civil Conversation*, we may observe a shift from retribution as action to
revenge as fantasy, which gives the appearance of mercy but preserves none
of its inward feeling—in this way, we are inching closer toward the phenomenon of civil vengeance.

George Puttenham's *The Arte of English Poesie* takes up the issue of revenge
for a distinctly English audience. Like Castiglione and Guazzo, Puttenham advocates restraint but also admits the necessity of vengeance in particular
cases: "And in a noble Prince nothing is more decent and welbesseming his
greatnesse, than to spare foule speeches, for that breedes hatred . . . Also not
to be passionate for small detriments or offences, nor to be a revenger of them,
but in cases of great injurie, and specially of dishonors: and therein to be very
sterne and vindicative, for that savours of Princely magnanimitie: nor to seeke
revenge upon base and obscure persons, over whom the conquest is not glorious, nor the victorie honourable."[29] Although Puttenham's focus remains on
delineating princely behaviors, his prescriptions extend implicitly to readers
as well. And because he signals his familiarity with the cultural legacy that contributes to private vengeance, he is better able to redirect his readers' behavior; for instance, to dissuade them from pursuing revenge in certain cases (e.g.,
taking revenge against inferior persons), he appeals to their honor—the same
honor that would spur them toward revenge in the first place. Broadly speaking, these literary examples balance a cultural investment in revenge with civil
safeguards and exemplify an early modern world in transition. But given that
these precautions do not entertain the effect of vengeance on sovereignty and
governance, these advisory texts go only so far in propelling the cultural shift

---

28. Stefano Guazzo, *The civile conversation*, trans. George Pettie (London: Richard Watkins, 1581),
N4v.

29. Puttenham, *The arte of English poesie*, Kk3r.

away from private retribution. To visualize this shift more fully, then, we now turn our attention to texts designed for other audiences.

Concurrent with the Tudor campaign against and suppression of private vengeance is the sixteenth-century explosion of conduct manuals that reflected a cultural fixation on civility. According to Anna Bryson, what instigated this development was "a preoccupation with the full-scale dramatization of social identity—a systematic attempt to relate rules of behavior to questions of individual personality, and a stress on what may be termed self-preservation or 'self-fashioning.'"[30] Insofar as conduct literature is predicated on the belief that "men and women can be *produced*,"[31] it seeks to "transform, subjugate, and produce the body it inscribes with the signs of civility."[32] To accomplish this objective, Norbert Elias explains, such texts cultivate shame as well as a heightened sensitivity to bodies and their impact on the social sphere.[33] Consequently, conduct formation emerges as less of a progressive narrative—that is, a general shaking off of barbarous infelicities to embrace gentility—and more "the product and precipitate of harsh, aversive conditioning in which male subjects cultivate anxieties about the very bodies they inhabit."[34] Even as I will argue that conduct literature participates in the cultural shift from private vengeance to the Tudors' centralized control of retribution, these texts are not necessarily uniform in their approaches to revenge. Yet in spite of their differences, they provide a collective sense of how young subjects were trained in civil vengeance. How, then, did these texts dissuade the Crown's most malleable subjects from retributive actions or words? What was the process by which vengeful tendencies were stamped out in young readers, especially given

---

30. Anna Bryson, *From Courtesy to Civility: Changing Codes of Conduct in Early Modern England* (Oxford: Oxford University Press, 1998), 108–9.

31. Ann Rosalind Jones, "Nets and Bridles: Early Modern Conduct Books and Sixteenth-Century Women's Lyrics," in *The Ideology of Conduct: Essays on Literature and the History of Sexuality*, ed. Nancy Armstrong and Leonard Tennenhouse (New York: Methuen, 1987), 39–72, quote from 41.

32. Barbara Correll, *The End of Conduct: "Grobianus" and the Renaissance Text of the Subject* (Ithaca, NY: Cornell University Press, 1996), 14. See also Gail Kern Paster, *The Body Embarrassed: Drama and the Disciplines of Shame in Early Modern England* (Ithaca, NY: Cornell University Press, 1993), 1–22. Humility, though it makes a less frequent appearance in scholarly discussions of conduct literature, is another consequence of the civilizing process. Yet early modern humility ought to be distinguished from the term's contemporary associations with self-effacement. As Jennifer Clement concludes in her nuanced study, early modern humility "can encompass both abject submission to God and qualified assertions of self-respect and agency" (*Reading Humility in Early Modern England* [Burlington, VT: Ashgate, 2015], 132).

33. Norbert Elias, *The Civilizing Process: Sociogenetic and Psychogenetic Investigations* (London: Blackwell, 2000).

34. Correll, *The End of Conduct*, 7.

the fact that childhood was and remains punctuated by episodes of sanctioned violence?

What prompts Roger Ascham to pen his manual for pedagogues, *The Scholemaster*, is an alarming trend at Eton wherein a number of young scholars were running away to avoid the frequent beatings enacted by their instructors. Ascham connects the physical abuse not to failed attempts at discipline per se but rather to the caprices of individual instructors. He writes: "For whan the scholemaster is angrie with some other matter, then will he sonest faul to beate his scholer: and though he him selfe should be punished for his folie, yet must he beate some scholer for his pleasure: though there be no cause for him to do so, nor yet fault in the scholer to deserve so."[35] When Ascham identifies the instructor's anger "with some other matter" as the source of the abuse, he connects a culturally acceptable practice of discipline to a misdirected mode of vengeance and, critically, also identifies the instructor's "pleasure" in venting his aggression on an undeserving subordinate.[36] By contrast, he advocates a "gentler" pedagogical approach, one in which young subjects are educated patiently and indoctrinated properly rather than driven from learning for fear of abuse. Addressing his fellow instructors, he outlines how they ought to handle their pupils' mistakes: "Chide not hastelie: for that shall, both dull his witte, and discorage his diligence: but [ad]monish him gentelie: which shall make him, both willing to amende, and glad to go forward in love and hope of learning."[37] His adjectival use of "gentelie"—only letters removed from "gentilitie"—reinforces the cultural connection between nobility and mild behavior, which is typified by an absence of vengeance.[38]

An emphasis on love, forgiveness, and nonaggression defines civility in much of the early modern conduct literature intended for children. In Thomas Paynell's translation of *De Civilitate Morum Puerilium*, Desiderius Erasmus proclaims: "The greatest parte of civilitie is (so thou faile not therein) easily to pardone other mens faultes: nor thou must love thy frend nevertheles, although he have certain rude manners and evil favored condicions: for ther are yet in

35. Roger Ascham, *The Scholemaster or Plaine and Perfite Way of Teachyng Children* (London: John Daye, 1570), C4r–C4v.

36. Chapter 2 will explore misdirected vengeance at greater length.

37. Ascham, *The Scholemaster*, C4r.

38. Gentleness and gentility were not the only values lauded by Renaissance instruction books; decorousness and eloquence were also valorized. And although early modern pedagogy formulated universal rules for decorous behavior and speech, as Julian Lamb argues, it struggled with an inability to define their precise contours or execution in specific contexts. See *Rules of Use: Language and Instruction in Early Modern England* (London: Bloomsbury, 2014).

other perfeccions dooe recompence the rudenes of their maners."[39] Given that a primary aim of conduct formation is the cultivation of neighborly love and, by extension, unflappable forbearance, it would seem that vengeance has no place in the process; instead, gentle tolerance and ready forgiveness appear as the apex of civility, a point that Erasmus stresses through his parenthetical note to the reader. And in contrast to the advice offered by Castiglione and Puttenham, he refuses to entertain an occasion that would merit retribution. Erasmus continues: "If thy frend do fail thorow ignorance in any thyng that semeth to bee of importaunce, it is civily done, swetelye and secretely to [ad]monish hym."[40] Here, he expands the requirements of civility to include the careful management of friends' behaviors, and because he understands ignorance, rather than malice, to be the origin of offense, infelicities are subsequently minimized. Taken in this light, how could another's failing move one to anger? It is instead an opportunity for reproof and instruction.

Of course rationalizations cannot always stave off angry responses. For such occasions, Francis Seager issues explicit warnings regarding fury and vengeance in *The Schoole of Vertue*:

> The hastie man wants never trouble
> His mad moody mynde his care doth double,
> And malyce thee move to revenge thy cause
> Dread ever god and daunger of the lawes,
> Do not revenge though in thy power it be
> Forgeve the offender being thine enemie.
> He is perfectly pacient we may repute plaine
> From wrath and furye himselfe can retrayne.[41]

To dissuade his young readers from retribution, Seager reminds them of the spiritual and material consequences and, much as Guazzo advised princes, urges children to restrain themselves from making use of their power to avenge themselves. But Seager's use of "retrayne" leads us to the heart of conduct formation: to "retrayne" oneself is a process that is importantly reflexive—the practice by which subjects not only learn new behaviors but also unlearn detrimental ones. Civility, characterized by a commitment to love, patience, and forgiveness, would seem thus far to offer no sanctuary to vengeful subjects. But even as conduct literature advises its readers against retribution and other

---

39. Desiderius Erasmus, *The Civilitie of Childehode*, trans. Thomas Paynell (London: John Tisdale, 1560), D2r.

40. Ibid., D2r–D2v.

41. Francis Seager, *The Schoole of Vertue* (London: Wyllyam Seres, 1557), C4v.

uncivil behaviors, I will argue that vengeful behaviors persist, and are not so much "retrayne[d]" but redirected along other paths. Although prohibitions against revenge aim to form a society with fewer acts of vengeance, what we will find is a society no less vengeful, particularly as it relates to the matter of social mobility.

Between the years of 1540 and 1640, English society underwent a "seismic upheaval of unprecedented magnitude," as Lawrence Stone observes, in which upward and downward social mobility occurred simultaneously.[42] "Those who lacked the title [of gentleman] were busy trying to acquire it," Ruth Kelso explains, and "those who had it were anxious to resist encroachment."[43] Although the fundamental class lines divided the aristocracy from everyone else, a division primarily established between those who engaged in manual labor and those who secured other modes of employment,[44] the distinction was muddled by the rapidity with which wealth, property, and land changed hands. For instance, rates of land sale and purchase reached their peak during the decade beginning in 1610—when rates were 250 percent higher than in the 1560s.[45] And between 1575 and 1625, more country-house building occurred than in any other fifty-year period; this constitutes, as Stone understands it, "significant proof of a 'rise of' the gentry."[46] Finally, we might also consider the increased numbers of peers (rising from 60 to 160), baronets and knights (from 500 to 1,400), and squires (from 800 to 3,000) during the period.[47] The upper classes trebled when the total population barely doubled,[48] and their numbers increased in part thanks to enterprising wholesale traders.[49] But the inclusion of inland and sea merchants was begrudging at best. "An exclusive sense of aristocratic identity," Frank Whigham writes, "was being stolen, or at least encroached upon, by a horde of young men not born to it."[50] As the ranks of the newly wealthy swelled, standards of living increased significantly

---

42. Lawrence Stone, "Social Mobility in England, 1500–1700," *Past and Present* 33 (1966): 16–55, quote from 16.

43. Ruth Kelso, "Sixteenth Century Definitions of the Gentleman in England," *Journal of English and Germanic Philology* 24, no. 3 (1925): 370–82, quote from 370.

44. Stone, "Social Mobility in England," 17.

45. Ibid., 33.

46. Ibid., 26.

47. Ibid., 24. See also Frank Whigham, *Ambition and Privilege: The Social Tropes of Elizabethan Courtesy Theory* (Berkeley: University of California Press, 1984), 9.

48. Whigham, *Ambition and Privilege*, 9.

49. Christopher Brooks, "Apprenticeship, Social Mobility and the Middling Sort, 1550–1800," in *The Middling Sort of People: Culture, Society, and Politics in England, 1550–1800*, ed. Jonathan Barry and Christopher Brooks (New York: St. Martin's Press, 1994), 52–79, quote from 60.

50. Whigham, *Ambition and Privilege*, 5.

and were due to higher agricultural prices, more commercial activity, and an increased demand for professional services supplied by greater numbers of educated men.[51] Conversely, the laboring classes increased in numbers as well, yet given the system of exploitation already set in place, their standards of living declined precipitously.

Despite the fundamental class distinctions between aristocrat and laborer, there can be no doubt that households existed between the two extremes. Yet the ones that fell between their polarized counterparts and were recognizable as such lacked a coherent class identity around which they might unite.[52] Even the very language used to describe middling status presaged discord. On the matter, Keith Wrightson observes: "Unlike the vocabulary of estates and degrees, which expressed distinctions within a unified social order, the language of 'sorts' was a terminology pregnant with actual or potential *conflict*. It aligned the learned against the simple, the richer against the poorer, the better against the meaner, vulgar, common, ruder or inferior sorts."[53] With the emergence of literate households who were neither laboring nor aristocratic, middling types were often eager to assert their civility in order to distance themselves from the "vulgar" masses below. Thus, conduct literature assuaged some of their anxiety by providing them with a veritable road map for their aspirational journeys.

As fluctuating social distinctions and redistributions of wealth contributed to social conflict, authors of early modern conduct literature navigated a precarious terrain as they addressed both middling and aristocratic audiences. While writers must necessarily admire the aristocracy's nobility—and they often signal this admiration by citing individual persons who inspire their works—they must also admit that nobility can be self-fashioned for their second group of addressees. It was a delicate balance to refrain both from offending the upper classes and marginalizing the middling audiences for whom these texts were produced. Indeed, the tacit questions—Who may have access to nobility? And on what grounds?—are answered in part by the prefatory materials of conduct literature. Or, at the very least, these introductions symptomatize a profound unease with an early modern England in flux. In his preface to *The Schoole of Good Manners*, William Fiston issues a dedication to

---

51. Stone, "Social Mobility in England," 26. For an examination of how models of sufficiency shift to accommodate more plentiful resources secured through, for example, colonial pursuits, see Hillary Eklund, *Literature and Moral Economy in the Early Modern Atlantic* (Burlington, VT: Ashgate, 2015).

52. Keith Wrightson, "'Sorts of People' in Tudor and Stuart England," in Barry and Brooks, *The Middling Sort of People*, 28–51, 44.

53. Ibid., 38.

the young Master Edward Harington with the following caveat: "Not as, though you needed any such instructions: for I am assured that you know and dayly practice, mo[re] and better than here are prescribed. But for that I esteeme you alreadie a patterne of vertuous good manners in the view of many others. I have thought good, to make you a patrone of this little schole, wher the rude and ignorant may (if they will) lerne some forme of fashions, by reading and practicing that here is proposed."[54] As Fiston engages in the *humilitas topos*, he takes convention one step further by elevating his young exemplar not only to a model for lower classes but also as their "patrone." And by emphasizing that the "rude and ignorant" must remedy their limitations, he shifts the responsibility for class organization from the mysterious workings of divine will (or the caprices of fortune) to issues of personal agency and ambition. If one endeavors to work hard, as the familiar lesson goes, one will encounter greater success. Yet from the vantage of laboring classes and middling sorts, this is, at best, an invitation to a proximate relationship to nobility, one in which they will learn "some forme of fashions," an approximation that leaves them still unschooled in those niceties that young Harington, the "patrone of this little schole," practices daily.

In *De Civilitate Morum Puerilium*—the most influential, widely translated, published, and imitated conduct book—Erasmus's relation to the concept of nobility, to the emergent democratization of the term, and to aristocrats themselves appears still more complicated.[55] The longevity of its success was in part due to its incorporation in sixteenth-century schools, prompting Franz Bierlaire to call it "the most esteemed school manual."[56] Like Fiston, Erasmus dedicates his work to a young nobleman whom he tutored: "So nowe I applye

---

54. William Fiston, *The Schoole of Good Manners* (London: J. Danter, 1595), A4r–A4v.

55. According to Anna Bryson, *De Civilitate* was the "most influential book on good manners" of the sixteenth century (*From Courtesy to Civility*, 29). Within a single year, it generated twelve editions and was translated into major vernacular languages (Franz Bierlaire, "Erasmus in School: The *De Civilitate Morum Puerilium*," in *Essays on the Works of Erasmus*, ed. Richard DeMolen [New Haven, CT: Yale University Press, 1978], 239–51, quote from 243). Its publication success spawned a number of imitative texts that include Richard West's *The Book of Demeanor*, Thomas Paynell's *The Civility of Childehoode*, William Fiston's *The Schoole of Good Manners*, Francis Hawkins's *Youths Behavior*, and Francis Seager's *The Schoole of Vertue* (Bryson, *From Courtesy to Civility*, 30–31). Although *De Civilitate* is considered one of his lesser works, Erasmus himself attests to the singular importance of his project in a letter to Budé: "For whoever may seek to render service only and not attract attention, the brilliancy of the material is less important than its utility. I will not reject any work . . . if I determine that it is useful in bringing about progress in studies. I do not write for Persius nor Laelius, I write for children and for the unlettered [pueris et crassulis scribuntur]" (Bierlaire, "Erasmus in School," 239).

56. According to school statutes in England, reading *De Civilitate* was expressly required in, for instance, Bury Saint Edmunds (1550), Winchester (between 1561 and 1569), and Bangor (1569), though its use was not limited to these particular cities or regions. See Bierlaire, "Erasmus in School," 242.

my selfe to thy childhode, and shall teache the maners of chyldren: Nat bycause thou nedest these prescriptes and rules, brought up at the begynnynge of an enfant amonge courtyers, after that obtaynyng so notable a mayster to fasshyon youthe rude and ignorante . . . but for that ende that all chyldren shall more couragyously lerne this thynges, because it is dedycate to the childe of great possessyon and of singular hope."[57] Although Erasmus trades in the usual conventions of modesty—conferring on his young addressee the duty of "fasshyon[ing] youthe rude and ignorante"—his prefatory address does not exonerate aristocratic readers. In the sentence's second clause, he insists, for example, that "all children" are in need of conduct training.

Yet subsequent passages do not resolve the dilemma posed by writing for two distinct audiences, and two contradictory claims arise: (1) that all children are in need of education, and (2) that common children in particular require this education. "It is semely and fytynge," Erasmus opines in a later portion of the preface, "that a man be well fasshyoned in soule, in body, in gesture, and in apparel: and in especyall it besemeth chyldren all maner of temper-aunce, and in especyall in this behalf noble mennes sonnes."[58] His frank in-structions for aristocratic youth suggest that they are beyond neither censure nor surveillance. In particular, I wish to focus on the parallel structure created by the twice-repeated "in especyall" and the two competing readings that struc-ture produces. In the first possibility, "in especyall" places the two categories (i.e., all children and noblemen's sons) in an equivalent position regarding ex-pectations for appropriate behavior. The other interpretation, however, posi-tions the second "in especyall" as a modification of the first group (i.e., all children) such that noble young men are expected to exhibit such courtesies above or beyond that of their middling counterparts. I belabor these details because the sentence symptomatizes the fundamental tension between inclu-sivity and particularity as these terms relate to expanding definitions of nobil-ity. Erasmus remains consistent in his inconsistency, for, as *De Civilitate*'s preface continues, he makes competing appeals to both aspiring and high-born youths while, perhaps more significantly, espousing a radical commitment to the democratization of nobility. He writes: "All are to be taken for noble, which exercyse their mynde in the lyberall science. Lette other men paynte in their shyldes Lyons, Egles, Bulles, and Leopardes: yet they have more of verye nobylyte."[59] By targeting the literal paint with which aristocrats distinguish themselves, he presents a tacit condemnation of the superficial trappings of

---

57. Desiderius Erasmus, *De Civilitate Morum Puerilium*, trans. Robert Whytyngton (London, 1532), A1v–A2r.

58. Ibid., A2v.

59. Ibid., A2v–A3r.

self-congratulatory nobility. As an alternative, then, he introduces the term "verye nobylyte" such that this true nobility is loosened from its aristocratic origins through an embrace of liberal science and elevated.

Though Erasmus invites his readers to take up the mantle of "verye nobylyte," the civilizing process he outlines is exhaustively comprehensive—no bodily occurrence is too private or too ludicrous to fall outside scrutiny. Addressing the courtesy issues posed by indigestion and flatulence, for instance, he acknowledges those who "teacheth that a chylde shal kepe in his nether wynde, his buttockes fast closed or clynged" but advocates instead for the discreet release of wind for health reasons.[60] "If thou may," he counsels, "go aparte do that a lone by thy selfe, if no[t] (after the olde proverbe) Let him close the fert under colour of a coughe."[61] The "extraordinary seriousness and the complete freedom with which questions are publicly discussed," Norbert Elias argues, "shows particularly clearly the shift of the frontier of embarrassment and its advance in a specific direction."[62] But these precepts do not normalize the bodily functions they govern; on the contrary, codification suggests how subjects are expected to internalize protocol such that they bear sole responsibility for not introducing embarrassment into the social sphere. As we will soon see, shame, disgust, and anxiety permeate the prescriptive discourse of conduct literature—and such uncomfortable feelings arise as the cost aspirational subjects must pay for their pursuit of "verye nobylyte."

At its ideal, civil formation is as exhaustive as it is self-sustaining, obliging its young adherents to be the strictest evaluators of their behavior. "A well-bred person," Erasmus urges, "should always avoid exposing without necessity the parts to which nature has attached modesty. If necessity compels this, it [undressing] should be done with decency and reserve, *even if no witness is present*. For angels are always present, and nothing is more welcome to them in a boy than modesty, the companion and guardian of decency."[63] Through the invocation of angels, he collapses whatever distinction may exist between the public and private domains, for all behavior occurs in a public one of sorts.[64]

---

60. Ibid., B1r.

61. Ibid., B1r–B1v.

62. Elias, *The Civilizing Process*, 111.

63. Quoted in ibid., 110. Emphasis mine.

64. Although the process of conduct formation necessarily demands a diminishing domain of privacy in favor of a public sphere, the notion of privacy in early modern culture was in flux. The prevailing critical assumption that the early modern world did not value privacy or could not access it may be traced back to Lena Cowen Orlin's *Private Matters and Public Culture in Post-Reformation England* (Ithaca, NY: Cornell University Press, 1994). David Cressy nuances this position by arguing that, while privacy did exist, the public and private domains remained "intermeshed" (*Birth, Marriage, and Death:*

But as he posits two contradictory claims in his hypothetical—"no witness is present" and "angels are always present"—he calls attention to the mechanisms of surveillance at the heart of conduct formation that enable the establishment of the perpetually public sphere: in the absence of visible witnesses, the civilizing process compels its subjects to manufacture them through imagination such that they export the duties of internal surveillance to another party. In so doing, conduct formation instantiates a fractured subjectivity—an acting subject paired with a fastidious judge.

Because the process of conduct formation necessitates one to remain perpetually under the rigors of self-evaluation, one does not even need an actual witness to register an inappropriate act. Perhaps it is for this reason that Francis Hawkins offers the following advice in *Youths Behaviour*: "When thou blowest thy nose, make not thy nose sound like a trumpet, and after, looke not within thine handkerchiefe."[65] In contrast to the matter of modesty in *De Civilitate*, the offense described in Hawkins's text is inappropriate not due to immorality but to its repugnance to others. He continues: "Take heed thou blow not thy nose as children doe, with their fingers, or their sleeves, but serve thy self of thy handkercher."[66] If we fail to register the irony of Hawkins's second sentence, it is because we have overlooked the designated audience of his publication: children. It is a strange moment, to be sure, when he admonishes his young readers to refrain from acting their ages, an aside that leads one to wonder whether Hawkins momentarily forgets his audience or if, in fact, the statement reveals the underlying logic of conduct formation: do not be yourself. To some extent, of course, that conclusion is of no great surprise; those who read conduct manuals aimed to transform themselves into someone better. But insofar as conduct formation is a mode of estrangement from oneself such that this other self may observe, evaluate, and modify behavior, it compels a psychic rupture in middling sorts.

Barbara Correll calls this estrangement "civil scopophilia," contending that "the subject of civility must both generate and incorporate the gaze of the other" to guarantee the success of civil formation.[67] In a similar vein, Lynn

---

Ritual, Religion, and the Life-Cycle in Tudor and Stuart England [Oxford: Oxford University Press, 1997], 476). More recently, Ronald Huebert challenges the critical consensus to argue that privacy was indeed valued by Shakespeare's contemporaries and that it was accessible for some (*Privacy in the Age of Shakespeare: Evolving Relationships in a Changing Environment* [Toronto: University of Toronto Press, 2016]).

65. Francis Hawkins, *Youths Behaviour, or Decency in conversation amongst men* (London: W. Wilson, 1646), 3.

66. Ibid.

67. Correll, *The End of Conduct*, 57.

Enterline refers to the phenomenon as "monitor monitorum."[68] For Enterline, a consequence of conduct formation is that "an intrapsychic scene is folded inward as a persistent interpsychic system" such that those who embody the split most fully are, ostensibly, the most civilized.[69] The private sphere dissipates to the extent that even the most solitary acts are always under scrutiny. Building on their incisive assessments, I wish to connect the individual effects of conduct formation to the broader social consequences of civil vengeance. Put simply, what is the relation between the civilizing process and civil vengeance? And how are the aspirational subjects who undergo this process subsequently shaping and shaped by civil society?

Lacan's "mirror stage" proposes one means by which we might both visualize the extended consequences of this interpsychic drama and return to the question of vengeance.[70] According to Lacan, this critical stage of human development occurs in infancy, yet its consequences extend into adulthood. When the infant is "unable as yet to walk, or even stand up, and held tightly as he is by some support, human or artificial, he nevertheless overcomes, in a flutter of jubilant activity, the obstructions of his support and, fixing his attitude in a slightly leaning-forward position, in order to hold it in his gaze, brings back an instantaneous aspect of the image."[71] The reflection that the infant apprehends in the mirror is his "Ideal-I," and the mirror constructs a solid, coherent subject that was, immediately prior, understood only as disconnected fragments. It is the mirror that grants the infant the semblance of coherence and mastery. Of greater significance, though, is that the feat is made possible by some kind of prop, and, as such, the achievement (i.e., standing) is wholly anticipatory. When the infant leans forward into the mirror, he leans forward into the future to generate an image of maturity he has yet to assume; Lacan describes it as "a drama whose internal thrust is precipitated from insufficiency to anticipation."[72] Though the moment is heralded with great "jubila[tion]" by the subject, it also "brings back" commensurate levels of anxiety. As an ongoing consequence of the developmental stage, the subject assumes "the armour of an alienating identity, which will mark with its rigid structure the

---

68. Lynn Enterline, *Shakespeare's Schoolroom: Rhetoric, Discipline, Emotion* (Philadelphia: University of Pennsylvania Press, 2011), 40.

69. Ibid.

70. For Gail Kern Paster, the Lacanian mirror stage is an apt framework to clarify the civilizing process as it "locate[s] shame socially [and] in the gaze of a desirable other." *The Body Embarrassed*, 18.

71. Jacques Lacan, "The Mirror Stage as Formative of the Function of the I as Revealed in Psychoanalytic Experience," in *The Norton Anthology of Criticism and Theory*, ed. Vincent B. Leitch et al. (New York: W. W. Norton, 2001), 1285–90, quote from 1286.

72. Ibid., 1288.

subject's entire mental development."[73] The "fragmented body"—that which the subject once inhabited—persists as a spectral threat, prompting terrifying dreams of bodily disintegration and of impenetrable egos disguised as fortresses. When awake, the subject engages in anxious defensiveness, an aggressive warding off of any possibility of slipping back into incoherence.

If we analogize the civilizing process to Lacan's mirror stage, as I am suggesting, ambitious early modern subjects also "recognize" themselves in conduct literature. Should readers exhibit proper conduct, as the seductive promise goes, they too may embody their ideal selves and claim "verye nobylyte." But even as they might experience temporary elation at their gains, negative emotions of fear and anxiety soon follow. Ever attentive to these fears, conduct literature deploys terrorizing caricatures of laboring classes to elicit these anxieties and to urge a stricter adherence to the precepts set forth in its pages. Yet scholarship on conduct literature largely elides this aspect.[74] Elias concludes that manuals "place no particular emphasis on social distinctions, if we disregard occasional criticism of peasants and small tradesmen."[75] Yet Erasmus's criticisms are not infrequent but recurrent, and his remarks are often characterized by a surprising amount of vehemence in De Civilitate as well as in the conduct literature it inspires. By designating laboring and trade classes as social scapegoats, he trains his readers to view them with aversion.[76] And the deliberate cultivation of disgust was not particular to Erasmus's work, for, as Natalie K. Eschenbaum and Barbara Correll argue, "Renaissance conduct books made disgust a second nature."[77] Indeed, the deployment of insulting stereotypes of peasants and small tradesmen—in particular fishmongers and carters—is requisite to the civilizing process, and they function as the proverbial bogeyman to steer middling sorts away from their backgrounds and toward the mirage-like possibility of social mobility.

---

73. Ibid.

74. For instance, although Barbara Correll rightly recognizes the aversive use of femininity and bestiality in conduct conditioning, her otherwise astute argument overlooks how the specter of the "vulgar" classes constitutes a significant component of this training in civility.

75. Elias, The Civilizing Process, 65.

76. Thanks to the recent turn to affect, disgust has enjoyed its own Renaissance, generating a number of studies preoccupied with the early modern world and beyond. For a comprehensive survey of revulsion in the period, see Natalie K. Eschenbaum and Barbara Correll, Introduction to Disgust in Early Modern English Literature (New York: Routledge, 2016), 1–20. See also Benedict Robinson, "Disgust c. 1600," English Literary History 81, no. 2 (2014): 553–83. For general studies of the emotion, see Carolyn Korsmeyer, Savoring Disgust: The Foul and the Fair in Aesthetics (Oxford: Oxford University Press, 2011); Colin McGinn, The Meaning of Disgust (Oxford: Oxford University Press, 2011); William Ian Miller, The Anatomy of Disgust (Cambridge, MA: Harvard University Press, 1997); and Sianne Ngai, Ugly Feelings (Cambridge, MA: Harvard University Press, 2005), 332–56.

77. Eschenbaum and Correll, Disgust in Early Modern English Literature, 5.

As he enumerates malpractices in *De Civilitate*, Erasmus leverages the presumed dichotomy between aristocratic and vulgar persons as well as their behaviors to dictate appropriate conduct for young men. Railing against the unseemliness of runny noses, he states: "Let nat the nose thrilles be full of snyvell lyke a sluttysshe persone: That vyce was noted in Socrates as a reproche. To drie or snytte thy nose with thy cappe or thy cote is all of the carte, upon thy sleve or thynne elbowe is propertie of fysshmongers."[78] Here, we might read "propertie" as a slant synonym for the absence of propriety as well as the way that a particular idea of propriety becomes property of certain classes. Insofar as offenses are categorized alongside specific occupations, the text fosters disgust in readers toward uncivil behavior, a disgust that extends implicitly to those in maligned forms of employment. And because conduct books reduce the sum of one's achievement to the careful practice of social mores, even Socrates's reputation as one of the founders of classical philosophy can do little to insulate him from long-standing charges of bodily incontinence and incivility.[79] Moreover, those who exhibit the physical condition that contributes to the malpractice—that is, nasal congestion—are described in status-laden terms that also intimate and encapsulate their moral failings. For instance, the use of "fishmonger," a term that serves as a euphemism for panderer, is perhaps the most blatant example in this passage.

But fishmongers and fleshmongers are not the only ones singled out; Erasmus returns again and again to carters as concomitant with grotesque incivilities. To thrust one's fingers into a dish of food is "the maner of carters," as is speaking in a "hye and clamorous" voice.[80] Offenses that include picking one's teeth and gesturing lewdly with one's knife are identified as the "maner [that] cometh all of the carte and hath in a maner a resemblaunce of madnesse."[81] While the term "carter" designates an occupation, it also denotes "a type of low birth or breeding; a rude, uncultured man, a clown" at this time.[82] Although *De Civilitate* does not clarify its use of the term—whether it refers to employment or caricature—this does not especially matter: the position of carter is inextricable from the panoply of "vulgar" class assumptions. Thus, in such instances, conduct literature insists on an essentialist relationship among behavior, employment, and class.

78. Erasmus, *De Civilitate Morum Puerilium* (1532), A4r–A4v.

79. On this, Erasmus appears to be in error, for Plato's *Dialogues* includes numerous jabs at the rounded shape of Socrates's nose, not its congested nature.

80. Erasmus, *De Civilitate Morum Puerilium* (1532), B8v, C8r.

81. Ibid., C3v.

82. See *OED*, s.v. "carter, *n.*," def. 1.

De Civilitate reinforces this essentialism by associating bestial behaviors with laboring and trade classes. To gnaw on bones at the dinner table, Erasmus writes, is to exhibit a likeness to "dogges," whereas "to pycke it with [one's] knyfe is good maner."[83] Here, aversive conditioning associates infelicities, which are already aligned with laboring classes, with animals; in this way, proper behavior emerges not only as the civil option, but also as the *human* option. For example, when Erasmus denounces winking, he writes: "It is unsyttynge to loke upon a man and wynke with the one eye: For what els is it but to make blynde hym selfe? Lette leave that gesture to the fysshes called Thynnes [tuna fish] and craftismen."[84] The force of his argument derives from the reader's presumed repugnance to "unnatural" behavior, and by associating the offense with craftspeople and tuna, a creature that does not even breathe air, *De Civilitate* insinuates that the laboring classes, in the guise of craftspeople, exist far removed from the category of the human. Gone are the gentle reproofs for which he advocated earlier in the text.

Because Erasmus valorizes civil behaviors by aligning their opposites with lower classes, his logic obliges middling sorts to repudiate not only offensive behaviors but also the people who are presumably emblematic of them. Indeed, it is not enough to refrain from committing malpractices; one must also tacitly abide by this class-based or, more precisely, employment-based repudiation. As such, the civilizing process places the ambitious in a double bind in which they must prove themselves and their gentility through their distance from lower classes and, in fact, from their own origins. As Julia Reinhard Lupton has shown, belonging costs us dearly. "Citizenship rites," she explains, "come into being by exacting some cancellation, sacrifice, or mortification of prior familial, regional, or cultic allegiances."[85] Conduct formation, the process by which one proves one's fitness for civil society, is a two-pronged mode of civil vengeance wherein subjects identify and disparage incivilities and, by extension, other people. Subjects enact revenge against others through condemnation in order to preserve their tenuous positions while also directing vengeance toward themselves and all those individual parts that must be met with shame and improved in order for subjects to claim "verye nobylyte."

But how does one reconcile the disparagement of laboring classes with the larger project of conduct literature to empower middling sorts? Why promulgate a broader understanding of nobility only to make explicit that other sorts are inherently barred from it? If, as I have proposed, the Lacanian mirror

---

83. Erasmus, *De Civilitate Morum Puerilium* (1532), C2v.

84. Ibid., A4v.

85. Julia Reinhard Lupton, *Citizen-Saints: Shakespeare and Political Theology* (Chicago: University of Chicago Press, 2005), 76.

stage is one way by which we might understand the psychic and social consequences of conduct formation, then we must also acknowledge that civil subjects grapple with the threat of slipping back into the chaos of the clumsy and vulgar. I would argue that this repudiation shores up civilized subjectivity and that it is motivated not by sheer snobbery per se but rather by anxious defensiveness. And the historical realities of early modern England bear out this anxiety. As Linda Woodbridge puts it, the fear that *"anyone* might suddenly become poor" weighed on many.[86] Patricia Fumerton proposes that "given the unexpected and intermittent nature of poverty's embrace, one would expect that especially for this lowest sector of housed society, uneasy identification with the 'vagrant' migrant/laboring poor could have been very strong."[87] Ian Archer corroborates these conclusions when he analyzes the participation of middling classes in local government, stating, "Their attitudes towards the poor were shaped by the awareness of the transitory nature of their own business fortunes."[88] And in his research on the parish of Aldenham, Hertfordshire, in the early seventeenth century, Steve Hindle found that nearly 35 percent of families were recorded as poor—and therefore able to collect poor relief—at some point during their marriage, whereas only 50 percent of families were deemed financially able to contribute to the parish poor rate.[89] The process of conduct formation obliges subjects to defend themselves against what they once were and what they might—at any point—inhabit once again. The pervasive fear of slipping (back) into poverty is not mere psychoanalytic conjecture but anchored in the material experiences of early modern households. Given the extraordinary economic, agricultural, and employment precariousness of the period, it seems hardly surprising that conduct literature demands a preoccupation with the minutiae of social niceties. How much more elegant it is to reduce the complexities of an emergent market economy and its consequences to the manner of cutting one's meat or of excusing oneself from a table. And how convenient it is to obscure the

---

86. Linda Woodbridge, *Vagrancy, Homelessness, and English Renaissance Literature* (Champaign: University of Illinois Press, 2001), 116.

87. Patricia Fumerton, *Unsettled: The Culture of Mobility and the Working Poor in Early Modern England* (Chicago: University of Chicago Press, 2006), 197. Elsewhere she explains: "By virtue of their personal investment in a mobile market—and all its unpredictable vagaries—such businessmen conceivably could have recognized themselves, however partially or fleetingly, in unsettled poor laborers" (151).

88. Ian Archer, *The Pursuit of Stability* (Cambridge: Cambridge University Press, 1991), 259. For an alternative reading, see Fumerton, *Unsettled,* 151.

89. Steve Hindle, *On the Parish? The Micro-Politics of Poor Relief in Rural England, c. 1500–1750* (New York: Clarendon Press, 2004), 337.

systematic exploitation of laboring classes by shifting the onus for their problems to individuals themselves. This, too, is civil vengeance.

In *The Scholemaster*, Roger Ascham witnesses the ease with which social regression occurs. Appalled by the behavior of a young child at a dinner party, he recalls with a palpable shudder:

> This last somer, I was in a Gentlemans house: where a young childe, somewhat past fower yeare olde, cold in no wise frame his tonge, to saie, a little shorte grace: and yet he could roundlie rap out, so manie ugle othes, and those of the newest facion, as som good man fourescore yeare olde hath never hard named before: and that which was most detestable of all, his father and mother wold laughe at it. I moche doubt, what comfort, an other daie, this childe shall bring unto them. This Childe using moche the companie of serving men, and geving good care to their taulke, did easelie learne, which he shall hardlie forget, all daies of his life hereafter.[90]

I cite the episode for two reasons. First, though the child "did easelie learne" unseemly language, his behavior reflects not his family's status, at least according to Ascham's interpretation, but that of their servants. Second, his mealtime outburst illustrates how impressionable subjects readily slip back into incivility. That is, the child's exposure to and expression of vulgarity mark him such that even appropriate training cannot disabuse him of the lessons learned in the company of servingmen. Given children's vulnerability to their environments, parents and pedagogues, he urges, must be all the more vigilant.

What escapes Ascham's attention, however, is the polyvalence of the parents' laughter. Though the laughter signals amusement at witnessing the incongruity of a cursing (aristocratic) child, it also intimates their presumption of an innate imperviousness to debasement. Whatever might escape from the mouth of their babe, it gives these parents no cause for concern: theirs is a most certain status. Because incivilities are attached so fixedly to the laboring classes in the early modern imaginary, the aristocratic privilege is one in which subjects are permitted to dabble in bad behavior without suffering social consequences. If the nobility presumes itself securely distant from vulgarity, that belief is grounded in an essentialist understanding of class divisions— entrenched divisions that cannot be overcome by nonchalant displays of social infelicity *or* the diligent execution of courtesy.

---

90. Ascham, *The Scholemaster*, F4v.

Conduct literature, by contrast, challenges these assumptions by assuring its readers that, if they take pains to learn and display proper etiquette, they too may claim some degree of nobility. In *De Civilitate*, Erasmus writes: "To suche as chaunce to be well borne it is then shame nat to be of lyke maners as their progenytours were. Whome fortune wylleth to be of common sorte, of lowe bloode, and uplandysshe, they must laboure the more to sette them selfe forthe with avauncement of good maners in that that fortune hath debarred them."[91] Although *De Civilitate* sets up the two groups in opposition, Erasmus appears to challenge social expectations through his admission that the nobility are not necessarily in possession of good manners—a remarkable claim that enables the social category to be made somewhat more accessible. And in emphasizing fortune's role in class stratification, he tacitly diminishes whatever unearned accolades might be associated with those of a higher birth. Under a more democratized notion of nobility, Erasmus extols those of "lowe bloode," those whom fortune has "willed" to be common, to renew their efforts to circumvent fortune. Yet even as their advancement hinges on their efforts, questions remain: How is fortune outsmarted? How do subjects outrun their social destiny? And who (or what) is benefited by such tales?

If we recall the Lacanian narrative on which I have relied to frame this dynamic, we will remember that subjects cannot converge with their ideal selves, and early modern social climbers can only approach nobility asymptotically. Like the maddening effects of the reflection in the mirror, subjects remain mired in inadequacy, and their achievements—whatever they might be and whenever they might arrive—are necessarily belated. Erasmus continues: "No man can chose to hymselfe father and mather or his country, but condycion wys, and maners any man maye countrefet."[92] Although he claims that nobility can be cultivated in those of modest standing, the use of "countrefet" undermines the performance, however convincing, of nobility. Given the term's undercurrent of dishonesty and fraudulence,[93] the exhibition of good manners emerges as part of an elaborate ruse, a social disguise employed to advance one's standing.[94] Even as *De Civilitate* enables the mobility of the aspirational, it reinforces class distinctions: good manners will never be the

---

91. Erasmus, *De Civilitate Morum Puerilium* (1532), D3r.

92. Ibid., D3r.

93. At this time, to counterfeit means "to make an imitation of"; "to forge"; "to adulterate"; "to disguise"; "to feign, pretend, simulate"; and "to make or devise (something spurious) and pass it off as genuine" (*OED*, s.v. "counterfeit, v.").

94. If we recall our initial discussion of *The Spanish Tragedy* and Second Citizen's compliment of Hieronimo ("This gentleness shows him a gentleman."), the difference between "show" and "countrefet" becomes all the more apparent. Even as "show" retains a connection to fictiveness, it is used here as proof, whereas "countrefet" is fundamentally inauthentic.

legitimate possession of the "common sorte." The best that they may assume is an imitation. And although he admits the influence of fortune in such matters, Erasmus shifts much of the onus to subjects themselves and their willingness to self-fashion. Insofar as individuals are presumed sufficiently agential to shift their social positions, I understand such advice as a potent example of civil vengeance, for it is precisely the fantasy of agency—that one could re-create oneself according to the models of noblemen and accrue status—that is systematically used against working and merchant classes. This agential fantasy displaces the material circumstances that more fully account for the predicament in which middling sorts find themselves in Elizabethan England. Civil vengeance functions against the aspirational, then, by terrorizing them with the presumed vulgarity of the lower sorts and their discomfiting proximity while extracting from them the surplus labor believed necessary to manage their destinies. As for those still lower sorts who languish in privation, the logic of civil vengeance is employed to hold them responsible for their unhappy lot too.

To visualize the tenacious fantasy of social mobility proffered by conduct literature and its cruel dissolution on the early modern stage, let us return to *The Spanish Tragedy* and to its conclusion, in which Hieronimo reveals his spectacle—that of his dead son and theirs—to the Spanish and Portuguese ruling elite. Too slowly do they realize that their kin are dead and that their kingdoms are left without heirs, and in the face of their dawning sorrow, Hieronimo makes his final point: "Oh, good words! / As dear to me was my Horatio / As yours, or yours, or yours, my lord, to you" (4.4.168–70). As he charts out correspondences here, this response recalls his earlier words to Bazulto and issues an invitation to a more equitable, sympathetic world. His grief for his lost Horatio does not exceed but matches that of the now grieving fathers and uncle, "for all as one are our extremities" (3.13.92). The 1603 Q5 version exaggerates further Hieronimo's presumed equivalence to the nobility. After his failed attempt to hang himself, he invites the other grieving men to hang themselves together such that the mingling of their bodies (i.e., putting their heads together in one noose) makes evident their unlikely unity in tragedy: "Come, and we shall be friends; / Let us lay our heades together: / See heere's a goodly nooze will hold them all."[95] In the mere invitation of friendship, Hieronimo takes as his premise that they are already of proximate social states, which has been achieved through their collective loss.[96]

---

95. Thomas Kyd, *The Spanish Tragedie* (London: W. W[hite], 1602), L4v.

96. On the relationship between social status and early modern friendship between men, see Alan Bray, "Homosexuality and the Signs of Male Friendship in Elizabethan England," in *Queering the Renaissance*, ed. Jonathan Goldberg (Durham, NC: Duke University Press, 1994), 40–61.

But Hieronimo's proposal—whether implicit as in the 1592 version or explicit in the 1603 Q5—is met with incredulity as the rulers refuse to equate their losses with that of this mad interloper.[97] Indeed, all that they can do is restate their central trauma ("Brother, my nephew and thy son are slain"; "My Balthazar is slain." "Why has thou murdered my Balthazar?" "Why hast thou butchered both my children thus?"). Given the too visible corpse of Horatio—indeed, the only body that is not misrecognized as living—the incomprehension that they display when confronted with Hieronimo's loss appears all the more myopic and galling.[98] It remains thoroughly unacknowledged. Like the laughter of the parents at Ascham's dinner party, Hieronimo's interlocutors issue a resounding "no"—no, we are not equal; no, your suffering is not as terrible as ours; no, our loss is indeed more grievous than yours.[99] The play's conclusion insists, then, on the inflexibility of these social divisions for Hieronimo, an otherwise model civil servant with his earnest, unassuming manner. His great mistake is in believing that a history of unimpeachable conduct could blur social distinctions. And the consequence of this double bind is utter madness. "Hieronimo runs mad," Kevin Dunn explains, "when he is forced, from above and below, to recognize his class and to discover that this class has defined itself as classless."[100]

As Kyd's play reflects the entrenchment of early modern social divisions, its performance extends this "lesson" to middling audience members as well. If we consider the material and psychic burdens shouldered by lower classes, we might understand the process of conduct formation—in addition to the backlash from nobility against aspirational types—as a mode of unceasing civil vengeance. Given the asymptotic, never-to-be-reached mirage of true nobility, the final words of Revenge—"I'll there begin their endless tragedy"—take on new significance. Although traditionally read as a reference to the vengeful punishments enacted in hell—that is, a pronouncement on the boundless nature of divine retribution—the line might also be understood as a comment on what social engineering, which is achieved partly through conduct literature, demands of both middling characters and audiences.

---

97. In Q5, the Viceroy responds with outage: "O damned Devill, how secure he is" (Kyd, *The Spanish Tragedie* [1602], L4v).

98. Attempting to chart the equivalence of their loss, Hieronimo explains once again: "O, good words! / As dear to me was my Horatio / As yours, or yours, or yours, my lord, to you. / My guiltless son was by Lorenzo slain, / And by Lorenzo and that Balthazar / Am I at last revengèd thoroughly, / Upon whose souls may heavens be yet avenged / With greater far than these afflictions" (4.4.168–75). I thank Kevin Dunn for bringing this point to my attention.

99. Analyzing the same scene, Katharine Eisaman Maus issues a devastating conclusion: "To their betters, Hieronimo and Bel-imperia do not count; that is, they do not constitute independent centers of consciousness that need to be taken seriously" (*Inwardness*, 67).

100. Dunn, "The Gestural Politics of Counsel," 55.

CHAPTER 2

Feeling Revenge

Emotional Transmission and Contagious Vengeance in Donne's *Deaths Duell*

> And experience shewes, that *blood will have blood*;
> for though the murtherer escape the hands of the civill
> Judge, yet the terror and vengeance of God doth
> ordinarily pursue him to destruction.
>
> —William Perkins, *A godly and learned exposition of
> Christs Sermon in the Mount*

> I'll there begin their endless tragedy.
>
> —Thomas Kyd, *The Spanish Tragedy*

Through its focus on conduct literature, the previous chapter established how young subjects were primed for civil vengeance. To propel the transition from a legacy of private vengeance to the monarchy's centralization of retribution, conduct literature, as I have argued, accomplished much of the requisite cultural work. And while conduct formation depends on intrasubjective violence and repudiation, Kyd's *Spanish Tragedy* advances this claim to visualize the cruel promise of social mobility and its reliance on the logic of civil vengeance. Turning now from an exclusive consideration of the nascent civil avenger, chapter 2 takes up the early modern religious community as an ideal group through which to identify ongoing training in the principles of civil vengeance. Though this chapter retains an interest in the individual, it also situates her within a religious context in order to gauge the affective interplay between subjects and the social body to which they belong. Specifically, this chapter asks: What is the effect of civil vengeance on the social body? What forms of vengeance are enabled by or flourish through this sociality?

On the matter of revenge, it would seem that early modern Protestant Christianity could not be more explicit: vengeance belonged only to God and his magistrates. Preaching to his congregation at St. Paul's, George Downame claimed that one who commits an act of revenge is "inspired with a satanicall spirit."[1] For Downame, Christ's message in the New Testament arrives as the well-timed antidote to this devilish incitement: "Christ would have us to be so farre from desire of revenge, that he would have us readie rather to receive a second injurie, than to revenge the former."[2] This Christian prohibition extended beyond acts of revenge to encompass vengeful desires as well—even the desire for divine retribution.[3] As William Tyndale cautions his readers in his "Prologue to the Book of Numbers," "Your prayer it must be accordige to goddes worde. Ye may not desyer god to take vengeaunce on him whom goddes worde teacheth you to pytye and to praye for."[4] Similarly regarding revenge as a "corrupt affection," Andreas Hyperius traces its origin to the sin of wrath and underscores the gravity of negative emotions through his citation of 1 John 3:15, writing, "Whether thou hast borne hatred and malice to anie man, *He that hateth his brother is a manslayer*."[5] Meekness, by contrast, as William Perkins counsels, "is a gift of Gods spirit, whereby a man doth moderate his affections of anger . . . it makes a man with patience and a quiet heart to beare GODS Judgements, and to put up injuries, and to beare wrongs, when occasion of revenge is given him."[6]

Such are the unwavering voices that lead scholars to conclude that early modern Christianity opposed vengeance in no uncertain terms.[7] Perhaps most famous is the pronouncement of Charles and Elaine Hallett that "the injunction [against revenge] was unequivocal,"[8] and Lukas Erne recently reiterates this perspective when he argues that Hieronimo's eventual demise in

---

1. George Downame, *Lectures on the XV. Psalme read in the cathedrall church of S. Paule* (London: Adam Islip, 1604), I3r.

2. Ibid., I2r.

3. See, for instance, Bowers, *Elizabethan Revenge Tragedy, 1587–1642*, 1st ed., 62–85; and Katharine Eisaman Maus, Introduction to *Four Revenge Tragedies: "The Spanish Tragedy"; "The Revenger's Tragedy"; "The Revenge of Bussy d'Ambois"; and "The Atheist's Tragedy"* (Oxford: Oxford University Press, 1995), ix–xxxi.

4. William Tyndale, "Prologue to the Book of Numbers," in *The Pentateuch* (Antwerp: Johan Hoochstraten, 1530), A7v.

5. Andreas Hyperius, *The true tryall and examination of a mans owne selfe wherein every faithfull Christian . . .* , trans. Tho[mas] Newton (London: John Windet, 1587), D2v.

6. William Perkins, *A garden of spirituall flowers* (London: W. White, 1610), F5r.

7. See Bowers, *Elizabethan Revenge Tragedy, 1587–1642*, 1st ed., 62–85; Hallett and Hallett, *The Revenger's Madness*; and Eleanor Prosser, *Hamlet and Revenge*, 2nd ed. (Stanford, CA: Stanford University Press, 1971), 44–52. Linda Woodbridge offers a welcome criticism of this misguided assumption in *English Revenge Drama*, 22–58.

8. Hallett and Hallett, *The Revenger's Madness*, 121.

The Spanish Tragedy is part of a "pattern that affirms rather than questions a Christian view of providence."[9] Michael Neill and Katharine Eisaman Maus take these injunctions in the religious archive at face value as well.[10] For instance, as Maus explicates how early modern morality and social codes existed at cross-purposes, she leaves aside the Church's complicated stance on revenge.[11] Linda Woodbridge emerges as a notable exception when she concludes that "the alleged Christian abhorrence of revenge proves, on closer inspection, a chimera."[12] Her provocation emboldens me to read against the grain in order to excavate a set of religious texts that complicate the binary structure of sanction and prohibition. When scholars examine these same materials with the expectation that vengeance is spectacular and physically violent, if not fatal, they miss the curious acrobatics that early modern writers perform to negotiate the social stakes of and cultural investment in revenge. If, as I propose, early modern vengeance was in the process of a radical shift, we must return to the religious archive and accustom our eyes to this refashioned revenge—that is, forms that afforded social traction to those who existed as exemplars of Christian devotion.

To pursue this line of inquiry, I rely on a collection of religious works that include the writings of William Perkins and Thomas Beard to demonstrate that vengeance—both personal and divine—is located squarely in the social realm and not peripheral to it. In the first half of the chapter, I argue that vengeance is permitted vis-à-vis orthodox behavior and that intersubjective violence is recoded as godly retribution. Civil vengeance is radicalized further in John Donne's final sermon, *Deaths Duell*, as I reconstruct the atmosphere created by the 1631 delivery of the sermon at Whitehall in the second part of the chapter. Though emotion was central to the delivery of the early modern sermon, the conversion from performance to print makes emotion and its diffuse effects less accessible. To hypothesize how scholars might recover an af-

---

9. Lukas Erne, *Beyond "The Spanish Tragedy": A Study of the Works of Thomas Kyd* (Manchester, UK: Manchester University Press, 2001), 111.

10. See Neill, "English Revenge Tragedy," 328–50.

11. Maus clarifies: "On the one hand, both Christianity and some classical moral codes popular in the Renaissance prescribed patience and non-aggression . . . On the other hand, a man's 'honour' in early modern England required him to retaliate swiftly for slights to himself, and to refuse to tolerate the abuse of his kin or dependents" (Introduction to *Four Revenge Tragedies*, x).

12. Consider, for instance, the antitheatrical tracts generated by seemingly inexhaustible Christian moralists (e.g., Philip Stubbes, John Rainolds, Gosson, and William Pryne) who offer another perspective regarding revenge in the early modern imaginary. Though these writers condemned theater on a great many grounds—pride, wrath, incest, arrogance, backbiting, treason, and sodomy— the prolific revenge tragedies that entertained audiences, as Linda Woodbridge observes, did not prompt them to condemn theater for its portrayals of vengeance or for inciting spectators to take the law into their own hands. See Woodbridge, *English Revenge Drama*, 34–35, 36.

fective archive and visualize the transmission of civil vengeance, I read his final sermon alongside early modern medical texts and contemporary research in affective neuroscience.[13] With these texts, I propose that the sermon's delivery introduced and circulated intensely negative emotions, and it is this transmission of negative emotions, I argue, that constitutes a mode of vengeance enacted on and circulated through social bodies. Consequently, Donne's final sermon exists as an unlikely medium through which civil vengeance is elicited and transmitted.

My reading of *Deaths Duell* revolves around the matter of inaccessible revenge and specifically explores the possibilities of aiming for an unreachable target as well as the consequent effects of this aim on the social body. Because vengeance is regularly conceptualized as a relationship between victim and perpetrator—in traditional plays, for example, this typically occurs on the level of the individual versus another subject or an oppressive institution—that perspective necessarily diminishes the complex and often contradictory power dynamics that structure everyday existence. Thus, to account for this complication, my second chapter suggests that civil vengeance may have less to do with intention and directionality. But what exactly does that mean? Put simply, it means that revenge gets out of hand. In the jumbled transfer of emotions and affects, subjects maintain less control over their targets as well as the trajectories of their revenge projects such that even intended targets may be missed or others might be taken as substitutes.

As I discussed in the book's introduction, although scholarship imagines vengeance and those inimitable lone avengers to lie on the social periphery, this conclusion ignores the permeation and transference of vengeance in the early modern religious world. Rather than insisting that retribution is antithetical to Protestant Christianity, traditional religious materials reveal their fundamental

---

13. Focusing on acoustics, architecture, and space, recent scholars have attempted to re-create early modern sermons as performances. See Peter McCullough, "Preaching and Context: John Donne's Sermon in the Funerals of Sir William Cokayne," in *The Oxford Handbook of the Early Modern Sermon*, ed. Peter McCullough, Hugh Adlington, and Emma Rhatigan (Oxford: Oxford University Press, 2011), 213–70; Emma Rhatigan, "Preaching Venues: Architecture and Auditories," in *The Oxford Handbook of the Early Modern Sermon*, 87–119; and Mary Morrissey, *Politics and the Paul's Cross Sermons, 1558–1642* (Oxford: Oxford University Press, 2011). See also the exemplary Virtual Paul's Cross Project, which relies on architectural modeling software and acoustic stimulation to re-create the listening experience of Donne's 1622 sermon at Paul's Cross ("Virtual Paul's Cross Project: A Digital Re-creation of John Donne's Gunpowder Day Sermon," North Carolina State University [5 November 2013], http://vpcp.chass.ncsu.edu). Bruce Smith inspired much of the recent turn to sound with his argument that the "artifacts that survive from early modern England ask to be heard, not seen" in his invaluable study, *The Acoustic World of Early Modern England* (Chicago: University of Chicago Press, 1999), 13.

compatibility. "Dearly beloved," writes St. Paul in that familiar letter to the Romans, "avenge not your selves, but rather geve place unto wrath. For it is written: Vengeaunce is myne, I wyll repay sayth the Lorde. Therfore, yf thyne enemie hunger, feede hym: yf he thirst, geve him drinke. For in so doing, thou shalt heape coales of fyre on his head" (Rom. 12:19–20). Most fascinating about this oft-cited passage is the manner in which it sanctions vengeful behaviors through orthodoxy. Whereas God lays claim to vengeance, the faithful also enact a "benevolent" vengeance by practicing the teachings of Jesus (e.g., feed the hungry, care for the sick); turning the other cheek offers the added benefit of "heap[ing] coales of fyre" on the head of one's enemy. Although St. Paul permits vengeance, the means by which one secures that end are rerouted through channels of acceptable Christian behavior.

As Erasmus describes how the devout might overcome their spiritual hindrances, he couches his approach in the language of godly vengeance: "Thou art provoked to voluptuousnes and pleasures of the body, consider thy imbesilitie, and withdraw thy mind the more from unlawful pleasurs and delectations, occupyinge thy selfe in vertuous operations and chaste meditacions. Thou art moved to covetouse: increase thy charitie and almes toward thy poore neibour . . . And so every temptacion shal be unto the[e] a revenging of a godly purpose, and increase of vertue & trewe devocion. And trewly ther is none so good and readye awaye to destroye and repell thy enemie as this."[14] Shifting the terms of the spiritual conflict to a battleground in which one may "destroye and repell thy enemie," Erasmus incentivizes Christian behavior through the rhetoric of vengeance; as in St. Paul's argument, good works carry the supplementary benefit of thrashing one's spiritual enemies. Yet Erasmus also reroutes charitable behaviors through the logic of revenge. That is, charitable acts do not amass value because they are in imitation of Christ or because they alleviate the suffering of a "poore neibour." They are valued because they incrementally contribute to the ongoing battle between God and the devil, and vengeance evolves into the most effective means by which one marshals forces for good. Put simply, charitable acts accrue value because they are apt substitutes for vengeance. In this manner, major voices of Protestant Christianity capitalize on and hone vengeful impulses rather than attempting to eradicate them. Furthermore, Erasmus suggests that some agency accrues to subjects who take revenge by following doctrinal dictates. For instance, provided the injured party extends forgiveness to the offender, early modern Christianity

---

14. Desiderius Erasmus, *A godly boke wherein is contained certayne fruitefull, godlye, and necessarye rules, to bee exercised and put in practice by all Christian souldiers lynynge in the campe of this worlde* (London: Wyllyam Seres, 1561), M8v–A1r.

does not require punishment to be tempered with mercy. As Christopher Hill has shown, the model of debt litigation recurs in early modern Christianity such that "[one] may not only sue his adversary, but pursue him to the death, and yet forgive him."[15] Thanks to the requisite act of forgiveness, vengeance is shorn bare of its personal motivations but remains identifiable in the rabidity of its pursuit. Within the bounds of orthodoxy, one is permitted the pleasures of retribution, yet the mode by which one achieves that end is not brute aggression but rather tyrannical goodness: civil vengeance. Revenge with a smile.

As the Church and its ministers might advocate for tyrannical goodness, religious materials also circulate threats of divine punishment, threats that guarantee God's righteous vengeance for the wrongs of the world. Such is the narrative to which Thomas Beard subscribes in *The Theatre of God's Judgments*. In his translation from Jean de Chassanion's *Histoires memorables des grans et merveilleux jugemens et punitions de Dieu*, augmented with excerpts from the works of John Foxe, Raphael Holinshed, and John Stowe, Beard assembles an archive of God's righteous punishments intended to "bridle and restraine" his readers' "impiety."[16] Situated within the rather humorless genre of "judgment literature," *Theatre* offers innumerable examples of divine vengeance wrought against figures major and minor.[17] Its spectacular acts of revenge, detailed in gruesome extravagance, prompt David Mikics to regard Beard's technique as "theatrical moralism" insofar as the ability to discourage sin is directly proportional to the hyperbolic manner in which these punishments are described.[18]

But even as we approach the familiar model of divine punishment, these instances of vengeance are anchored to a social context or, more precisely, are wrought through civil agents, which resituate divine retribution in the social sphere. The narratives themselves also serve to reinforce the integrity of the social body. A few moments from *Theatre* will illustrate what I mean. Depicting the demise of Nestorius, a former bishop of Constantinople who put forth heretical notions regarding Christ's humanity, Beard writes: "So [having] turned upside downe that whole groundworke of our salvation, [Nestorius] escaped no more the just vengeance of God, then all other heretikes did: for first

15. Quoted in Woodbridge, *English Revenge Drama*, 89.

16. Thomas Beard and Thomas Taylor, *The theatre of Gods judgements wherein is represented the admirable justice of God against all notorious sinners* (London: S. I. and M. H., 1642), A1r.

17. John Foxe's *Book of Martyrs* is part of the genre. See also Beth Lynch, *John Bunyan and the Language of Conviction: Studies in Renaissance Literature* (Cambridge: D. S. Brewer, 2004), 104.

18. David Mikics, *The Limits of Moralizing: Pathos in Subjectivity in Spenser and Milton* (Lewisburg, PA: Bucknell University Press, 1994), 152.

hee was banished into a farre countrey, and there tormented with a strange disease: the very wormes did gnaw in pieces his blasphemous tongue, and at length the earth opened her mouth, and swallowed him up."[19] Prior to the punishment's description, Beard reiterates divine intervention as the episode's governing premise such that the following details—the Church leaders who ordered Nestorius's banishment, the worms that enacted the gruesome occurrence of *contrapasso*, and finally, the earth that ultimately silenced him—materialize only in the service of his argument. Insofar as Beard's logic hinges on a fundamental distortion of natural phenomena (e.g., vermiculation and decomposition), it substitutes human interactions and natural events for divine retribution. That is, unconnected events one might otherwise regard as precarious are revealed to function in accordance with God's will, thanks to the heavy-handed narrative. As Beard reminds his readers that Nestorius is no more exemplary than "all other heretikes" punished by God, he affirms the constancy, the delicious predictability, of divine vengeance, and each instance makes visible that larger pattern.

Though Beard makes liberal use of substitution as the means by which he reconstructs this history, vengeance is mediated explicitly through human agents as he relays other tales. Citing a Scottish cardinal who accused a rowdy audience of interrupting his sermon and later hanged them as heretics, Beard depicts the cardinal's comeuppance with palpable relish: "But ere long the cruell Cardinall found as little favour at another butchers hands, that slue him in his chamber, when hee dreamed of nothing lesse, and in his Cardinals robes hanged him over the wall to the view of men. And thus God revenged the death of those innocents, whose bloods never ceased crying for vengeance against their murder, untill he had justly punished him in the same kind, and after the same fashion which he had dealt with them."[20] With great satisfaction, Beard champions the violence wrought not by an official appointee of God (i.e., a sovereign or magistrate) but by an unnamed "butcher"—an act that runs counter to orthodox stances on vengeance. Although the term implies the brutality of the cardinal's murderer, early modern valences suggest other possibilities: the word referred most immediately to one who slaughters animals for food but also extended to executioners.[21] Because these two possibilities were better established when *Theatre* was published than the colloquialism with which we are now most familiar, Beard's reference to "butcher"

---

19. Jean de Chassanion and Thomas Beard, *The theatre of Gods judgements: or, a collection of histories out of sacred, ecclesiasticall, and prophane authours concerning the admirable judgements of God upon the transgressours of his commandements* (London: Adam Islip, 1597), G5r.

20. Ibid., E3v.

21. See *OED*, s.v. "butcher, n."

is not pejorative but speaks to the ways in which the unnamed murderer was simply fulfilling his duties. Even though the individual was not technically a magistrate of God, he becomes as much retroactively because his actions enable the fruition of a divine plan. To add further credence to this interpretation, we should note that, while Beard refers initially to the unnamed murderer as a "butcher," he seamlessly substitutes God in the sentence that follows.

In reading these strange episodes from *The Theatre of God's Judgements*, it is less my point that certain forms of fitting or appropriate violence are always already in the service of divine vengeance, though that is, of course, in line with the operational logic here. Rather, such transactions substitute intersubjective violence for divine retribution, and thus locate the operations of vengeance within a social context, even—or especially—when that vengeance is referred to as divine will. Shifting the focus from the actual realities of lawlessness, private vengeance, vigilantism, and murder, Beard's narrative fixes readers' attention on the revelation of a divine master plan, one that may materialize only through a social body. Although these crimes also imply the breakdown of that body as well as a wanton disregard of law, reading the acts through the optic of divine vengeance imbues them with godly purpose and meaning. What could otherwise be understood as a rupture in the social fabric (i.e., violence among subjects that results in death) is recuperated through this account of godly retribution; thus, such narratives enforce the façade of social stability.

As divine vengeance makes meaning from ostensibly senseless violence, it also exhibits remarkable endurance. In *A Godly and Learned Exposition of Christs Sermon in the Mount*, William Perkins contemplates the long-term consequences of adultery in the form of vengeance visited on one's descendants:

> [Adultery] bringeth Gods vengeance upon the posteritie: and therefore *Job* calleth it *a fire which shall devoure unto destruction*: yea, the greatnesse of Gods punishment upon Adulterers, partly in this life, and principally after death, may plainely shew the greatnesse of this sinne . . . And the place where they stood [towns of Admah and Zeboiim], it made a poole of poysoning water unto this day. And although the Lord doe not shew such extraordinary revenge against sinne, yet his wrath is a consuming fire against whole families, townes, and kingdoms, for this sinne; though *David* repented of his Adulterie, yet for that very sinne, *the sword must not depart from his house for ever.*[22]

22. William Perkins, *A godly and learned exposition of Christs Sermon in the Mount* (Cambridge: Thomas Brooke and Cantrell Legge, 1608), G8r–G8v.

Even as Perkins establishes that divine vengeance visits future generations, he discourages reading the punishment as excessive by equating its "greatnesse" with the sin such that this equivalence renders it commensurate and just. Yet there is another narrative that competes with the first. Through the "poole of poysoning water," Perkins draws a temporal connection from the biblical sites of Admah and Zeboiim to the moment in which he writes in 1608, one in which the water *still poisons*. But just as soon as one might marvel at God's "extraordinary revenge," Perkins assures his audience that such a conclusion is incorrect, as if trying to stave off heretical interpretations of unjust punishment. By contrast, he argues that what animates the extensive destruction of "whole families, townes, and kingdoms" is God's wrath kindled by the sin of adultery. Yet the distinction between "extraordinary revenge" and "wrath" is not altogether convincing, and, to add further fuel, Perkins leaves us with David's penitence juxtaposed against the specters of his three dead sons (i.e., Amnon, Absalom, and Adonijah), who are killed by the "sword [that] must not depart from his house for ever." I make use of this passage to draw a line from the meditations on divine vengeance as unceasing to explore the unmistakable discomfort with which these punishments are reported.

At other moments, ordinary vengeance can be pressed into the service of godliness. In *A Garden of Spirituall Flowers*, Perkins identifies revenge as one of the seven signifiers of true repentance. He explains: "That is, the penitent man is so offended with the sin hee hath committed, that hee will be revenged of himselfe for it, as for example, if hee have offended in gluttony, he will revenge himselfe by fasting two or three daies after; if he have offended in whoredome, hee will be revenged of his lusts bewayling of them ever after: and so of other sinnes. By these [signes] it may appear what true repentance is."[23] My point here is less that Christian voices explicitly encourage revenge as a means by which the devout repent thoroughly, even as the discovery is of interest. Rather, I want to isolate two tacit characteristics of revenge present in the passage that will occupy the remainder of this chapter: shifting targets and constitutive excess. Regarding the first trait, Perkins moves steadily from "revenged of himselfe" to "revenge himselfe" and concludes with "revenged of his lusts," thereby shifting the specific targets of vengeance in subsequent clauses. Whereas in the first example the subject himself is the target of his penitential revenge, the second implies revenge on behalf of oneself, while, in the final example, "his lusts" are the targets of revenge. The inconsistency in Perkins's argument is made all the more peculiar if we consider how explicitly he outlines the mechanisms of revenge, offering, as he does, a few concrete

---

23. Perkins, *A garden of spirituall flowers*, D6v–D7r.

examples to clarify his claims. Indeed, I read the slippage between these targets of revenge as symptomatic of a confused purpose of vengeance, that
revenge itself has an unpredictable trajectory. Perhaps it is from this unpre-
dictability that the second characteristic of revenge—constitutive excess—
arises here as well because one is compelled to cast a wider net in order to
secure ever-shifting targets. For Perkins, revenge generates a disproportionate
exchange. One episode of gluttony yields two to three days of fasting, while
sexual impropriety urges the offending subject to mourn his sin "ever after."
The latter example means, then, that revenge persists for an indefinite period
of time and well beyond the temporal perimeters of the original transgression. It is with these two elements of revenge in mind—shifting targets and
constitutive excess—that I now turn to *Deaths Duell* to examine the relationship among civil vengeance, substitution, and the transmission of intensely
negative feelings.

On 25 February 1631, John Donne preached his final sermon to an audience
at Whitehall that included King Charles I and the Court.[24] There, a cadaver-
ous Donne meditated on the unceasing nature of death mere weeks before
his own in a Lenten address that Evelyn M. Simpson describes as a "strange
mingling of intense devotion to Christ with a gloomy morbidity of fancy
which delights in picturing the physical corruption of the body with the ac-
companiment of worms and dust."[25] Biological death, as Donne informed
his auditors, is not a tidy conclusion to worldly sufferings but rather "an *entrance* into the *death of corruption* and *putrefaction* and *vermiculation* and *incineration* and dispersion in and from the *grave*, in which every dead man dyes
over againe."[26] As Donne links together postmortem humiliations, his sermon
subscribes to an accretive logic, generating excess that tries the imagination
yet proves elusive on the printed page. "More than any of his other sermons,"
Ramie Targoff insists, "*Deaths Duell* reminds us again and again that the text
we have received is merely a script of what was originally a live performance."[27]
Whatever might have been conveyed through oral delivery—tone, gesture, and

---

24. For an explanation of the confusion surrounding the date of John Donne's final sermon, see
Jonquil Bevan, "*Hebdomada Mortium*: The Structure of Donne's Last Sermon," *Review of English Studies* 45, no. 178 (1994): 185–203, esp. 188n8. Donne died several weeks later on 31 March 1631.

25. Evelyn M. Simpson, *A Study of the Prose Works of John Donne*, 2nd ed. (Oxford: Clarendon
Press, 1948), 10.

26. Donne, *Deaths Duell, or a Consolation to the Soule, against the Dying Life, and Living Death of the
Body* (London: Thomas Harper, 1632), C3v. Even though *Deaths Duell* was not the original title, it is
convenient to refer to the sermon by its publication title. Subsequent references to *Deaths Duell* are
from this edition unless otherwise noted.

27. Ramie Targoff, *John Donne, Body and Soul* (Chicago: University of Chicago Press, 2008), 156.

emotion—is lost in the conversion of performance to print.[28] And insofar as the deployment and management of emotion are integral to the act of preaching, I consider how scholars might approach print for an ampler sense of the emotional fabric so indispensable to the sermon's delivery.[29] Making use of affect contagion—the "bioneurological means by which particular affects are transmitted from body to body"—I argue that Donne's delivery transmitted intensely negative emotions (i.e., anxiety, disgust, and anger) as well as their physiological markers (e.g., increased heart rate and release of hormones).[30] Specifically, I contend that secreted chemical signals spread emotion, noting that early modern medicine recognized the phenomenon as well. Because considerations of affect offer a broader palette of interpretive possibilities, or, as Adam Frank concludes, "thinking about affect can change what counts as material and what material might do," the chapter argues implicitly for the value of ephemera—vengeful feelings and their grave effects in the material world.[31]

Insofar as Donne's delivery spreads these emotions throughout his congregation, my subsequent reading reveals missed targets of revenge to be part of civil vengeance. Put another way, this section elaborates my conception of civil vengeance to include circulated, even misdirected, aggression that may erupt outside willfulness or intention. Even so, civil vengeance is shown to be intractable from the social sphere, for this revenge must be transmitted through and among social bodies. What characterized civil vengeance in the writings of Beard and Perkins—specifically, the ever-shifting targets of revenge and constitutive excess—is unmistakably amplified in *Deaths Duell*.

---

28. As Arnold Hunt states, early modern sermons were "oral performances whose virtue was deemed to lie precisely in their oral nature, but exist for us today only in written and printed form" (*The Art of Hearing: English Preachers and Their Audiences, 1590–1640* [Cambridge: Cambridge University Press, 2010], 59). Some early modern ministers regarded print sermons as attenuated forms of these oral performances. See, for instance, Edward Willan, *Six Sermons* (London: Printed for R. Royston, 1651), E4v; and Samuel Hieron, *Three Sermonsful of Necessarie Advertisements, and Gracious Comforts, for All Those Whose Care Is to Worke Out Their Owne Salvation with Feare and Trembling* (London: B. Alsop., 1616), A2r. See also James Rigney, "Sermons into Print," in *The Oxford Handbook of the Early Modern Sermon*, 198–212, esp. 201 and 203.

29. Central to the early modern sermon is, as Kate Armstrong argues, the "creation and expression of strong emotion," and she urges scholars to "attempt to re-create [them] in order to understand fully sermons of this period" ("Sermons in Performance," *The Oxford Handbook of the Early Modern Sermon*, 120–36, esp. 135). See also Debora K. Shuger, *Sacred Rhetoric: The Christian Grand Style in the English Renaissance* (Princeton, NJ: Princeton University Press, 1988).

30. Anna Gibbs, "After Affect: Sympathy, Synchrony, and Mimetic Communication," in *The Affect Theory Reader*, ed. Melissa Gregg and Gregory J. Seigworth (Durham, NC: Duke University Press, 2010), 186–205, quote from 191.

31. Adam Frank, "Some Avenues for Feeling," *Criticism* 46, no. 3 (2004): 511–24, quote from 511.

To balance current scholarship on affect with an early modern understanding of emotion, I offer a brief clarification of my terminology.[32] I use "emotion" as a contemporary equivalent to "passions" and "affections," which some early modern writers regarded as synonyms.[33] Emotion, as I define it, transforms and concretizes the constellation of precognitive sensations and feelings into language. But in the process of translation, there are impressions and sensations that remain unobserved, unconscious, and consequently unconverted into language. That remainder is affect, the "specific physiological responses that then give rise to various effects, which may or may not translate into emotions."[34] Even as I distinguish emotion from affect, the boundary between the two was porous in the early modern world. Brian Cummings remarks that "the passions" resemble affect insofar as the former "occupied an uneasy borderland between the mental and the bodily, the rational and the physiological."[35] Allison P. Hobgood contends that the distinction between affect and emotion, characteristic of contemporary affect theory, rests on notions that are "wholly post-Cartesian and, thereby, entrenched in a division between psychology and physiology, conscious feeling and unconscious sensation that was . . . only just barely coming to fruition" in the early modern world.[36] And because humoral theory shaped medical perceptions of the human body and its sensations, subjects most likely experienced emotion as

---

32. For recent discussions of affect in early modern studies, see Steven Mullaney, *The Reformation of Emotions in the Age of Shakespeare* (Chicago: University of Chicago Press, 2015); Ronda Arab, Michelle M. Dowd, and Adam Zucker, eds., *Historical Affects and the Early Modern Theater* (New York: Routledge, 2015); Amanda Bailey and Mario DiGangi, eds., *Affect Theory and Early Modern Texts* (New York: Palgrave, 2017); and Bradley Irish, *Emotion in the Tudor Court: Literature, History, and Early Modern Feeling* (Evanston, IL: Northwestern University Press, 2018). Yet even benign feelings may generate division and sow discord in the early modern world; see, for example, Katherine Ibbett, *Compassion's Edge: Fellow-Feeling and Its Limits in Early Modern France* (Philadelphia: University of Pennsylvania, 2017).

33. Gail Kern Paster, Katherine Rowe, and Mary Floyd-Wilson, eds., Introduction to *Reading the Early Modern Passions: Essays in the Cultural History of Emotion* (Philadelphia: University of Pennsylvania Press, 2004), 1–20, esp. 2. According to Susan James, passions are "generally understood to be thoughts or states of the soul which represent things as good or evil for us, and are therefore seen as objects of inclination or aversion" (*Passions and Action: The Emotions in Seventeenth-Century Philosophy* [Oxford: Oxford University Press, 2000], 4). For a brief overview of the classification systems inherited by early modern subjects, see ibid., 4–8.

34. Elizabeth Wissinger, "Always on Display: Affective Production in the Modeling Industry," in *The Affective Turn: Theorizing the Social*, ed. Patricia Ticineto Clough and Jean Halley (Durham, NC: Duke University Press, 2007), 231–60, quote from 232.

35. Brian Cummings, "Animal Passions and Human Sciences: Shame, Blushing, and Nakedness in Early Modern Europe and the New World," in *At the Borders of the Human: Beasts, Bodies, and Natural Philosophy in the Early Modern Period*, ed. Erica Fudge, Susan Wiseman, and Ruth Gilbert (London: Palgrave Macmillan, 1999), 26–50, quote from 26.

36. Allison P. Hobgood, *Passionate Playgoing in Early Modern England* (Cambridge: Cambridge University Press, 2015), 5–6.

"an ongoing, dynamic process not an occasional, static state."[37] Even though early modern conceptualizations of emotion surely inhabit affect more readily than current models, I adhere to a flexible distinction for clarity's sake. Insofar as emotion is sensation codified by language, autonomic aspects of emotion—heartbeats and rates of breathing, for example—remain unaccounted for, and it is precisely these physiological markers, I will argue, that facilitate the transmission and circulation of emotion in Donne's congregation. And this transference of negative emotion through the social body—deliberate, accidental, or some combination thereof—both constitutes and complicates the matter of civil vengeance.

Despite its reputation for severity, early modern Protestant preaching recognized emotion as the means by which ministers effected spiritual transformation.[38] Emotional appeals enabled preachers to achieve their primary religious objectives, which included, according to Debora K. Shuger, "awakening a rightly ordered love" in their addressees and "redirecting the self from corporeal objects to spiritual ones."[39] Although the manner and intensity of emotional displays depended largely on the region and, by extension, Puritan influence, it was widely acknowledged that preachers ought to engage the emotions of their auditors.[40] Because nonverbal modes of communication were believed most apt in "conveying inward the affections," preaching handbooks encouraged ministers to make careful use of them.[41] As Jeffrey Knapp notes, these texts also exhorted ministers to incorporate theatrical techniques into their preaching such that many pursued playacting as part of their clerical training.[42]

Yet a minister's authentic feelings remained central to the project of emotional management. This belief stemmed in part from Quintilian's classical rule that, in order for speakers to elicit emotion from their audiences, they must first experience the intended emotion.[43] Preaching handbooks stressed a minister's significance in crafting an emotional and consequently spiritually persuasive atmosphere. In *The Arte of Prophecying: Or, A Treatise concerning the Sacred and Onely True Manner and Methode of Preaching*, Perkins opines: "Wood,

---

37. Ibid., 12.

38. Hunt, *The Art of Hearing*, 81–82.

39. Shuger, *Sacred Rhetoric*, 138.

40. Hunt, *The Art of Hearing*, 90.

41. Ibid., 84. For a secular treatise on hand gestures, see John Bulwer, *Chirologia, or the Naturall Language of the Hand* (London: Tho[mas] Harper, 1644).

42. Jeffrey Knapp, *Shakespeare's Tribe: Church, Nation, and Theater in Renaissance England* (Chicago: University of Chicago Press, 2002), 2.

43. Quintilian, *Institutes of Oratory: Or, Education of an Orator*, trans. John Selby Watson (London: George Bell and Sons, 1891), 427.

that is capable of fire, doth not burne, unless fire be put to it: and he must first be godly affected himselfe, who would stirre up godly affections in other men. Therefore what motions a sermon doth require, such the Preacher shall stirre up privately in his owne mind, that hee may kindle up the same in his hearers."[44] Hyperius envisions another dynamic between the preacher and his congregation in *The Practis of Preaching, Otherwise Called the Pathway to the Pulpet*: "Before all thinges it is very necessary that hee which speaketh, doe conceyve such lyke affections in his mynde, and rayse them upp in himself, yea, and (after a sorte) shewe them forth to be seene unto others, as hee coveteth to bee translated into the myndes of his auditors."[45] Though both regard the minister as the origin of emotion, Perkins presumes that his auditors possess the requisite materials for combustion. Hyperius, by contrast, imagines a form of mental implantation in which the preacher's affections are not elicited but "translated" in his audience. Hyperius's model affords the minister greater control over and responsibility for the spiritual well-being of his flock, while Perkins's version boasts a more reciprocal relationship. Yet despite these differences, both arguments rest on an underlying assumption that emotions are readily transmitted between the early modern pulpit and pew, and this assumption remains foundational to the claims that I will make later regarding the transmission of negative emotion and civil vengeance.

Sermons themselves offer some evidence of how ministers directed the emotions of their congregations. In the case of Donne, he crafted his sermons to uplift the sorrowful, hearten the downtrodden, and reprimand the recalcitrant.[46] In a 1625 sermon at St. Paul's, he states: "God hath accompanied, and complicated almost all our bodily diseases of these times, with an extraordinary sadnesse, a predominant melancholy, a faintnesse of heart, a chearlesnesse, a joylesnesse of spirit, and therefore I returne often to this endeavor of raising your hearts, dilating your hearts with a holy Joy, Joy in the holy Ghost, for *Under the shadow of his wings*, you may, you should, *rejoyce*."[47] In a sermon for the Earl of Exeter in 1624, Donne champions the Church of

---

44. William Perkins, *The Arte of Prophecying: Or, A Treatise concerning the Sacred and Onely True Manner and Methode of Preaching* (London: Felix Kyngston, 1607), K3v.

45. Andreas Hyperius, *The Practis of Preaching, Otherwise Called the Pathway to the Pulpet conteyning an Excellent Method How to Frame Divine Sermons, and to Interpret the Holy Scriptures according to the Capacitie of the Vulgar People*, trans. John Ludham (London: Thomas East, 1577), 43r.

46. Anita Gilman Sherman posits that Donne "takes it for granted that his audience is subdued and depressed," and so he aims to uplift and remind his listeners of the redemptive power of Christ ("Donne's Sermons as Re-enactments of the Word: A Response to Margret Fetzer," *Connotations* 19, no. 1–3 [2009/2010]: 14–20, quote from 15–16).

47. Donne, *The Sermons of John Donne*, ed. Evelyn M. Simpson and George R. Potter, 10 vols. (Berkeley: University of California Press, 1954), 7:68–69.

England and its vitality: "Religion is not a *melancholy*; the spirit of God is not a *dampe*; the Church is not a *grave*," he reminds his audience. "It is a *fold*," he insists, "it is an *Arke*, it is a *net*, it is a *city*."[48] Even death is described in consolatory terms: "This life shall be a gallery into a better roome, and deliver us over to a better Country."[49] Whether Donne's audiences were convinced by his declarations or not is another matter entirely and one that cannot be settled with any degree of certainty. Yet evidence from even this compressed sample suggests his repeated attempts to urge perseverance and optimism on his auditors.

What a marked contrast, then, is his final sermon, *Deaths Duell*.[50] With one foot in the grave, Donne refuses the redemptive stance that characterizes his earlier sermons and presents his audience with a ghoulish memento mori.[51] He writes:

> We must al passe this *posthume* death, this *death* after *death*, nay, this death after buriall, this *dissolution* after *dissolution*, this death of *corruption* and *putrifaction*, of *vermiculation* and *incineration*, of *dissolution* and *dispersion* in and *from* the *grave*, when these bodies that have beene the *children* of *royall parents*, and the *parents* of *royall children*, must say with *Job, Corruption thou art my father*, and *to the Worme thou art my mother and my sister*. *Miserable riddle*, when the *same worme* must bee *my mother*, and *my sister*, and *myselfe*. *Miserable incest*, when I must bee maried to my *mother* and my *sister*, and bee both *father* and *mother* to my *owne mother* and *sister*, *beget* and *beare* that *worme* which is all that *miserable penury*; when my *mouth* shall be *filled* with *dust*, and the *worme* shall *feed*, and *feed sweetely* upon me.[52]

Ample are the horrors on which the passage lingers such that one could almost concede Stanley Fish's provocative claim that "Donne is sick and his poetry is sick" or T. S. Eliot's derisive description of Donne as the "Reverend

---

48. Ibid., 6:152.

49. Ibid., 3:203.

50. Although the manuscript is not known to have survived, several scholars insist that Donne prepared it for press and intended its posthumous publication. See Helen Gardner, "Dean Donne's Monument in St. Paul's," in *Evidence in Literary Scholarship: Essays in Memory of James Marshall Osborn*, ed. René Welleck and Alvaro Ribeiro (Oxford: Clarendon Press, 1979), 29–44, esp. 34; Bevan, "*Hebdomada Mortium*," 188; and Donne, *Sermons*, 10:275–76.

51. Although Donne incorporates macabre descriptions in a few earlier sermons, his final sermon persists as an anomaly. On the curiously anti-redemptive qualities of *Deaths Duell*, see Judith H. Anderson, "Body of Death: The Pauline Inheritance in Donne's Sermons, Spenser's Maleger, and Milton's Sin and Death," in *Rhetorics of Bodily Disease and Health in Medieval and Early Modern England*, ed. Jennifer Vaught (Farnham, UK: Ashgate, 2010), 171–92.

52. Donne, *Deaths Duell*, D2v–D3r.

Billy Sunday of his time, the flesh creeper, the sorcerer of emotional orgy."[53] Analytic readings only multiply the terrors. Attending to the peculiar placement of "sweetely," for instance, Kimberly Johnson observes how the "decomposing body is registered as a material artefact, one that is fully available to the suite of perceptual senses," as Donne's auditors are summoned "to reflect on the flavour of a corpse."[54]

Yet it is not the sermon's preoccupation with putrefaction that animates its affective charge. Rather, the exquisite tension that Donne identifies as inherent to decomposition generates the effect, a process that collapses distinctions and violates boundaries, while simultaneously preserving those same categories (e.g., relationships and identity) in the postmortem universe. Metamorphosing *"my mother*, and *my sister*, and *myselfe"* into a perverse trinity, he cloaks both bigamy and incest in the holy sacrament of marriage. At other moments, Donne collapses yet reifies notions of identity that include gender as he alternately imagines his corpse squarely as himself and also as the worm that both *"beget*[s] and *beare*[s]." But he can only achieve the requisite revulsion by presupposing that a worm with its obscene, defiling mouth possesses a mother and sufficient sentience to be distressed by the macabre affair. To accomplish this, Donne's rhetoric relies on a synecdochic connection between the future worm and the current addressee such that the former maintains an essential quality of the latter.

Winding worms and wombs together in another passage, Donne explains how both come to signify death: "Our very *birth* and entrance into this life is, *exitus à morte*, an *issue from death*, for in our mothers *wombe* wee are *dead so*, as that wee doe *not know* wee *live*, not so much as wee doe in our *sleepe*, neither is there any *grave* so close, or so *putrid a prison*, as the *wombe* would be unto us, if we stayed in it *beyond* our time, or dyed there *before* our time. In the *grave* the *wormes* do not kill us, wee *breed* and *feed*, and then *kill* those wormes which wee our selves produc'd."[55] As Donne diminishes the distance between the suffocating enclosure of the womb and the grave, he characterizes fertility as inherently monstrous. The corpse bears an unsettling congruence to the pregnant body insofar as it generates and nourishes the worms that, in an

---

53. Stanley Fish, "Masculine Persuasive Force: Donne and Verbal Power," in *Soliciting Interpretation: Literary Theory and Seventeenth-Century English Poetry*, ed. Elizabeth D. Harvey and Katharine Eisaman Maus (Chicago: University of Chicago Press, 1990), 223–52, quote from 223; and T. S. Eliot, "Lancelot Andrewes," in *Selected Essays: New Edition* (New York: Harcourt, Brace, 1950), 289–300, quote from 292.

54. Kimberly Johnson, "The Persistence of the Flesh in *Deaths Duell*," in *Shakespeare Up Close: Reading Early Modern Texts*, ed. Russ McDonald, Nicholas D. Nace, and Travis D. Williams (London: Bloomsbury, 2012), 64–69, quote from 66.

55. Donne, *Deaths Duell*, B3r–B3v.

approximation of infanticide, it then kills. In this way, his sermon contaminates life with the corporeal threats of death and decay.

But to what end does Donne depict these grotesqueries, generating feelings of revulsion and despair in the process? It would seem that he does so to edify his audience. Discussing the efficacy of aversive conditioning in the early modern world, Barbara Correll explains that it functions by associating feelings of disgust with undesirable behaviors such that desired ones are "performed without reflexivity."[56] Corpses, as Cynthia Turner Camp observes, not only inspire aversion but also urge subjects to contemplate their actions: "Dead flesh and its volatile thingness circumvent rational intellection to strike at the hindbrain, generating in the viewer a horror, pity and ethical self-reflection capable of generating true renovation."[57] As Donne elicits disgust from his Whitehall audience, reason demands that he does so to persuade them toward improved behavior. Indeed, what distinguishes the sermon from other genres of public speech, Jeanne Shami notes, is the focus on "moving and persuading hearers to spiritual conversion."[58] To achieve this, the sermon progresses through "stages of penitence or consolation" before the minister brings the devout to "a kind of emotional resolution or catharsis."[59] It ought to follow, then, that Donne dwells on decomposition to move his auditors toward an equally dramatic but critically redemptive conclusion. Yet this is the point at which his motives seem altogether muddled, for neither a change in heart nor in behavior will stave off the horrors that he has predicted for his audience and himself. To make use of Camp's phrasing, "true renovation" does nothing to mitigate Donne's frightful prophecy. As the heightened rhetoric spurs a peculiar kind of purposelessness, other questions surface: Why would a minister terrify his audience? What is produced by foregrounding the inability to temper a most distressing outcome? And how does all of this relate to the matter of vengeance?

To explore the mechanisms by which emotions might have circulated in Donne's 1631 audience and their connection to civil vengeance, I turn now to bioneurological models of affect contagion and their early modern analogues. Insofar as this chapter understands circulated feelings as a form of civil vengeance, I must first explain the mechanisms by which emotional transmis-

---

56. Correll, *The End of Conduct*, 24.

57. Cynthia Turner Camp, "The Temporal Excesses of Dead Flesh," *Postmedieval* 4, no. 4 (2013): 416–26, quote from 425.

58. Jeanne Shami, "The Sermon," in *The Oxford Handbook of John Donne*, ed. Jeanne Shami, Dennis Flynn, and M. Thomas Hester (Oxford: Oxford University Press, 2011), 318–37, quote from 325.

59. Hunt, *The Art of Hearing*, 81.

sion occurs. Mimicry, a largely unintentional mode of communication that underpins social interactions, is perhaps most familiar as a mode of affect contagion.[60] Mimicry functions such that the movements, gestures, and facial expressions exhibited by an actor stimulate identical neural networks of spectators (or companions) as if they were performing the action themselves.[61] As Anna Gibbs argues, "sympathetic modes of communication not only persist alongside linguistic modes but they also inhabit and actively shape them."[62] Another mode of affect contagion occurs via chemical signals, or pheromones, which are processed in the nasal cavity.[63] Teresa Brennan contends that individuals modify an environment through the chemical signals they emit, and those who come into contact with the environment undergo changes as a result.[64] "The transmission of affect, if only for an instant," Brennan writes, "alters the biochemistry and neurology of the subject. The 'atmosphere' or the environment literally gets into the 'individual.'"[65] In the process of respiration, individuals inhale atmosphere, made up of substances that include pheromones, and in response to these chemical signals but without awareness of that response, subjects exhibit autonomic and behavioral changes.[66] Following these effects, individuals feel anxious or aroused, joyful or enraged. Thus, the transmission of affect relies on environment, individual human bodies, and their concomitant biological reactions.

Although the world of Donne may seem incompatible with contemporary neuroscience, accounts of affect contagion are readily observable in early

60. Gibbs, "After Affect," 186–205. See also Ulf Dimberg, Monika Thunberg, and Sara Grunedal, "Facial Reactions to Emotional Stimuli: Automatically Controlled Emotional Responses," *Cognition and Emotion* 16, no. 4 (2002): 449–71.

61. Gibbs, "After Affect," 196. For scholarship that underscores the connection between mimicry and emotional contagion, see Elaine Hatfield, Richard L. Rapson, and Yen-Chi L. Le, "Emotional Contagion and Empathy," in *The Social Neuroscience of Empathy*, ed. Jean Decety and William Ickes (Cambridge, MA: MIT Press, 2009), 19–30; and Veronika Engert, Franzika Plessow, Robert Miller, Clemens Kirschbaum, and Tania Singer, "Cortisol Increase in Empathic Stress Is Modulated by Emotional Closeness and Observation Modality," *Psychoneuroendocrinology* 45 (2014): 192–201.

62. Gibbs, "After Affect," 199.

63. Pheromones are secreted chemical signals that communicate with and enact changes in members of the same species. Recent scientific studies suggest that pheromones cause significant autonomic and behavioral changes in human subjects without stimulating their olfactory receptors. Pheromones are not "smelled" but exert their effects through the vomeronasal system in the nasal cavity, which includes the VNO organ, the vomeronasal-terminalis nerves, and the hypothalamic and limbic system structures. See Bernard I. Grosser, Louis Monti-Bloch, Clive Jennigs-White, and David L. Berliner, "Behavioral and Electrophysiological Effects of Androstadienone, a Human Pheromone," *Psychoneuroendocrinology* 25, no. 3 (2000): 289–99; and Kathleen Stern and Martha K. McClintock, "Regulation of Ovulation by Human Pheromones," *Nature* 392, no. 6672 (12 March 1998): 177–79.

64. Teresa Brennan, *The Transmission of Affect* (Ithaca, NY: Cornell University Press, 2004), 69.

65. Ibid., 1.

66. Ibid., 69.

modern culture and have been amply documented.[67] By reviewing such accounts, we can visualize the mechanisms of affect contagion as understood by Donne and his contemporaries.[68] Helkiah Crooke's *Microcosmographia, A Description of the Body of Man* presents an early modern analogue to the process that Brennan calls "chemical entrainment," in which pheromones transmit affects that may then lead to particular emotions. Crooke writes: "Even as our spirites are refreshed and exhilarated with sweete savours, not by apprehending the s[c]ent of them; but by receiving a thinne ayrie vapour from them whereby the spirites are nourished, enlightened and strengthened."[69] Here, Crooke draws a causal link between emotion (i.e., "spirites") and scent such that pleasing smells, though not consciously recognized, prompt discernible changes in mood.

But scent was believed to influence not only emotions but also the corporeal body. Addressing the early modern scorpion theory—the belief that smelling a basil plant would produce a scorpion in one's brain—Crooke postulates that undetectable elements or "seedes" in the environment penetrate the body via respiration, initiating radical physiological changes:

> That an odour attayneth really unto the braine may be proved; because such odours do sometimes helpe and sometime hurt. The detriment seemeth not to proceed from the odour but from the quality of the subject which accompanieth the odour, that is, the exhalation . . . Neither doeth the quality onely of exhalation affect the braine, but sometimes some seedes of the very substance of bodies that are of subtle partes are transported in the exhalation, which setling in the braine brings foorth fearefull accidents and strange effects, as it did in him who smelling oft upon Basill had a Scorpion bred in his braine. It is therefore necessary we should beleeve that the odour is really *perceived* by the organ.[70]

For Crooke, an odor's qualities derive from the subject's "subtle partes" that are transported in the process of respiration. His usage of "fearefull accidents" and "strange effects" implies a relationship to affect in which the subject is not wholly agential, that affects, in other words, may potentially hijack the body. Though the scorpion theory is as imaginative as it is inaccurate, its persistence suggests an underlying belief that our environments affect us, and we, in turn,

---

67. See, for example, the scholarship of James, Brennan, and Hobgood.

68. For studies on early modern smell, see Jonathan Gil Harris, *Untimely Matter in the Time of Shakespeare* (Philadelphia: University of Pennsylvania Press, 2009), 119–40; and Holly Dugan, *The Ephemeral History of Perfume: Scent and Sense in Early Modern England* (Baltimore: Johns Hopkins University Press, 2011).

69. Helkiah Crooke, *Microcosmographia, or, a Description of the Body of Man* (London: William Jaggard, 1615), 251; and Brennan, *The Transmission of Affect*, 9.

70. Crooke, *Microcosmographia*, 712.

possess the ability to affect our environments.[71] And insofar as the early modern world attributes great power to smell, it presupposes not impervious bodies but rather ones that are malleable, fluid, and partially constituted by their surroundings. Indeed, this is a world receptive to contagious affect in a way that would be corroborated and refined by modern science centuries later.

Because both contemporary affect theory and early modern theorizations of smell propose that emotions are diffused through and elicited by environments, I turn now to the atmosphere Donne creates in his delivery of *Deaths Duell* and read it as an example of civil vengeance. Writing from the perspective of Donne's audience, Targoff describes the event as coercive participation in "a confrontation for which we have had no warning, and in which we may not have been prepared to engage."[72] The squeamishness extends to scholars who, if they make mention of the sermon's peculiar qualities, transmute them into something else altogether.[73] Although Simpson and John Carey acknowledge the macabre aspects in *Deaths Duell*, they focus on psychological assessments of the author.[74] Donald Ramsay Roberts acknowledges that there is "more than a tinge of morbid absorption in the physical decay" but does not pursue further its effects.[75] In his examination of Donne's remarks on death in public address, Arnold Stein omits any mention of such matters.[76] Still other critics insist on the sermon's redemptive message. James R. Keller, for instance, interprets Donne's unsavory preoccupations in light of alchemical science, while Felecia Wright McDuffie reads them as inflected by medieval philosophies of bodily resurrection.[77] And although Targoff concedes that the sermon's "alarming intensity . . . may indeed make the flesh creep," she insists that its eschatological message—Christians will be resurrected with all their parts intact—is a "forceful affirmation of resurrection."[78] Collectively speaking,

---

71. Michael Hardt, "Foreword: What Affects Are Good For," in Clough and Halley, *The Affective Turn*, ix–xiii, esp. ix.

72. Targoff, *John Donne, Body and Soul*, 161.

73. For a notable exception, see Blaine Greteman, "'All This Seed Pearl': John Donne and Bodily Presence," *College Literature* 37, no. 3 (2010): 26–42, esp. 35.

74. According to Simpson, one of Donne's major psychological shortcomings was his "morbid obsession with the idea of death" (*A Study of the Prose Works*, 65). John Carey speculates that Donne "enjoyed giving his congregation the horrors," and that "terror afforded him a histrionic triumph" (*John Donne: Life, Mind, and Art* [New York: Oxford University Press, 1981], 134).

75. Donald Ramsay Roberts, "The Death Wish of John Donne," *PMLA* 62, no. 4 (1947): 958–76, quote from 963.

76. Arnold Stein, "Handling Death: John Donne in Public Meditation," *English Literary History* 48, no. 3 (1981): 496–515.

77. James R. Keller, "The Science of Salvation: Spiritual Alchemy in Donne's Final Sermon," *Sixteenth Century Journal* 23, no. 3 (1992): 486–93; and Felecia Wright McDuffie, *To Our Bodies Then We Turn: Body as Word and Sacrament in the Works of John Donne* (New York: Continuum, 2005), 85.

78. Targoff, *John Donne, Body and Soul*, 161.

scholarship has avoided a confrontation with the internal contradiction of *Deaths Duell*: that the sermon diffuses an unarticulated and unresolved anxiety through the congregation, an affect at odds with the emotions it presumably sought to inculcate.

After all, to believe Targoff's recuperative claim, one must overlook the fact that redemption is relegated to one sentence in *Deaths Duell*: "And by *recompacting* this *dust* into the *same body*, and *reanimating* the *same body* with the *same soule*, hee shall . . . establish me into a life that shall last as long as the *Lord of life* himselfe."[79] As Donne repeats "same" three times, he reinforces an early Christian belief in material continuity, the notion that resurrected bodies will comprise their *"same"* earthly parts. But, as Targoff herself observes, the material continuity extends only to Donne insofar as he concludes the sentence with a singular first-person pronoun.[80] Although the shift focuses the audience on his diseased body displayed before them, it also excludes them from God's redemptive promise. Indeed, by minimizing the sermon's focus on resurrection, Donne manipulates the emotions of his auditors, directing them toward intense feelings of paralysis and anxiety as well as thwarting their expectations for his homily. And as the sermon generates an intense fear of an unceasing *"death* after *death**," Donne changes the chemistry of the environment and effects accompanying bioneurological changes in his addressees.

Undeterred by the presence of Charles I in his audience, Donne imagines the postmortem indignities reserved for a sovereign: "That the *Monarch*, who spred over many nations alive, must in his dust lye in a corner of that *sheete of lead*, and there, but so long as that lead will laste, and that privat and *retir'd man*, that thought himselfe his owne for ever, and never came forth, must in his dust of the grave bee published, and (such are the *revolutions* of the *grave*) bee mingled with the dust of every high way, and of every dunghill, and swallowed in every puddle and pond. This is the most inglorious and contemptible *vilification*, the most deadly and peremptory *nullification* of man, that wee can consider."[81] As Hamlet did before an aghast Claudius, Donne conjures a nightmare of class-crossing that is produced through the synecdochic relationship between dust and monarch. "High way" and "dunghill" emerge as metonyms for commoners, and the latter term mingles the dust of the revered sovereign with waste. His remains, coterminous with the sovereign himself, become fodder for all that lives in "puddle and pond," while "every" underscores the humiliating democratization of his body. When Donne substitutes

---

79. Donne, *Deaths Duell*, D4r–D4v.
80. Targoff, *John Donne, Body and Soul*, 172.
81. Donne, *Deaths Duell*, D3v.

"man" for "monarch," he universalizes the degradation such that the emotions generated on behalf of the sovereign—outrage, repugnance, anxiety, shame—extend to audience members themselves.

As Donne declares the biological process of decomposition to be the "most inglorious and contemptible *vilification* . . . that wee can consider," he moves his auditors to indignation with his characteristic reliance on the superlative. But to whom or what does Donne direct that indignation? The answer to this question puts us back within reach of civil vengeance. He writes: "Truely the consideration of this *posthume Death*, this death after buriall, that after God (with whom are the *issues of death*) hath delivered me from the *death* of the *Wombe*, by bringing mee into the *world*, and from the manifold deaths of the *world*, by laying me in the *grave*, I must dye againe in an *Incineration* of this *flesh*, and in a dispersion of that dust."[82] Here, God delivers us from two deaths: death in the womb (through birth) and the "manifold deaths of the *world*" (through death). In life and in death, God rescues his own, and the parenthetical—a variation of the refrain to which his sermon is devoted ("Unto God the Lord belong the issues of death" from Psalm 68:20)—reinforces this conclusion.[83] But inconsistencies arise in the final independent clause that trouble a tidy reading. What (or who) compels "me" to die again in the process of decomposition? And might these subsequent deaths complicate Donne's prior claims? Although the passage's parallel structure connects the "from" and "by" prepositional phrases, we might also read or—as his audience did—hear another association within the unwieldy sentence: "By laying me in the grave, I must die again in an incineration of this flesh, and in a dispersion of that dust."[84] If we then read "by laying me in the *grave*" as dependent on the clause that follows it, we encounter the unexpected presence of a misplaced modifier. Within the logic of the passage, "I" do not lay myself in the grave; God does. This grammatical and syntactical confusion obscures the fact that the one who delivers is also the one who compels "me" to die again. Put another way, God's deliverance of "me" from the "manifold deaths" is also that which obliges "me" to undergo the subsequent deaths of incineration and dispersion. And it is these subsequent deaths to which he devotes the bulk of his sermon, focusing not on the eventual reprieve but on excruciating humiliation.

---

82. Ibid.

83. Donne selected the sermon's scripture; see Targoff, *John Donne, Body and Soul*, 162.

84. Indeed, the 1633 publication encourages reading the passage as two independent clauses, for there are two spaces, rather than one, immediately preceding the "by laying me" phrase—spacing consistent with the usage of semicolons, colons, and periods in the manuscript. See *Deaths Duell, or A Consolation to the Soule, against the Dying Life, and Living Death of the Body* (London: B. Alsop and T. Fawcet, 1633), C4v.

Donne's fastidious attention to the postmortem treatment of Christ's body only exacerbates the issue, and I offer two passages below for comparative analysis. Addressing what preserved Christ's body, Donne concludes, "This *incorruption* then was not in *Josephs gummes* and *spices*, nor was it in *Christs* innocency, and *exemption* from *originall sin*, nor was it . . . in the *hypostaticall union* . . . Wee looke no further for *causes* or *reasons* in the *mysteries* of *religion*, but to the *will* and pleasure of *God* . . . *Christs* body did *not see corruption*, therefore, because *God* had *decreed* it shold not."[85] Shortly thereafter, Donne turns his attention to our predicament: "'Tis true that original sinne hath induced this corruption and *incineration* upon us; If wee had not sinned in Adam . . . we had had our *transmigration* from this to the other world without any *mortality*, any *corruption at all*."[86] Given their proximity in *Deaths Duell*, these passages reveal a curious disparity. Although the stain of original sin precludes our transmigration without corruption, the absence of it in Christ was not what preserved his physical body. Rather, it was, according to Donne, the *"will and pleasure of God."* The incongruity becomes more apparent in the second passage. There in the first clause, "we" are the objects on whom original sin acts, and this construction allows "us" to cede much of our responsibility for this punishment. Whereas "we" is the active subject in the second clause, "we" errs only symbolically in the failure of Adam. Donne does not locate, in other words, the justification for the punishment in sins actively committed by his auditors. And this absent justification only intensifies the horrors of vermiculation on which he meditates. At the same time, he makes no mention of God here—in stark contrast to the first passage—as if to diminish his agency in the situation, even as, according to the logic he has set forth, God bears responsibility for this consequence. As a result, then, there is a tacit sense throughout these passages that a wrong, some kind of injustice, is being perpetuated which Donne seems to process during the sermon.

In coercing auditors into meditating on the inevitable violence visited on the good and bad alike, *Deaths Duell* transmits a frightful vision about which one can do nothing. Thanks to the rhetorical energy Donne devotes to the inevitability of postmortem horrors, he moves his audience to great outrage, grief, and dread on behalf of abused monarchs, for those who have already passed and, ultimately, for themselves. To elicit these dramatic reactions, he depicts an unceasing punishment in vertiginous detail and then, abruptly, pulls his addressees back from the precipice of heretical outrage with the orthodoxy of the psalm's refrain. That is, the tension exists between the sermon's

---

85. Donne, *Deaths Duell*, D1r.
86. Ibid., sig. C4r.

fixation on decay, the attendant anxiety arising from this reality, and finally, the repeated reminder that God is in charge of death. Though he could deliver us from this postmortem nightmare, he does not. It is neither his will nor pleasure to choose otherwise. Even as Donne articulates no explicit criticism, the scaffolding for it is nevertheless visible.

However, this is not to suggest that Donne puts forth a deliberately heretical stance or that he intentionally inflicts negative emotions on his audience. If we can approach *Deaths Duell* unimpeded by assumptions of authorial intentionality or notions of what sermons ought to do, we can visualize more clearly what the text accomplishes in terms of civil vengeance and how it circulates ugly feelings. As for what Donne may have gained from dwelling on unpleasantries, let us consider a detail from Sigmund Freud's *Beyond the Pleasure Principle* to illuminate the triangulation among God, minister, and congregation: "It can also be observed that the unpleasurable nature of an experience does not always unsuit it for play. If the doctor looks down a child's throat or carries out some small operation on him, we may be quite sure that these frightening experiences will be the subject of the next game; but we must not in that connection overlook the fact that there is a yield of pleasure from another source. As the child passes over from the passivity of the experience to the activity of the game, he hands on the disagreeable experience to one of his playmates and in this way revenges himself on a substitute."[87] In his analysis of the savage play of small children, Freud proposes by way of digression at least three items of interest for our examination of vengeance in *Deaths Duell*. First, he identifies how hierarchal power structures may prohibit a "wronged" individual from taking vengeance. A child may retaliate against the doctor with as much success as Donne might have had against God. The second point is a consequence of the first: the hierarchal challenges of avenging oneself are then channeled into the social interactions with one's peers, be they "playmates" or congregants. An out-of-reach target does little to quell the impulse toward revenge, yet lateral replacements are readily available. That is, Freud's anecdote informs my notion of substitutive vengeance. Even as the revenge dynamic and its causal agent (i.e., the doctor's visit) may be obvious to curious onlookers, there is nothing to suggest in his account that the children themselves are aware of or intending retribution, and this observation brings me to my final point: one need not be conscious of one's vengeful inklings in order to transmit civil vengeance. Whereas Freud's child works through physical revenge in her reenactment of the frustrating business of a doctor's visit,

---

87. Sigmund Freud, *Beyond the Pleasure Principle*, trans. and ed. James Strachey (New York: W. W. Norton, 1989), 16–17.

Donne's emotional vengeance operates along a similar, though not identical, logic. If he experienced great anxiety concerning his looming death, he might have "mastered" that trepidation and terror by passing it along to his congregation in the same way. As I have traced how Donne both reifies and erases God's culpability for the postmortem punishments that await all, regardless of behavior or belief, *Deaths Duell* reveals profound ambivalence and deep frustration. And in the near-obsessive rehearsal of this logic before his auditors along with his diminished focus on redemption, he transfers negative emotions that cannot be directed toward God. Thus, the actual target of aggression (i.e., God) is missed, and the social body serves as both proxy and vehicle for this contagious vengeance.

Hypothesizing how revulsion, terror, and even vengeance might be transmitted throughout Donne's congregation is a risky endeavor because these claims are impossible to substantiate fully. And audiences—early modern or otherwise—are not monoliths but are composed of individuals. Remarking on the "personal nature of sensations and feelings" of early modern audiences, Bruce R. Smith writes, "They are the possessions of individuals . . . and cannot be generalized."[88] To complicate matters further, we might also consider Sara Ahmed's argument that a subject's orientation to the object in question determines her consequent emotions and thereby accounts for the uneven, contingent process of transmission.[89] Furthermore, there is much that scholars are unable to verify regarding the sermon's delivery. One cannot know the particular gestures that Donne deployed on that day, even as we have records that indicate gesture-laden sermons were characteristic of his delivery style. One cannot discern individual responses to *Deaths Duell* or determine the Whitehall pulpit from which he preached.[90] One cannot know fully how the crowd's atmosphere felt or even smelled.

Despite our temporal distance from that Friday afternoon in 1631, artifacts remain that reveal something of the environment as well as of Donne's effect on his audience. Proposing that Donne's excellence as a preacher derived from his aptitude for extralingual communication, poet and clergyman Jasper Mayne apostrophizes:

---

88. Bruce R. Smith, *Phenomenal Shakespeare* (Malden, MA: Wiley-Blackwell, 2010), 7.

89. Sara Ahmed, "Happy Objects," in Gregg and Seigworth, *The Affect Theory Reader*, 29–51.

90. Donne would have preached either from the King's Chapel pulpit or the outdoor pulpit. Because, as Peter McCullough argues, Lenten sermons took the place of plays as attractive public events for Londoners, it is likely that Donne preached his final sermon in the outdoor "Preaching Place," which held at least 2,000 individuals (*Sermons at Court: Politics and Religion in Elizabethan and Jacobean Preaching* [Cambridge: Cambridge University Press, 1998], 134). See also Targoff, *John Donne, Body and Soul*, 176–77.

Yet have I seene thee in the pulpit stand,
Where wee might take notes, from thy looke, and hand;
And from thy speaking action beare away
More Sermon, then some teachers use to say.
Such was thy carriage, and thy gesture such,
As could divide the heart, and conscience touch.
Thy motion did confute, and wee might see
An errour vanquish'd by delivery.[91]

I invite us to read Mayne's curious phrase "thy speaking action" as an admission that Donne's gestures themselves communicate in a manner not unlike the chemical signals released by him and his audience. And, insofar as the nonverbal expressions "beare away" more sermon than other ministers might preach, Mayne indicates their depth, worth, and reach. In particular, it is his "looke" and "hand," not the spoken text, that prompt his audience's notetaking, while his "carriage" and "gesture" stimulate spiritual transformations (i.e., "errour vanquish'd"). From the perspective of affect theory, we know that his body language had the capacity to stimulate the neural networks of his congregation as well. By marveling at the efficacy of Donne's extralingual communication, Mayne reveals to us the relevance of these subtle modes: posture, look, gestures, or even pheromones.

In his description of the delivery of *Deaths Duell*, Donne's biographer Izaak Walton extends another artifact to us: "And when to the amazement of some beholders he appeared in the Pulpit, many thought he presented himself not to preach mortification by a living voice, but mortality by a decayed body and dying face. And doubtlesse many did secretly ask that question in *Ezekiel, Do these bones live?*"[92] Here, Walton represents Donne's appearance as a speaking action insofar as the sermon's efficacy is achieved through the arresting spectacle of a living corpse in the pulpit. Though attenuated, his voice withstood the rigors of preaching, as he transmitted something beyond the sermon's text to his audience. "After some faint pauses in his zealous prayer," Walton recalls, "his strong desires enabled his weake body to discharge his memory of his preconceived meditations . . . Many that then saw his teares, and heard his hollow voice, professing they thought the Text prophetically chosen, and

91. Jasper Mayne, "On Dr. Donnes Death," in *Poems*, by John Donne (London: Printed by M[iles] F[lesher], 1633), Eeer–Eee2v, quote from Eee2r.

92. Izaak Walton, *The Life of John Donne, Dr. in Divinity, and Late Dean of Saint Pauls Church London* (London: J. G., 1658), F2v. For an interrogation of Walton's familiarity with Donne, see Jessica Martin, *Walton's Lives: Conformist Commemorations and the Rise of Biography* (Oxford: Oxford University Press, 2011), 169.

that *Dr. Donne had preach't his own funerall Sermon.*"[93] For Walton, Donne's "strong desires" propel the sermon's delivery as if the emotional surplus overcomes the limitations of his fragile body. What captures Walton's attention in particular are the tears and hollow quality of Donne's voice, and, like Mayne, he attends less to the sermon's content and more to its emotional delivery.

In *Treatise of the Affections, or, The Soules Pulse Wherby a Christian May Know Whether He Be Living or Dying*, Essex minister William Fenner issues a defense of emotional sermon deliveries. By eliciting the congregation's affections or emotions, Fenner maintains, a minister produces not only physical but also spiritual transformations: "Yea, the affections make humours, bloud, spirits, members, even bones and all the body for to suffer. Hence it is, when a man sets his affections upon God, *his feare*, the feare of God makes him *tremble*, his *Love*, the love of God makes him to *weepe for his sinnes.*"[94] Perhaps it is for a similar reason that Donne explicitly demands his audience to weep in *Deaths Duell*: "If thou didst any thing that needed Peters teares, and hast *not shed them*, let me be thy *Cock*, doe it now, Now, thy *Master* (in the unworthiest of his servants) *lookes back upon thee*, doe it now."[95] As Donne himself was crying, if Walton's account is to be trusted, his admonishment compels his congregation to mimic his affective performance and thereby effects a transference in his addressees that makes use of both the sermon's text (i.e., the specific command to weep) and its delivery (i.e., Donne's own tears).

It is also significant that Donne's command presupposes that the mark of one's spiritual transformation is gauged not by words of prayer or promise but by one's affective display. Though many preachers believed this to be true of weeping, early modern medicine, an unlikely ally, corroborates the perspective as well. In *Microcosmographia*, Crooke explains that tears are produced

> when we rub our eyes, or by the coldnesse of the ayre, or by the winde, or by some griefe of minde and weeping fit; at which times they drop out like plentifull sweate, or rather like a bubling streame through those holes which we saide before were formed in the terminations of the brims of the eye-lids: for at such times the muscles of the face and of adjacent parts doe contract themselves sometimes with wayling and mourning sometimes without; sometimes the Respiration being cut off in the middest with a sobbing stay and the voice broken about the

---

93. Walton, *The Life of John Donne*, F3r.

94. William Fenner, *Treatise of the Affections, or, The Soules Pulse Wherby a Christian May Know Whether He Be Living or Dying* (London: R. H., 1642), B3r–B3v.

95. Donne, *Deaths Duell*, F4v.

top of the *Larynx*, yea sometimes quite intercepted: and thus is this matter of the teares moved by Expression.[96]

In approaching crying as a wholly mechanical phenomenon, one generated by either external or internal stimulation, Crooke's formulation refuses the possibility that tears could be disingenuous, that they could be accessories to a studied performance. Despite the constitutive uncertainty of what prompts another's tears—for one's sins? for lacking the requisite distress for these sins? because others cry? for an unrelated event or person altogether?—weeping appears as a reliable indicator of internal turmoil in the early modern world. The critical leap that Donne makes is that emotions and their affective displays function as the guarantors of inward belief; they afford access to truth. Furthermore, insofar as "expression" or "some griefe of minde" might cause tears, the passage underscores the complex interaction between the physical body and private feeling, connecting the ephemerality of emotions to respiration, facial contortions, vocal muscles, and eye movements. In the production of tears, grief is just as pressing and potent as a foreign object in one's eye, and tears bridge the internal world of private feeling and the external atmosphere of Whitehall and its congregation. In this manner, Crooke signals the imbrication of the physical and emotional bodies in the early modern world.

Insofar as Donne points his congregation to something beyond the text and demands that his audience supplement the sermon with their tears, he draws attention to what exists beyond the sermon's linguistic content. Even as affect theory cannot grant us access to that ephemeral moment of delivery—the tears cried by Donne and his congregation have long since dried—this methodological approach enables us to visualize that possibility most clearly. As we expand our object of study to circulated emotions and sensations, we also foster our capacity to engage the ephemera of some forms of civil vengeance and visualize their consequences. By aligning civil vengeance with emotional contagion, I offer a mode by which one could transmit uncomfortable feelings through language and, unconsciously, through physiological responses to words, gestures, tone, and atmosphere. Contagious vengeance, then, positions revenge as a disease—rather than a willful desire or intended action—that can be contracted by and disseminated throughout the social body. And the communicability of civil vengeance pushes it beyond arithmetic retaliation, complicating the elegance of a quid pro quo exchange. Moreover, the communicability of civil vengeance also means that its targets do not remain stable—we see this most explicitly in the manner in which Donne "misses"

---

96. Crooke, *Microcosmographia*, 539–40.

God and makes use of his congregation as a proxy. Building on this foundation in my next chapter, I explore how the logic of revenge sanctions and manifests as preemptive violence enacted by a social body against a minoritized group. And insofar as community ties are strengthened in the sharing of negative affects—that is, social groups cohere through negative affects and acts—civil vengeance also functions as that which proves one's membership to a local community or emergent nation-state.

CHAPTER 3

Fantasizing about Revenge
Vagrancy and the Formation
of the Social Body in
Shakespeare's *2 Henry VI*
and Nashe's
The Unfortunate Traveller

Idleness, Robert Burton declares in *The Anatomy of Melancholy*, is "the *malus genius* of our nation."[1] The early modern world regarded the vice as symptomatic not only of psychological and physical maladies but also of spiritual ones. In fact, much of the anxiety it provoked was distinctly Protestant, its origins located in Martin Luther's writings,[2] and religious doctrine reaffirmed the cultural intolerance of idleness and, by extension, vagrancy.[3] Consider Adam Hill's 1593 sermon at Paul's Cross:

> Idlenesse is an other sinne which crieth for vengeance, against which *Paul* thus writeth: *Wee command you in the name of Christ Jesus, that ye withdraw your selves from every Brother which walketh inordinately, and not after the institution he hath received of us: for ye your selves know, how yee ought to follow us, for we behaved not our selves inordinately amongst you; neither tooke wee bread of any man for nought, for wee wrought with labour and travaile* . . . *For wee heard that there were some amongst you which walke inordinately and*

---

1. Burton, *The anatomy of melancholy*, 53. Elsewhere Burton writes: "There is no greater cause of Melancholy than idlenesse, *no better cure than businesse*" (6).

2. As Paola Pugliatti explains, because Luther associated begging with Catholic pietism, he aimed to abolish it in favor of establishing poor relief (*Beggary and Theatre in Early Modern England* [Aldershot, UK: Ashgate, 2003], 60).

3. Examples include the following letters from St. Paul: 2 Thessalonians (3:6–12) and 1 Thessalonians (4:9–11).

worke not at all, but are busie bodies: therefore them that are such, we com-
maunde and exhort by our Lord Jesus Christ, that they worke with quietnesse,
and eate their owne bread.[4]

Exemplified by an unwillingness to "labour and travaile" for one's own bread, the sin of idleness manifests itself as the immoderate walking of these "busie bodies." While the vagrants' perceived parasitism marks them as social antagonists, their precarious status is reinforced further by scriptural dictates that advise the faithful to "withdraw" from their peripatetic brethren. That is, Hill's interpretation of St. Paul's letter promotes a fractured social body and ongoing segregation as punishment for uncooperative members.

But the admonishment is easier preached than practiced, particularly as one considers the relationship of the vagrant to the body politic. In *A Treatise of the Vocations, or, Callings of Men*, William Perkins laments the consequences of their presence in England: "It is a foule disorder in any common wealth that there should be suffered rogues, beggars, vagabonds; for such kind of persons commonly are of no civil societie or corporation, nor of any particular Church: and are as rotten legges, and armes, that droppe from the bodie. Againe to wander up and downe from yeare to yeare to this ende, to seeke and procure bodily maintenance, is no calling, but the life of a beast: and consequently a condition or state of life flatte against the rule; That every one must have a particular calling."[5] By citing the triumvirate of parasitism—rogues, beggars, and vagabonds—Perkins isolates them from the good subjects who rightly belong and contribute to the commonwealth. Indeed, these individuals are defined solely by their not-belonging, interpreted not only as antisocial but also inhuman. Victims of their parasitism are implicit yet extensive: all those associated with the commonwealth suffer from the vagrant. His next simile, which compares them to gangrenous appendages and aligns them with contagion, emphasizes the degree to which they incapacitate the social body and the subsequent difficulty with which the commonwealth attempts to free itself from the encumbrance. While Perkins focuses on the broad effects of individual shortcomings, Burton connects the psychological ailment of melancholy and its origin of idleness to widespread disruptions of the nation-state: "Yet amongst many Roses some Thistles grow, some bad weeds and enormities which much disturbe the peace of this Body politike, and Eclipse the honor and glory of it . . . The first is idlenesse by reason of which wee have

---

4. Adam Hill, *The crie of England A sermon preached at Paules Crosse in September 1593* (London: Ed. Allde, 1595), E1r–E1v.

5. William Perkins, *A Treatise of the vocations, or, Callings of Men* (London: John Legat, 1603), B5v–B6r.

many swarmes of rogues and beggers, thieves, drunkards, and discontented persons, many poore people in all our Townes."[6] By invoking the language of plague and pestilence through his use of "swarmes," Burton emphasizes, as Perkins did before him, both the debilitating effects and the contagious quality of idleness perpetuated by vagrant types.

I begin with this brief cultural foray to gain some sense of the vagrant—a figure aligned with biological disease and social death, a persistent harbinger of discord and decay—and his place within the early modern imaginary. As I turn from an analysis of how individual subjects are trained in and exercise the principles of civil vengeance to the modes by which civil vengeance organizes the social body, this chapter marks a pivot point within the book as a whole. In what follows, I unpack how the vagrant foments social cohesion and even the project of nation-building. For instance, we might look to Burton's deliberate invocation of "our Townes" and how he creates a sense of belonging, a community between the writer and his readers to the exclusion of the intractably idle. Benedict Anderson's concept of "imagined communities" is of relevance here as he underscores the singular importance of fantasy: "[The community] is *imagined* because the members of even the smallest nation will never know most of their fellow members, meet them, or even hear of them, yet in the minds of each lives the image of their communion."[7] But the imaginative connections that sustain communities and their members also fuel the dynamics of social exclusion. Because social cohesion is achieved in part through exclusion, I begin by illustrating how English civil society organizes itself against a so-called parasitic Other while, paradoxically, keeping that vulnerable group in close proximity as an effective scapegoat. For the social problems imagined to be caused by the excluded population—problems that include the consumption of limited resources, crime, and terrorism— normative society justifies its poor treatment of vagrants as retribution. To elaborate the triangulation of vengeance, fantasy, and social cohesion, I read episodes of vagrancy in Shakespeare's *2 Henry VI* through the optic of Giorgio Agamben's concept of the *homo sacer*. The fantasy of victimhood on the part of normative society produces vagrant bodies, I argue, that are constructed to withstand extreme forms of labor and punishment, and the resulting bodies then sustain an expanding nation-state. My reading of Thomas Nashe's *The Unfortunate Traveller, or The Life of Jack Wilton* reveals the dynamic at work on the international stage in the novel's attempts to define early

6. Burton, *The anatomy of melancholy*, 52.

7. Benedict Anderson, *Imagined Communities: Reflections on the Origin and Spread of Nationalism*, rev. ed. (London: Verso, 2006), 6.

modern Englishness against not only the Continent but also cosmopolitanism, which it classifies as a form of vagrancy.

Civil vengeance remains a critical aspect of the formation of the social body, and this chapter specifically concerns itself with fantasy and temporality. By attending to how the fantasy of victimhood is deployed to legitimize injustice against a minoritized group, my chapter also disrupts the traditional teleology of vengeance. The typical temporal logic dictates that one takes revenge for an act that has occurred in the past, and it is precisely this causal relationship in which an injustice precipitates the revenge act that distinguishes retribution from "ordinary" acts of aggression. But in examining the early modern cultural relationship to vagrancy, we will see that vengeance is not always the second item in this equation. If individuals cultivate a fantasy of victimhood—if they believe that others plague them or even that they might—this fantasy entitles them to preemptive retaliation: vengeance that masquerades as "just" punishment, especially when the punitive action aligns with the interests of the state. And it is through the vengeance taken against the vagrant that civil society coalesces.

With this in mind, I wish to return once more to Adam Hill's sermon in which he declares that idleness is a sin that "crieth for vengeance." In the book of Genesis, it is the blood of the murdered Abel that first "crieth for vengeance" to God, and for his misdeed, Cain is condemned to roam unceasingly; scriptural precedent then establishes vagrancy as fitting vengeance for the most terrible of crimes. When Hill argues that idleness similarly merits revenge, it is not that he equates the sin with murder per se but that he gestures toward the early modern belief that those who embodied the sin of idleness (i.e., vagrants) were also presumed to harbor the most criminal impulses: theft, violence, murder, and sedition. Put simply, idleness is never merely idleness but always, as Burton asserts, the nurse to and symptom of all other vices. Given the cultural assumption that vagrants harmed or would harm normative society, such seditious elements deserved commensurately severe punishments from this perspective. Therefore, what Hill's sermon proffers is preemptive vengeance, a concept that will be elaborated further and refined in other cultural materials examined in the chapter.

To whom does the term "vagrant" refer? Derived from the Latin *vagari* (i.e., to wander), the terms "vagrant" and "vagabond" were often used interchangeably in the early modern world, even as they provoked confusion from a legal standpoint.[8] The "gross imprecision" of early modern law, Paul Slack writes,

---

8. Although both terms were used in Tudor and Stuart royal proclamations, "vagabond" was more widely used under James I. It is of note, too, that vagabond and vagabondage have slightly more

"defined vagrancy as 'wandering' or 'loitering' and designated houses of correction for people who were 'idle' or 'disorderly.'"[9] Under this capacious definition, subjects were divided further into the categories of deserving poor and "sturdy beggars," who were presumed sufficiently able-bodied to secure gainful employment. Those who were compelled to rely on charity due to infirmity were provided with licenses and permitted to beg in public areas, while the remainder were targets of local and national authorities. For the sake of consistency, I rely on the term "vagrant" to denote individuals who, lacking homes and consistent employment in fixed locations, move in search of work. Such individuals might also engage in begging (with or without a license) as well as extralegal activities. Insofar as these subjects exist on the social periphery and are often disconnected from normative familial structures, they remain especially vulnerable to physical, emotional, psychic, and legal violence. And although my literary examples of vagrancy are male characters, that reality is not representative of the many female subjects who were categorized as vagrants by London authorities.[10] Finally, I take seriously Paul Cefalu's twofold caution against celebrating vagrancy for its "misrule" and dissociating it from its socioeconomic origins; for this reason, I do not champion the vagrant as a figure of subversion or antisocial antagonism.[11] Instead, I aim to consider how fantasies of victimhood and vengeance attach themselves to this character and consolidate a social body through revenge by anchoring the ensuing discussion of vagrancy to the historical-cultural context from whence it emerges. Agamben's elaboration of the *homo sacer*, or the one "who *may be killed and yet not sacrificed*," provides a valuable framework in explicating the construction of the social body in relation to the vagrant.[12] Existing peripheral to human and divine law, the *homo sacer* "is included in the juridical order . . . solely in the form of its exclusion (that is, of its capacity to be killed)."[13] By attending to the liminality of these twinned figures, vagrant

---

negative connotations. For a discussion of the terms' valences, see Woodbridge, *Vagrancy, Homelessness, and English Renaissance Literature*, 28–30.

9. Paul Slack, *Poverty and Policy in Tudor and Stuart England* (London: Longman, 1988), 91.

10. Despite many excellent studies of early modern vagrancy, they almost uniformly envision their subjects to have been male. As Fiona McNeill argues in her valuable corrective, the masculine preoccupation obscures the "sexually and socially deviant single women in early modern London, who [were] always clustered at the bottom of the socioeconomic layer" (*Poor Women in Shakespeare* [Cambridge: Cambridge University Press, 2007], 154).

11. Paul Cefalu, *Revisionist Shakespeare: Transitional Ideologies in Texts and Contexts* (New York: Palgrave Macmillan, 2004), 26.

12. Giorgio Agamben, *Homo Sacer: Sovereign Power and Bare Life*, trans. Daniel Heller-Roazen (Stanford, CA: Stanford University Press, 1998), 8.

13. Ibid.

and *homo sacer*, we can explore more fully how civil vengeance animates the social body.

Under Tudor and Stuart rule, vagrancy increased substantially, and historians have gauged the increase from evidentiary sources that include census records, poor relief records, arrest reports made to the Privy Council, firsthand accounts (e.g., observations of William Harrison, John Stow, and Phillip Stubbes), rogue literature, records from workhouses (e.g., Bridewell), and even constables' accounts.[14] Moreover, both Elizabeth I and James I penned numerous proclamations against vagrancy, and Elizabethan law, in particular, underwent a series of revisions as it refined punishments designed to curb the social issue.[15] But exact numbers are more difficult to come by. Because early modern poor relief was administered at the parish level, such records are imprecise and often incomplete. By the conclusion of Elizabeth's reign in 1603, D. M. Palliser estimates that vagrancy increased by 35 percent.[16] The London records at Bridewell document an explosion in vagrancy three times that of the city's overall population.[17] Arthur Kinney notes that the Queen's Privy Council executed a series of watches, designed to apprehend vagabonds and send them home. One such search, whose 1569 occurrence is documented in the British Museum, yielded approximately 13,000 petty criminals.[18] Yet while English sovereigns and their representatives expounded endlessly on the gravity of the matter, the observations of foreign diplomats in their correspondence home do not corroborate these perspectives.[19] Given the significant variance in the estimates I cite, one should remember that they reveal only one aspect of the historical narrative, and a limited one at that. What we might safely conclude, then, is that an undeniable increase in vagrancy proved a sufficient nuisance that English authorities enforced increasingly severe penalties.

---

14. The usefulness of these archives varies widely. Consider Slack's caveat regarding arrest records and the "selective enforcement" of vagrancy laws: "[Justices and constables] certainly did not punish all poor wanderers as vagrants. Neither, on the other hand, did they punish as vagrants people who could be convicted of some other crime" (*Poverty and Policy in Tudor and Stuart England*, 92).

15. Andreas Hyperius's *The regiment of povertie*, which influenced the development of Elizabethan Poor Law, urges interrogation as a technique to discern the undeserving poor from "verie penurie" and criminalize them (*The regiment of povertie*, trans. Henry Tripp [London: F. Coldock and H. Bynneman, 1572], 33v).

16. William C. Carroll, *Fat King, Lean Beggar: Representations of Poverty in the Age of Shakespeare* (Ithaca, NY: Cornell University Press, 1996), 21.

17. Slack, *Poverty and Policy in Tudor and Stuart England*, 93.

18. Arthur Kinney, "Afterword: (Re)presenting the Early Modern Rogue," in *Rogues and Early Modern English Culture*, ed. Craig Donne and Steve Mentz (Ann Arbor: University of Michigan Press, 2004), 361–81, esp. 363. Frank Aydelotte first cited the presence of the 1569 artifact in the British Museum in *Elizabethan Rogues and Vagabonds* (Oxford: Clarendon Press, 1913), 4.

19. Carroll, *Fat King, Lean Beggar*, 39.

What factors contributed to the unprecedented increase in vagrancy? Traditionally, scholars have cited three major cultural shifts: the enclosure movement; the dispersion of feudal retainers; and the dissolution of monasteries, which administered relief to the poor without discrimination.[20] Agricultural patterns played a role as well, as seasonal laborers moved to locate work for the spring and summer months, and in years of failed harvests, the numbers of arrested vagrants increased substantially.[21] Exacerbating the food shortage, grain prices increased during periods of insufficiency, while successive outbreaks of the plague, influenza, and typhus disrupted economic and familial structures, sending many into the streets to beg. In addition, England's population growth, rates of inflation, and wages out of pace with inflation impacted poverty levels, thereby increasing the number of placeless persons.

In a 1615 proclamation, James I reveals a fleeting familiarity with the cultural factors that contribute to vagrancy, which he regards as a dire social problem that breeds "an unreadinesse in the Countrey." For the precipitous rise in vagrancy and its consequences for England, he places the onus on the nobility, admonishing them to "live in the steps and examples of their worthy Ancestours, by keeping and entertaining Hospitalitie, and charitable relieving of the poore according to their estate and meanes." As James exports the duties of the now-absent monasteries to his noblemen, he reprimands them for their inhospitality and reminds them they are not "borne for themselves, and their families alone, but for the publique good and comfort of their Countrey."[22] This is one occasion—and an altogether rare one at that—in which a sovereign does not distinguish between so-called sturdy beggars and the deserving poor. Consequently, the proclamation remains an inadvertent admission that the problems posed by vagrancy were generated by a complex set of factors within the larger social matrix.

But unsurprisingly, cultural criticisms of vagrants were most often leveled at the individual. The criminalization of vagrancy was the starkest example of dominant attitudes insofar as the law targeted and held subjects responsible for structural inequity. Moreover, these laws exacerbated the very issues that they were presumed to address.[23] Summarizing the legal matter with characteristic wit, Linda Woodbridge writes: "Why should there be laws

20. Aydelotte, *Elizabethan Rogues and Vagabonds*, 14–17.

21. Slack, *Poverty and Policy in Tudor and Stuart England*, 95.

22. James I, "His Majesties Proclamation, requiring the Residencie of Noblemen, Gentlemen, Lieutenants, and Justices of Peace, upon their chiefe Mansions in the Countrey, for the better maintenance of Hospitalitie, and discharge of their duties [Newmarket, 9 December 1615]," in *Stuart Royal Proclamations*, 1:356–58.

23. Slack, *Poverty and Policy in Tudor and Stuart England*, 100.

against vagrancy? Because vagrants are criminals. How do we know they are criminals? Because vagrancy is a crime."[24] It was this tautology that drew the eye of the law to an unprecedented number of mobile persons, and by criminalizing those subject to the vagaries of socioeconomic conditions, legal changes, and even weather fluctuations, the state shifted responsibility to individuals.

While Elizabethan Poor Law created the crime of vagrancy, those who wandered were also associated with a threatening lawlessness. The vagrant's presumed criminality ranged from petty theft to sexual assault and murder, while vast criminal networks were believed to organize wandering subjects.[25] Their suspected ties to seditious and foreign groups prompted James I to enforce licensing to distinguish peddlers from vagrant imposters in a 1618 proclamation: "And whereas under colour of using the said Trade [of peddler], many Rogues and idle wandering persons, carrying about trifles in the habite of Pedlers or Pettie-Chapman, so misbehave themselves, as they are indeed no other but Sturdy Beggars, theeves, and absolute dissolutes, and many of them being of no Religion, or infected with Poperie, carry abroad and disperse superstitious Trumperies, unknown and unsuspected, to the prejudice and wrong of Us and Our loving Subjects."[26] Insofar as the disreputable group is "infected" with Catholicism, they are to some extent presented as victims, but this passivity does not inhibit them from functioning as carriers, as in the etiological models of biological disease, who then spread "Poperie" throughout the kingdom. Catholicism was not the only infection they were presumed to carry, for the vagrant, as William Carroll notes, "was tarred with every brush . . . and inflated into a repulsive bogeyman haunting the state."[27] The early modern fear of terrorism was directed against the vagrant, and this fear had pronounced material effects on those suspected of arson and plague-spreading in both England and throughout the Continent.[28] Following the 1666 Great Fire in London, for instance, British authorities took additional precautions to protect themselves from vagrants who were believed to function

<hr>

24. Woodbridge, *Vagrancy, Homelessness, and English Renaissance Literature*, 4.

25. This erroneous assumption has trickled down to contemporary scholars. For instance, Slack concludes that "recent research shows beyond doubt, however, that poor wanderers made a large contribution to criminality in early modern England" (*Poverty and Policy in Tudor and Stuart England*, 92). Divorcing vagrancy from criminality, Woodbridge debunks the myth that rogue pamphlets reflect actual lives of vagrants.

26. James I, "A Proclamation inhibiting all persons after Bartholomewtyde next, to use the Trade of a Pedler or Pettie-Chapman, unlesse they be Licenced according to a course lately taken by Us in that behalfe [Windsor Castle, 6 July 1618]," in *Stuart Royal Proclamations*, 1:393–95.

27. Carroll, *Fat King, Lean Beggar*, 36.

28. Johannes Dillinger, "Terrorists and Witches: Popular Ideas of Evil in the Early Modern Period," *History of European Ideas* 30, no. 2 (2004): 167–82, esp. 172.

as pyromaniac mercenaries for both Quakers and Catholics.[29] One cannot overemphasize the vertiginous chasm between paranoid cultural perceptions and the historical reality of vagrancy.

Beyond criminality, vagrants were coupled with biological contagion, an association borne out in much of the period's literature.[30] In her analysis of disease discourse in early modern London, Margaret Healy writes that "metonymic associations elide readily into metaphors, and the marginal poor tend to become synonymous with stench, filth, and plague."[31] For instance, the ragged clothing of the mobile poor was presumed to offer little in the way of protection from disease such that their overly permeable exteriors enabled them to unwittingly carry the plague to new geographic sites.[32] In 1604, James Manning takes the logic of contagion a step further by posing the following rhetorical question to his readers: "May not [vagrants] be condemned for murtherers, which having plague soares will presse into companies to infect others, or wilfully pollute the ayre, or other meanes, which others are daily to use, and live by?"[33] Relying on the fiction of deliberate "plague-spreaders," Manning invests them with agency for their proximity to an otherwise healthy body politic such that they could be prosecuted for murder and consequently executed for existing on the margins. Absent from the discourse is an acknowledgment of alternative explanations for plague outbreaks in England (i.e., increased trade, travel, and colonization). Thus, by marrying contagion to the "willful" vagrant, Manning elides the social reasons for the appearance of both

---

29. See, for example, Johannes Dillinger, "Organized Arson as a Political Crime: The Construction of a 'Terrorist' Menace in the Early Modern Period," *Crime, History, and Societies* 10, no. 2 (2006): 101–21, esp. 103. See also Frances E. Dolan, "Ashes and 'The Archive': The London Fire of 1666, Partisanship, and Proof," *Journal of Medieval and Early Modern Studies* 31, no. 2 (2006): 383–86; and Penny Roberts, "Arson, Conspiracy and Rumour in Early Modern Europe," *Continuity and Change* 12, no. 1 (1997): 9–29.

30. The trope of vagrant as embodied corruption permeates even twentieth-century scholarship. In *Elizabethan Rogues and Vagabonds*, Aydelotte writes: "Instead they [rogues and vagrants] went about spreading as best they might the discontent which was in the air" (52). In characterizing such individuals as active carriers of "discontent," Aydelotte tacitly associates them with sedition and social unrest—precisely that with which early modern audiences would have associated them as well.

31. Margaret Healy, *Fictions of Disease in Early Modern England: Bodies, Plagues and Politics* (New York: Palgrave Macmillan, 2001), 93.

32. Woodbridge, *Vagrancy, Homelessness, and English Renaissance Literature*, 178. Healy notes that the careful enforcement of vagrancy laws was part of London's attempts to contain the epidemic (*Fictions of Disease in Early Modern England*, 155). Expressing support for urban quarantines based on class standing, Thomas Lodge writes that city officials ought to bar "any of those to enter their Citty that come from such places as are suspected, except they be men of note, of whose prudence and securitie they may be assured . . . but for such as are vagabonds, masterlesse men, and of servile and base condition, for such I say, they ought not to be admitted" (*A Treatise of the Plague* [London: Thomas Creede and Valentine Simmes, 1603], F1v).

33. James Manning, *Complexions Castle* (London: John Legat, 1604), A1v.

the plague and the vagrant, seizing instead on the fantasy of fully agential in-dividuals.

The association with contagion is not only biological but also figurative. "Like most parasites," Carroll writes, "the beggar was often represented as both a carrier and an instance of 'infection' and 'disease,' an unnatural and deviant flaw in the body politic whose 'natural' state was supposedly one of health."[34] So when Francis Bacon bemoans the vagrant's presence as a "bur-then, an eye-sore and a scandal" as well as a "seed of peril and tumult in a state," his language is not unhinged hyperbole but a revelation of the imbri-cation of vagrancy and contagion in the early modern imaginary.[35] To be clear, my purpose in reviewing these early modern cultural fantasies is not to debunk them; scholars who include A. L. Beier, William Carroll, and Linda Woodbridge have amply proven them to be the pernicious fictions they were. Rather, I approach these cultural materials and the attitudes they reveal—in particular, normative society's tenacious belief in its victimhood—as partici-pating in the broader phenomenon of civil vengeance directed against the va-grant. These materials represent, in other words, the phantasmatic scaffolding on which fantasies of the vagrant are constructed. In what follows, we will see how episodes of personal revenge are mediated by the production of va-grant bodies and the fantasies attached to them such that the excessive vio-lence done to these bodies is rationalized preemptively.

In its depiction of the leadership failures of King Henry VI and the machina-tions of dissatisfied nobles, Shakespeare's *2 Henry VI* chronicles the events that culminate in the Wars of the Roses. Even as political conflict is the central pre-occupation of *2 Henry VI* as well as the tetralogy it forms, the play remains troubled by the social question of what to do about vagrancy. The play's first example, which involves petitioners attempting to contact the Lord Protector (Duke of Gloucester), illustrates how the practice of enclosure benefits land-owners at the expense of the laboring classes beneath them. In an attempt to deliver their supplications to the Duke of Gloucester, two petitioners approach the Queen and the Duke of Suffolk. Though the Second Petitioner recognizes Suffolk and tries to withhold the petition from him, the imperious Suffolk con-fiscates it, reading aloud: "What's here? 'Against the Duke of Suffolk for en-closing the commons of Melford'! How now, Sir Knave?" (1.3.23–25).[36]

---

34. Carroll, *Fat King, Lean Beggar*, 7.

35. Francis Bacon, *An Account of the Life and Times of Francis Bacon*, ed. James Spedding (London: Trübner, 1878), 651.

36. All references are to William Shakespeare, *Henry VI, Part II*, in Greenblatt et al., *The Norton Shakespeare*, 203–90. This text is based on the 1623 First Folio.

Although the petitioners are not vagrants per se—or, more precisely, not yet—enclosing formerly common land was a major contributor to the rise in early modern vagrancy. To deflect his culpability for the unfortunate gaffe, the Second Petitioner emphasizes his representative status in the suit: "Alas, sir, I am but a poor petitioner of our whole township" (1.3.26–27). On behalf of her beloved Suffolk, an incensed Queen Margaret responds thusly: "And as for you that love to be protected / Under the wings of our Protector's grace, / Begin your suits anew and sue to him. [*She tears the supplication*] Away, base cullions! Suffolk, let them go" (1.3.41–44).[37] Here, Shakespeare takes a practice with which early modern audiences are themselves familiar and places it in an earlier and therefore anachronistic context.[38] In so doing, the text guides its readers' sympathies toward the laboring classes by showcasing their lack of recourse, and insofar as Suffolk and Margaret exhibit unrestrained disdain for their subjects, a disdain that at its core is directed at Gloucester, they are marked as antagonists to the Crown, to justice, and to the common care of the most vulnerable.

The second moment that frames the text's stance on vagrancy involves the formerly absent Gloucester as one of its principal figures. Here, the lame Simon Simpcox and his wife arrive at the court in celebration of the return of Simon's sight, thanks to the "miraculous" intervention of St. Alban. Even before they offer their account, the surname alone—a portmanteau composed of "simple" and "coxcomb," that is, caps often worn by jesters—hints at their humble origins. Although King Henry unequivocally rejoices at the news ("Now God be praised, that to believing souls / Gives light in darkness, comfort in despair!"), Gloucester maintains his skepticism. To prove his suspicions correct and to expose the couple as frauds, he asks Simpcox to name the individuals present and the colors they wear. Though Simpcox identifies colors with no difficulty, he protests that he cannot name the individuals who wear them. From Gloucester's perspective, the incongruity confirms his fraudulence. He retorts:

If thou hadst been born blind
Thou mightst as well have known our names as thus
To name the several colours we do wear.
Sight may distinguish colours, but suddenly
To nominate them all—it is impossible.

---

37. In the Q1 (1594) version, Suffolk tears up the supplication.

38. Henry VI reigned from 1422 to 1453, whereas the enclosure practice occurred in England during the sixteenth and seventeenth centuries.

Saint Alban here hath done a miracle.
Would you not think his cunning to be great
That could restore this cripple to his legs again?

(2.1.130–37)

To demonstrate the extent of the improbable miracle, Gloucester calls for a parish official to whip Simpcox until he moves his legs. As the whipping continues, he can no longer brook his punishment and runs away in an attempt to halt the pain. Gloucester then orders the mayor to whip both husband and wife "through every market-town" until they are returned to Berwick, their original home. Such a punishment—the whipping coupled with the return of the Simpcoxes to their origins—was routinely reserved for vagrants.[39]

I start with an examination of these two episodes for several reasons. Taken together, the scenes suggest the manner by which 2 Henry VI orients readers and audience members to the pressing question of early modern vagrancy. More specifically, the scenes intimate the precariousness with which subjects lived amid changing laws and aristocratic caprice. Because both episodes structurally hinge on Gloucester—his critical absence and presence—the play deploys him as a moral compass of sorts, one who can discern those worthy of sympathy and succor. Among the petitioners who suffer the economic consequences of enclosure, he is perceived to be an ally of the "deserving poor," and it is precisely this position that enables him to reveal the fraudulence of the Simpcox couple—that is, "sturdy beggars" who feign vulnerability and prey upon sympathies to feed off the labor of others—without appearing too severe. In so doing, Gloucester represents relatively orthodox Tudor and Stuart stances on vagrancy that admit the presence of those in need and make some accommodations for their unfortunate circumstances.[40]

But there are other vagrant groups who, from the perspective of the emerging nation-state, constitute grave threats well beyond social parasitism. Consider, for instance, Queen Elizabeth I's 1594 proclamation in which she denounces sturdy beggars alongside Irish traitors. She begins by observing the "multitude of able men, neither impotent nor lame, [who] exact money continually upon pretense of service in the wars without relief, whereas many of

<hr />

39. Whipping posts cropped up throughout London in response to 1598 legislation, which replaced the 1593 consequences for vagrancy of ear-boring and death. See Healy, Fictions of Disease in Early Modern England, 93.

40. For instance, Elizabeth's 1591 proclamation licensed Hugh Euance and his family to beg after their household and goods were destroyed in a fire. See "Licensing Collections for Hugh Euance [Westminster, 11 May 1591]," in Tudor Royal Proclamations, vol. 3, The Late Tudors (1588–1603), ed. Paul L. Hughes and James F. Larkin (New Haven, CT: Yale University Press, 1969), 81–82.

them never did so serve.["]41 She then turns her attention to another group who appear in the guise of the first but are in fact Irish rebels who "cannot have any good meaning towards her majesty, as of late hath been manifestly proved in some already taken that have secretly come into the realm with full purpose, by procurement of the devil and his ministers, her majesty's enemies, and rebels on the other side [of] the sea, to endanger her majesty's noble person."42 By linking the two groups in terms of their outward appearance and by their proximity in the proclamation, Elizabeth I ratchets up the threats posed by vagrancy, threats that include not only parasitism but also Catholic sabotage, sedition, and resistance to the expansion of empire.

Read in concert, these framing moments from 2 Henry VI also showcase the manner in which vagrant (or proto-vagrant) bodies are used for other kinds of work beyond physical labor. In the first exchange, Suffolk and Margaret's outburst against the Second Petitioner stems from their conflict with Gloucester such that the petitioners emerge as the objects on which the two may vent their frustrations. In the second, vagrant bodies provide fodder for amusement as the spectacle of the whipped Simpcox and his ironized "miracle" provokes laughter from onlookers. And insofar as both scenes suggest the ubiquity of material concerns, they pave the way for the social issues vocalized by the larger than life Jack Cade.43 Although some characters perceive the Simpcox episode as comical, it resists the traditionally tidy closure of comedy. Not laughter but misery concludes the scene, as the wife confesses to Gloucester, "Alas, sir, we did it for pure need" (2.1.157). Her final words meet with no reaction from other characters, yet they nevertheless stand as an unacknowledged remnant of the material circumstances that compelled them to engage in deception in the first place—able-bodied or otherwise. There is a need, but its articulation is neither sufficiently addressed nor refuted by the play or its characters.

Leaving aside the chaotic consequences of Jack Cade's politics for the moment, the issues he articulates are hardly illegitimate. In one invective against the social structure that consigns commoners to "live in slavery," he identifies literacy—and, by extension, Lord Saye—as a chief cause of that social oppression: "Thou hast appointed justices of peace to call poor men before them

---

41. Elizabeth I, "Ordering Arrest of Vagabonds, Deportation of Irishmen [Hampton Court, 21 February 1594]," in *Tudor Royal Proclamations*, 3:134.

42. Ibid., 135.

43. On this note, Thomas Cartelli observes that "garbled though they may be, the people's grievances are not, in any event, first expressed in the context of Cade's rebellion" ("Jack Cade in the Garden: Class Consciousness and Class Conflict in 2 Henry VI," in *Enclosure Acts: Sexuality, Property, and Culture in Early Modern England*, ed. Richard Burt and John Michael Archer [Ithaca, NY: Cornell University Press, 1994], 48–67, quote from 58).

about matters they were not able to answer. Moreover, thou hast put them in prison, and, because they could not read, thou hast hanged them when indeed only for that cause they have been most worthy to live" (4.7.34–39). As Cade evokes the legal privileges reserved for readers of Latin, he suggests how law and, more broadly, literacy do not work to protect the laboring classes but only to exploit them further. Even as Lord Saye is an inappropriate target for these structural grievances, what Cade points to is a legal system in which the cards are always already stacked against the poor and uneducated masses.[44] Elsewhere, Cade berates his followers who are tempted by Henry VI's offers of clemency and, to deter them from switching sides, details the network of social, corporeal, economic, and sexual oppression they will continue to face if they yield: "I thought ye would never have given out these arms till you had recovered your ancient freedom. But you are all recreants and dastards, and delight to live in slavery to the nobility. Let them break your backs with burdens, take your houses over your heads, ravish your wives and daughters before your faces" (4.7.167–72). Though Cade is the unruly mouthpiece for social criticisms of the ruling classes, he also implicates the laboring classes, should they fail him, as complicit in their own oppression.

While representing the concerns of the laboring poor, Cade is simultaneously cast as a vagrant by the play's characters. Indeed, as soon as we are introduced to him and his untidy band of rebels, he is marked as such by satirical asides that puncture his self-aggrandizement. These quips, such as those found in the following exchange, associate him with criminality and specifically vagrancy.

> CADE: Valiant I am—
> WEAVER: A must needs, for beggary is valiant.
> CADE: I am able to endure much—
> BUTCHER: No question of that, for I have seen him whipped three market days together.
> CADE: I fear neither sword nor fire.
> WEAVER: He need not fear the sword, for his coat is of proof. (4.2.47–54)

As the Weaver introduces beggary, though not necessarily a crime in and of itself under Elizabethan Poor Law, his qualification of Cade's beggary as "valiant" or "able-bodied" subsequently positions the latter as a criminal "sturdy beggar." Following the established logic of the insult, the Butcher's aside re-

---

44. Ibid., 61. Thomas Dekker corroborates Cade's accusation when he cites the "Lawyers griding of the poore" as a sin that courts God's ire in the form of plague outbreaks (*News from Graves-end: Sent to Nobody* [London: T[homas] C[reede], 1604], D2r).

fers to one of the corporal punishments reserved for able-bodied vagrants (i.e., whipping), while the Weaver's second aside may refer to the matted dirt of Cade's coat—that his clothing is consistent with vagrancy—and offers protection from the sword due to its impenetrable layers of filth.

If Cade is associated with vagrancy, how, then, do we understand his later speeches that veer into hyperbole and nightmare?[45] Although his blunt assessments of aristocratic privilege are not altogether incorrect, whatever credibility he might have established in articulating them is deflated by his subsequent words. Now posing a serious threat to a beleaguered crown, Cade voices the most monstrous fantasies of unchecked power: "The proudest peer in the realm shall not wear a head on his shoulders unless he pay me tribute. There shall not a maid be married but she shall pay to me her maidenhead, ere they have it. Married men shall hold of me *in capite*. And we charge and command that their wives be as free as heart can wish or tongue to tell" (4.7.110–15). As others have observed, Cade does not desire to abolish private property and the hierarchies that enforce it but rather aspires to be the sole arbiter of property. Moreover, his seemingly fantastical words are literalized instantly with the summary execution of a sergeant who accuses one of Cade's followers of sexually assaulting his wife. Whatever sympathies one might harbor for the poor and downtrodden are soon soured by his perversions of justice. As a result, scholars have traditionally relegated him to one of the following frameworks: comedian,[46] amalgam of various historical figures,[47] or political vehicle.[48] Of Cade's metamorphosis, Richard Wilson writes that he turns into a "cruel, barbaric lout, whose slogan is 'kill and knock down' and whose story,

---

45. Supplying one possible answer to that question, Stephen Greenblatt refracts Jack Cade's chaos through the haze of current U.S. politics (*Tyrant: Shakespeare on Politics* [New York: W. W. Norton, 2018], 35–52).

46. Stephen Longstaffe writes how the likely acting of Will Kemp would have established the performance "not simply as parody, but metaparody" ("'A Short Report and Not Otherwise': Jack Cade in *2 Henry VI*," in *Shakespeare and Carnival: After Bakhtin*, ed. Ronald Knowles [New York: St. Martin's Press, 1998], 13–35, quote from 26). See also Chris Fitter, "'Your Captain Is Brave and Vows Reformation': Jack Cade, the Hacket Rising, and Shakespeare's Vision of Popular Rebellion," *Shakespeare Studies* 32 (2004): 173–219; and Richard Wilson, *Will Power: Essays on Shakespearean Authority* (Detroit: Wayne State University Press, 1993).

47. Stuart Hampton-Reeves, "Kent's Best Man: Radical Chorographic Consciousness and the Identity Politics of Local History in Shakespeare's *2 Henry VI*," *Journal of Early Modern Cultural Studies* 14, no. 1 (2014): 63–87; and Ellen C. Caldwell, "Jack Cade and Shakespeare's Henry VI, Part II," *Studies in Philology* 92, no. 1 (1995): 18–79.

48. See Walter Cohen, *Drama of a Nation: Public Theater in Renaissance England and Spain* (Ithaca, NY: Cornell University Press, 1985); and Stephen Greenblatt, "Murdering Peasants: Status, Genre, and the Representation of Rebellion," in *Representing the English Renaissance*, ed. Stephen Greenblatt (Berkeley: University of California Press, 1988), 1–29.

as 'the architect of disorder,' is one long orgy of scatological clowning, arson, and homicide, fuelled by an infantile hatred of literacy and law."[49]

Though I do not necessarily disagree with Wilson's memorable assessment, I understand Cade's metamorphosis as a reflection of the delusions that attach themselves to historical vagrants. He looms large as a literary bogeyman, terrorizing England with theft, depravity, and violence—vices that also associate him with vagrancy. And as he foments sedition, infecting others with his plague of treachery and menacing the Crown, this, too, connects him with the vagrant. Breathing new life into the fantasies attached to peripatetic bodies, he animates them on stage for early modern audiences. But of course such imaginings reveal less of the vagrant and more of the culture in which such hallucinations flourished. Reading Cade as a literary manifestation of the early modern fantasy, then, we may consider more fully the terror that the figure inspires in normative society. Indeed, the social paranoia prompted by the vagrant suggests a society invested in its victimhood, one that sees itself perpetually held in the thrall and at the mercy of ragged misfits.

To pursue that line of inquiry, we must ask the following question: What does the fantasy of early modern victimhood, which is prompted by the vagrant, permit civil society to do? To address that first requires a brief digression into Agamben's conceptualization of the sovereign and his power in relation to the figure of the *homo sacer*. Distinguishing the two, Agamben writes, "The sovereign is the one with respect to whom all men are potentially *homines sacri*, and *homo sacer* is the one with respect to whom all men act as sovereigns."[50] That is, all subjects are rendered equally vulnerable before the sovereign, and the ensuing precariousness is fundamental to and constitutive of early modern subjectivity but is nevertheless borne disproportionately by certain bodies. As a visible outlier, the vagrant emerges as one such body. But all membership in the social-political sphere is intrinsically conditional and may be revoked at any time by the sovereign. Faced with this untenable position of precariousness, normative members align themselves, I argue, with the manifestation of sovereign power,[51] the power that reduces subjects to bare life and expels them from the social body into the "zone of indistinction between the human and the animal."[52] The desire to disavow this discomfiting reality and collective vulnerability accounts at least in part for this alignment.

Of course in aligning oneself with the sovereign, one cannot put on a crown, collect taxes, and enact law. In one sense, the fantasy of victimhood is authentic

---

49. Wilson, *Will Power*, 30.

50. Agamben, *Homo Sacer*, 84.

51. Of course their normativity is also born out of this alignment.

52. Agamben, *Homo Sacer*, 106.

yet displaced, existing as little more than a flimsy disguise that allows civil society to perpetuate preemptive punishment. This is how the collective rallies around victimhood as a fantasy that provides the space within which to exercise aggression with impunity. Yet from the dynamic arises a mode of vengeance divorced from its traditional quid pro quo exchange and appearing instead in the guise of justice and equity. To accomplish that, civil society feigns limited agency or nonagency when, in matter of fact, its members maintain the agential position throughout as lesser sovereigns-by-proxy. Here we find the quintessence of civil vengeance: though targeted aggression is launched against specific individuals, that aggression is strenuously disavowed, and the aggressor—be it state, institution, or individual—preserves the moral high ground vis-à-vis its disingenuous disavowal. One enjoys the singular pleasures of aggression without attracting social or religious disapproval ordinarily reserved for raw displays of vengeance. In the case of the early modern vagrant, civil society benefits from perpetuating this dynamic, from putting the vagrant to work, literally and symbolically. And given that civil society reaps the economic benefits from the creation and subsequent marginalization of vagrants, the willingness to see itself as victimized, rather than benefiting from vagrancy, adds insult to injury: to appropriate the moniker of victim is to extend existing political, social, economic, and moral privileges. In order to visualize the temporal phenomenon I describe here and how it relies on a fantasy of victimhood, I turn now to the fatal exchange between Cade and Alexander Iden.

When we meet Cade for the final time, it requires no stretch of imagination to apprehend his vagrancy. Beside himself with hunger and unable to hide in the woods any longer, he leaps over a brick wall, itself emblematic of enclosures, to "eat grass or pick a sallet." The absurdity of the situation, that the raging Cade is rendered prostrate with hunger, would not go unnoticed by audiences. Through the reference to "sallet," a pun on food and a soldier's helmet, he gestures toward the "systematic injustices of which [his hunger] is symptomatic: injustices that extend from the ranks of ambitious lords to those of dispossessed veterans."[53] Furthermore, the grass and uncultivated herbs he selects would have exercised, in accordance with humoral theory and herbal wisdom of the time, a sedative effect through their inherently cooling properties.[54] That is, even if he posed a threat, his choice of food signals both desperation and pacification. I emphasize these details to argue that the Cade with which we are now confronted is a ghost of his former self, an attenuated

53. Hillary Eklund, "Revolting Diets: Jack Cade's 'Sallet' and the Politics of Hunger in *2 Henry VI*," *Shakespeare Studies* 42 (2014): 51–62, quote from 59.
54. Ken Albala, *Eating Right in the Renaissance* (Berkeley: University of California Press, 2002), 110, 176.

man, no more than a mere vagrant who, in the earlier words of William Perkins, lives the "life of a beast." Cade *pace* Agamben inhabits little more than bare life, that is, *"life exposed to death,"* life that remains particularly vulnerable to sovereign violence.[55]

Iden, by contrast, is plump with good fortune and fancies himself a friend to the poor:

> Lord, who would live turmoilèd in the court
> And may enjoy such quiet walks as these?
> This small inheritance my father left me
> Contenteth me, and worth a monarchy.
> I seek not to wax great by others' waning,
> Or gather wealth I care not with what envy;
> Sufficeth that I have maintains my state,
> And sends the poor well pleasèd from my gate.
>
> *(4.9.14–21)*

As his name's homologous connection to "Eden" would imply, he enjoys a bucolic existence. Distinguished from wealthy landowners who fatten their estates at the expense of the laboring classes, he positions himself in tacit opposition to those who, like the Duke of Suffolk in the first act, enclose common land. And insofar as he sets up an equivalence between his "small inheritance" and a monarchy, Iden regards himself as a benevolent sovereign of his estate. But even as he "sends the poor well pleased," his Eden is a restricted one with its walls and gates to prevent those same individuals from unlawful trespass.

However magnanimous Iden casts himself in this initial speech, his subsequent response to Cade's unauthorized presence insinuates its stark limits.

> Why, rude companion, whatsoe'er thou be,
> I know thee not. Why then should I betray thee?
> Is't not enough to break into my garden,
> And, like a thief, to come to rob my grounds,
> Climbing my walls in spite of me the owner,
> But thou wilt brave me with these saucy terms?
>
> *(4.9.28–33)*

---

55. Agamben, *Homo Sacer*, 88.

Indeed, if readers know that Iden is good, it is only because he tells us as much. Yet noting the discrepancies between how he envisions Cade's transgressions, one sees that he makes much of a relatively minor offense. Although Iden insists that Cade "break[s] into [his] garden," "climb[s] [his] walls," and "rob[s] [his] grounds," Cade has been lying down in the grass, feasting on it and other herbs as the stage directions corroborate.[56] Through the performative use of pronouns in each line, Iden establishes enclosures, underscoring his ownership and Cade's trespass by consequence, and his subsequent victimhood through the endurance of such outrageous offenses. I belabor these details to distinguish the play's reality of Cade from Iden's perception of him. And as the Quarto's stage directions stipulate that Iden is accompanied by at least five followers and that Iden and Cade enter simultaneously from two different doors, "this simultaneity works," Chris Fitter points out, "not only to generate fear for a hopelessly outnumbered fugitive, but to undermine Iden from the moment he begins speaking."[57]

As the gap between Iden's self-assessment and the realities of the play widens, we catch a glimpse of what is to be gained through the reliance on the fantasy of early modern victimhood. Although he states that he is loath to fight the exhausted vagrant, he nevertheless soundly thrashes him to his death. Because Cade's vagrancy and illegal trespass mark him as persona non grata in the social-political world, his precarious status consequently entitles Iden to murder him. What the initial rationale behind Cade's murder reveals is a truth that, by now, should surprise no one: some bodies are deemed constitutively expendable. When Iden discovers the true identity of his seditious trespasser, he congratulates himself on his honorable triumph while Cade, taking advantage of the only means available to inflict insult, taunts him: "Farewell, and be proud of thy victory . . . For I, that never feared any, am vanquished by famine, not by valor" (4.9.69–72). Given that it was Cade's martial prowess that first attracted the Duke of York—"In Ireland have I seen this stubborn Cade . . . / And fought so long till that his thighs with darts / Were almost like a sharp-quilled porcupine"[58]—his words are not simply sour grapes but rather a sensible explanation for his opponent's unseasonable triumph. Never one to ignore the impotent invectives of a dying man, Iden retorts:

---

56. As Fitter observes, when Iden gestures to *his* walls, he gestures toward the very walls of the theater, and his confident possession is undermined by the audience's reality ("'Your Captain Is Brave,'" 209–10).

57. Ibid., 209.

58. In the extended passage, York states: "In Ireland have I seen this stubborn Cade / Oppose himself against a troop of kerns, / And fought so long till that his thighs with darts / Were almost like a sharp-quilled porcupine; / And in the end, being rescued, I have seen / Him caper upright like a wild Morisco, / Shaking the bloody darts as he his bells" (3.1.360–66).

How much thou wrong'st me, heaven be my judge.
Die, damnèd wretch, the curse of her that bore thee!
And [*stabbing him again*] as I thrust thy body in with my sword,
So wish I might thrust thy soul to hell.
Hence will I drag thee headlong by the heels
Unto a dunghill, which shall be thy grave,
And there cut off thy most ungracious head,
Which I will bear in triumph to the King,
Leaving thy trunk for crows to feed upon.

(4.9.73–81)

As in earlier speeches, he relies on the singular subject and singular possessive pronouns to emphasize how Cade's transgressions are, at the heart, against him (e.g., "How much thou wrong'st me"). In fact, what prompts this violence is the reminder that, had Cade been well fed, Iden would have met his end such that his consequent outburst stems from vanity and piqued pride—not defense on the part of England and his king. This is not well-intentioned patriotism but rather petty vengeance from a man who refused salad to the starving.

What the interaction also exemplifies is how personal vengeance becomes enmeshed within larger political structures. In particular, personal vengeance becomes legitimized by or disguised through appeals to nationalism. If we revisit Iden's initial refusal to fight—"Nay, it shall ne'er be said while England stands / That Alexander Iden, an esquire of Kent, / Took odds to combat a poor famished man" (4.9.39–41)—we see how he stakes his refusal to fight Cade in England's stability. I am not proposing that the incongruity between Iden's statement and fatal action puts England into danger, of course, but rather that his formulation discloses the imbrication of personal honor, private revenge, and national identity. And insofar as we see firsthand how Iden's rhetoric works to retroactively justify his actions against Cade—his discovery of the interloper's identity functions to prove the righteousness of his attack on him—*2 Henry VI* illustrates what I identify as a retroactive component to civil vengeance. Although Iden's behavior toward Cade may appear as unrestrained dominance rather than revenge, my chapter understands this violent assertion of power and retaliation as connected, not in opposition. Put simply, retaliation is the cover for violent assertions of power, and preemptive, excessive aggression goes best unchecked when it can be said to protect the king and country.

But what is often elided in discussions of Iden's apostrophe is that he expends his vitriol on an already-dead Cade. The disproportionate violence inflicted on Cade's corpse is deemed justifiable retaliation through the enduring belief in his commensurately dangerous presence. In commanding a deceased subject to die and punctuating the imperative with postmortem stab wounds, he presumes a kind of too-liveliness of Cade that is not eradicated in biological death. He subscribes to a fantasy in which the vagrant remains larger than life, *even in death*. As Iden stabs the corpse, he acts out his fervent wish of thrusting his soul to hell; he imagines, in other words, inflicting an unceasing punishment of eternal damnation. Instead, he satisfies himself with an appropriation of state justice in the act of decapitation, functioning as its de facto representative. And Iden's appropriation of state justice is amply rewarded insofar as King Henry extends to him a knighthood and a thousand marks, even as what moves him to murder is not the reason for his reward.[59]

Still, I want to linger on Cade's savage conclusion and consider what else permits Iden to indulge in this display of unmitigated violence. Because the fantasy of victimhood is sufficient to initiate and sustain repeated revenge acts, it disrupts the traditional teleology of vengeance. Moreover, the violence done to Cade's body is in proportion to the too-liveliness that he and vagrants like him are presumed to exhibit; the uncertain status of the vagrant precipitates an excessively violent response. If the vagrant, with his peripatetic movement and "busie bodie," is too enduring, then civil society allows itself a concomitant punishment to corral this subject into a more static existence. And indeed it did. Such enduring subjects held great value for England's imperial-capitalist projects precisely because they were presumed to withstand beyond-the-pale violence. It is this logic that enables incorrigible vagrants to be incarcerated in workhouses, or to be shipped off for the punishing work of colonial endeavors, or, in the case of Cade, to serve the political machinations of the nobility. After all, it was the Duke of York who manipulated him into fomenting a rebellion against King Henry VI in order to eventually claim the throne for his own family.

Thus, what contributes to Cade's death most immediately are not only his illegal trespass and his unrepentant theft of food but also the very system that creates property as well as its attendant legal and social privileges. While the paranoid notions of the vagrant are made to work for England, the violence of Cade's murder is also retroactively justified through the rhetoric of stability (e.g., enclosures) and vagrancy. Without enclosures, without ownership, without the uncompromising privileges of protecting one's property even if it results in the death of another, Iden's actions would be neither laudable nor legal. The fact that Cade is the outward leader of the rebellion emerges as the

---

59. See the exchange between King Henry and Iden in 5.1.64–82.

retroactive justification for his murder. But details matter not because vagrants—perceived as perpetual threats—are lives that do not matter. Like the *homo sacer*, vagrants can be killed but not murdered, for they distinctly don't count. And while all subjects are vulnerable before the sovereign—that is, all subjects are able to be killed, according to Agamben—this collective precariousness is exported to and concentrated in the vagrant. In killing Cade, Iden arrogates the sovereign prerogative, and disavows both his vulnerability and culpability. In knighting Iden for his deeds, King Henry VI reinforces the positive consequences of that social dynamic and symbolically confers a virtual kernel of his sovereignty. At the intersection of enclosures, vagrancy, and rebellion, Shakespeare reveals the deathly consequences of civil vengeance as it structures the social body.

How early modern England positioned itself on an international stage was inextricable from its domestic issue of vagrancy. As Kathleen Pories contends, vagrants "embodied a symbolic problem because they were taken to represent a malfunctioning country."[60] The visible poor are the ocular proof of England's inadequacies and emblematic of schisms in the body politic. Even beyond their symbolic import, vagrants seemed to pose a material threat to the monarch. Roger Manning relates an anecdote in which Elizabeth was passing through Islington in January 1582 when scores of beggars surrounded her carriage. The incident was sufficiently alarming, he surmises, because "William Fleetwood, recorder of London, was ordered to begin a sweep of masterless men the same day. The campaign lasted about ten days and netted several hundred vagrants—100 being taken in a single day. The beggars in Islington were easily located because they were wont to huddle together for warmth among the brick kilns in the village."[61] Although the eerie encounter and speedy government response might be read as indicative of the vagrant's perceived threat to the nation-state through Elizabeth's person qua England, it is nevertheless difficult to reconcile that interpretation with the pathetic image of groups huddled around brick kilns in the middle of winter.

If vagrants reflect the uncharitable underside of English politics and policies, they are also that against which England defines itself. And if enacting civil vengeance against these individuals facilitates social bonding between

60. Kathleen Pories, "The Intersection of Poor Laws and Literature in the Sixteenth Century: Fictional and Factual Categories," in *Framing Elizabethan Fictions: Contemporary Approaches to Early Modern Narrative Prose*, ed. Constance C. Relihan (Kent, OH: Kent State University Press, 1996), 17–40, quote from 18.

61. Roger Manning, *Village Revolts: Social Protest and Popular Disturbances in England, 1509–1640* (Oxford: Oxford University Press, 1988), 169.

normative members, we might reasonably expect this dynamic to play out on the global stage as well. With this hypothesis in mind, I turn now to Thomas Nashe's *The Unfortunate Traveller, or The Life of Jack Wilton* to explore how England constructs its fantasy of the nation-state. Because vagrancy is connected to empire, nationalism, and foreign policy, I want to begin with a text that moves us beyond England's borders yet also gets us to the heart of Englishness. Vengeance is featured prominently in *The Unfortunate Traveller* as well, and it intersects with demonstrations of nationalism—a matter I will explore more fully in later pages. But first I want to establish how the novel reclassifies cosmopolitanism as vagrancy.

Insofar as the exuberant novel chronicles the movements of its narrator (Jack Wilton), taking us to France, Italy, Germany, and the Netherlands, and back to England, the narrative enacts a kind of peripatetic movement traditionally associated with vagrancy. What sets off our unlikely protagonist for the Continent is a deadly outbreak of the sweating sickness in England. As I have argued already, the plague and vagrancy are coterminous, and *The Unfortunate Traveller* puts that connection on full display.[62] Wilton explains: "Let me quietly descend to the waning of my youthful days, and tell a little of the sweating sickness that made me in a cold sweat take my heels and run out of England. This sweating sickness was a disease that a man then might catch and never go to a hot-house. Many masters desire to have such servants as would work till they sweat again, but in those days he that sweat never wrought again. That scripture then was not thought so necessary which says, 'Earn thy living with the sweat of thy brows,' for then they earned their dying with the sweat of their brows."[63] Plague times, as Wilton makes clear, are periods of social and religious upheaval, opportunities to discard perspectives that are no longer applicable. Even religion is subject to the state of exception instantiated by the plague such that its edicts can be dismissed casually as "not . . . so necessary." Here, hard work heralds not efficiency but certain death, and insofar as fever (i.e., sweating) is the chief symptom of infection, Wilton tacitly links pathogenicity to exertion in his multiple references to the disease as a "sweating sickness." By focusing attention on the laboring classes—as it is the servants, not their masters, who succumb to death—he depicts the deadly illness as the ironic yet logical conclusion to a Protestant work ethic.

---

62. While Wilton's health is preserved, the sentence's formulation suggests that, insofar as he escapes in "a cold sweat," his exhibition of anxiety is identical to the symptoms of disease, and in this way he functions as a potential carrier.

63. Thomas Nashe, *The Unfortunate Traveller, or The Life of Jack Wilton*, in *The Unfortunate Traveller and Other Works*, ed. J. B. Steane (London: Penguin Books, 1985), 251–370, quote from 273.

But Protestant values and scripture are not the only items debilitated by the outbreak, for the minds who gave rise to conventional modes of illness management are revealed to be no more than quacks: "Galen might go shoe the gander for any good he could do; his secretaries had so long called him divine that now he had lost all virtue upon earth. Hippocrates might well help almanack-makers, but here he had not a word to say: a man might sooner catch the sweat with plodding over him to no end, than cure the sweat with any of his impotent principles."[64] The fathers of medicine, now found to be wholly ineffectual, also exacerbate the plague insofar as the effort involved in understanding Hippocrates's text brings the reader perilously close to contracting the disease. Even as there is precious little Wilton holds sacred (at least at this point in the text), he censures them and their adherents with a particular vehemence that suggests how significant disease leaves society in an uproar and unfit to combat these frightful challenges.

Not surprisingly, the apocalyptic times upend the traditional hierarchy on which early modern society relied: "Cooks that stand continually basting their faces before the fire, were now all cashiered with this sweat into kitchen stuff. Their hall fell into the King's hands for want of one of the trade to uphold it."[65] Although Wilton incorrectly traces the origins of the disease to overheating, in so doing, he draws an explicit causal relationship between labor and disease such that the laboring classes are most vulnerable to the outbreak. The outrageousness of the outbreak is encompassed in the hyperbolic claim that the sovereign would be responsible for his own kitchen, thanks to the swiftly successive deaths of his servants. Moreover, the only pains taken to prevent its spread are in the service of royalty. "It was high treason," Wilton recalls with characteristic wryness, "for a fat gross man to come within five miles of the Court."[66] If, as he concludes in his revisionist account of English disease, hard work is the most certain means to sudden death, vagrancy and aristocracy are the safest options. It is Wilton's good fortune to pursue the former and impersonate the latter.[67]

Though Wilton may be easily characterized as a vagrant himself—no home of which to speak, no employment, perpetual movement, and liberal acquaintance with various rogues—*The Unfortunate Traveller* broadens the definition of vagrancy to encapsulate travel abroad, which was customary for educated young men of certain means, and cosmopolitan attitudes. Most significantly, the novel brands those with the means to travel as vagrants, or, put another

---

64. Ibid., 275.
65. Ibid., 273.
66. Ibid., 274.
67. Jack Wilton famously impersonated his master, the Earl of Surrey, during his time abroad.

way, it extends vagrancy beyond abject poverty and ambiguous criminality. Even as definitions of cosmopolitanism remain contentious, I use the term to refer to an existence unconstrained by and unattached to national mores, allegiances, preferences, or politics.[68] Alan B. Farmer details the fractured nature of "cosmopolite" in the early modern world, as it most immediately referred to "citizens of the world" who sought self-improvement in the form of study and travel abroad.[69] But others, often Protestant writers, took umbrage at the licentious influences of their Continental counterparts and deployed the term as shorthand for "base sinner[s] who delight in worldly pleasures like fighting, feasting, cheating, and whoring."[70] In revising vagrancy to include travel and cosmopolitanism, Nashe's novel focuses on the construction of England's identity as a nationalistic fantasy that is both isolated from and simultaneously indebted to its global competitors.[71]

This identity construction is revealed most explicitly in the form of an extended condemnation of cosmopolitanism situated in the latter part of the novel, an episode that represents one of the lengthiest passages in the entire text. An exiled English earl who lives in Italy lectures the itinerant Wilton:

> Countryman, tell me, what is the occasion of thy straying so far out of England to visit this strange nation? If it be languages, thou may'st learn them at home; nought but lasciviousness is to be learned here. Perhaps, to be better accounted of than other of thy condition, thou ambitiously undertakest this voyage: these insolent fancies are but Icarus' feathers, whose wanton wax, melted against the sun, will betray thee into a sea of confusion.
>
> The first traveller was Cain, and he was called a vagabond runagate on the face of the earth. Travel (like the travail wherein smiths put wild

68. See, for instance, Crystal Bartolovich, "Utopian Cosmopolitanism," *Shakespeare Studies* 35 (2007): 47–57; Bryson, *From Courtesy to Civility*; Alan B. Farmer, "Cosmopolitanism and Foreign Bodies in Early Modern England," *Shakespeare Studies* 35 (2007): 58–65; Andrew Griffin, "Thomas Heywood and London Exceptionalism," *Studies in Philology* 110, no. 1 (2013): 85–114; Jonathan Gil Harris, "The Time of Shakespeare's Jewry," *Shakespeare Studies* 35 (2007): 39–46; David Scott Kastan, *A Will to Believe: Shakespeare and Religion* (Oxford: Oxford University Press, 2014), 11n13; and Brian C. Lockey, "Catholics and Cosmopolitans Writing the Nation: The Pope's Scholars and the 1579 Student Rebellion at the English Roman College," in *Representing Imperial Rivalry in the Early Modern Mediterranean*, ed. Barbara Fuchs and Emily Weissbourd (Toronto: University of Toronto Press, 2015), 233–54.

69. Farmer, "Cosmopolitanism and Foreign Bodies in Early Modern England," 61.

70. Ibid.

71. On the connection between English identity and style, Joseph Campana writes: "[Wilton's] peregrinations expose Nashe's attempt to define what it means for an English man to write in English prose at the turn of the seventeenth century" ("The State of England's Camp: Courtesans, Curses, and the Violence of Style in *The Unfortunate Traveller*," *Prose Studies* 29, no. 3 [2007]: 347–58, quote from 349).

horses when they shoe them) is good for nothing but to tame and bring men under.

God had no greater curse to lay upon the Israelites, than by leading them out of their own country to live as slaves in a strange land. That which was their curse, we Englishmen count our chief blessedness. He is nobody, that hath not travelled: we had rather live as slaves in another land, crouch and cap and be servile to every jealous Italian's and proud Spaniard's humour, where we may neither speak, look nor do anything but what pleaseth them, than live as freeman and lords in our country.

He that is a traveller must have the back of an ass to bear all, a tongue like the tail of a dog to flatter all, the mouth of a hog to eat what is set before him, the ear of a merchant to hear all and say nothing. And if this be not the highest step of thraldom, there is no liberty or freedom.[72]

In referring to Cain as both "traveller" and "vagabond runagate on the face of the earth," the earl aligns vagrancy and travel to formulate a connection between Continental travel, prized by the ambitious and privileged as a mode of improving themselves, and the vagrancy so condemned by Tudor and Stuart monarchs. And because the text links these two activities—that cultured travel is little more than godless wandering—*The Unfortunate Traveller* proffers an implicit triangulation of vagrancy, cosmopolitanism, and nation-building. Thus, if wandering is associated with God's punishment of the Israelites, then England emerges as the proverbial promised land. And to be genuinely English is not to flaunt one's familiarity with foreign customs but to remain faithful to those of one's home. That specifically English customs are not described is beside the point (at least for now). For the earl, any travel beyond that blessed isle is inescapably unfortunate.

As the earl addresses specific European countries, he enumerates their faults in predictable detail. In particular, he deflates the supposition that one could learn anything of substance while abroad as well as those persons who find England lacking:

What is there in France to be learned more than in England, but falsehood in fellowship, perfect slovenry, to love no man but for my pleasure, to swear *Ah par la mort Dieu* when a man's hams are scabbed? For the idle traveller, I mean not for the soldier, I have known some that have continued there by the space of half-a-dozen years, and when they come home they have hid a little wearish lean face under a broad French hat,

---

72. Nashe, *The Unfortunate Traveller*, 341.

kept a terrible coil with the dust in the street of their long cloaks of grey paper, and spoke English strangely. Nought else have they profited by their travel, save learnt to distinguish of the true Bordeaux grape, and know a cup of neat Gascoigne wine from wine of Orleance. Yea, and peradventure this also, to esteem of the pox as a pimple, to wear a velvet patch on their face, and walk melancholy with their arms folded.[73]

In this satire of French customs, the earl evinces disdain for both the cultural capital of Continental travel and the insistently irksome performances of cosmopolitanism once on English soil by emptying them of their significance. Or, more specifically, the earl reveals their meager gains to be little more than an accumulation of knowledge that extends only to a superficial familiarity with wine and the contraction of a raging case of syphilis, signaled by his reference to a "velvet patch" used to disguise necrotic flesh. As he ventriloquizes an aggressively nationalist stance, one that denigrates other countries and all those who have contact with them, he espouses a rhetoric that reinforces how cosmopolitanism plagues the nation-state. Englishness, even as the earl never articulates its definition, is consequently diluted by the exposure to foreign mores and the too liberal embrace of them.

It's tempting to disregard the episode, to chalk his words up to the frustration and palpable homesickness of the banished or even as one of the many bizarre anecdotes that pepper the novel. Moreover, there is always the problem of taking anything seriously or ascribing some kind of message, especially a didactic one, to *The Unfortunate Traveller*. In the grand tradition of satire, everything—especially those values held most dear—is scrutinized, emptied out, and laughed at.[74] But insofar as Nashe devotes pages to the earl's diatribe, *The Unfortunate Traveller* privileges the perspective, in spite of its hyperbole, as subsequent pages corroborate. If the earl is a voice of an emergent English nationalism, this "wisdom" is recognized only belatedly. When Wilton manages to extricate himself from the monologizing earl, he confides in the reader: "Here's a stir, thought I to myself, after I was set at liberty, that is worse than an upbraiding lesson after a breeching. Certainly if I had bethought me like a rascal as I was, he should have had an Ave Marie of me for his cynic exhortation. God plagued me for deriding such a grave fatherly advertiser. List the worst throw of ill lucks. Tracing up and down the city to seek my courtesan . . ."[75]

73. Ibid., 344.

74. Emily King, "Dirty Jokes: Disgust, Desire, and the Pornographic Narrative in Thomas Nashe's *The Unfortunate Traveller*," in *Disgust in Early Modern English Literature*, ed. Natalie K. Eschenbaum and Barbara Correll (New York: Routledge, 2016), 23–37.

75. Nashe, *The Unfortunate Traveller*, 347.

Between the second and third sentences, Wilton shifts to a retrospective position in which he makes sense of his astonishingly bad fortune, which immediately follows his meeting with the earl, as punishment for not heeding the unsolicited advice. And by using the term "plague," he returns us to the problem that was the origin of his peripatetic journey. He then literalizes the vagrant's itinerant path as he "trace[s] up and down the city" in search of his beloved courtesan, Diamante.[76] In so doing, Wilton reveals his prior intransigence and wrongheadedness in the face of the earl's excellent advice.

What prompts him to embrace the nationalism of the truculent earl and return to England is an encounter with the grotesqueries of Italian revenge. In contrast to the straightforward act of English dueling, Italianate vengeance is typified by elaborate intrigues that culminate in spectacularly violent ends; this is the revenge with which early modern theatrical audiences were preoccupied.[77] The complicated story, which Cutwolfe divulges before his execution, is as follows. In his three-year quest to avenge the death of his brother (Bartol), Cutwolfe has hunted the notorious banditto Esdras of Granado. Upon his capture, Esdras begs Cutwolfe to spare his life, offering himself up for torture, mutilation, and even blasphemy in order to postpone his death. Appearing to accept Esdras's proposition, Cutwolfe urges him to renounce God and issue his contempt for Christianity. After Esdras erupts in a sacrilegious deluge, Cutwolfe bids him open his mouth wide and promptly shoots him to death with a pistol.

From the English perspective, the episode is emblematic of Italianate revenge, as its vengeance is excessive and prolonged rather than immediate—after all, it took years for Cutwolfe to even catch up to Esdras. And what Cutwolfe achieves is not only revenge through murder but also the satisfaction of damning Esdras's soul to hell for all eternity: he accomplishes the elusive goal of inflicting unending revenge on his adversary. But beyond its consistency with Italian revenge, the episode connects nationalism to vengeance. Once Cutwolfe concludes his tale before the Italian villagers who have congregated to witness his execution, he calls forth to them: "This is the fault that hath called me hither; no true Italian but will honour me for it. Revenge is the glory of arms and the highest performance of valour; revenge is whatsoever we call law or justice. The farther we wade in revenge, the nearer

---

76. Her name, which is not only foreign insofar as it derives from the French past participle of *diamanter*, is also synonymous with artifice. The *OED* defines diamanté as "material to which a sparkling effect is given by the use of paste brilliants, powdered glass or crystal." The artificial jewels of costume jewelry are examples. See *OED*, s.v. "diamanté, *n*."

77. Bowers, *Elizabethan Revenge Tragedy, 1587–1642*, 2nd ed., 47–56.

come we to the throne of the Almighty."[78] Though vengefulness may be next to godliness in Cutwolfe's blasphemous construction, he appeals specifically to his countrymen through a nationalist rhetoric ("no true Italian") in which their stance on vengeance is the gauge for their patriotism. Thus, *The Unfortunate Traveller* offers revenge as a litmus test to distinguish nation-states and their cultural values.

Even as the onlookers repudiate Cutwolfe's association of vengeance with Italian identity, their behavior only confirms his claim as they cry, "Executioner, torture him, tear him, or we will tear thee in pieces if thou spare him!"[79] The outcry is peculiar for a number of reasons, not least of which is that Cutwolfe's death sentence has already been determined, and there is nothing to suggest that the executioner retains the power to remit it. Therefore, the commands of the rapacious mob emerge as simultaneously threatening and superfluous. Moreover, the description of Cutwolfe's execution puts into question the very notion of Italian justice insofar as state punishment and (Italian) vengeance exist in an uncomfortable proximity, lending credence to his claim that "revenge is whatsoever we call law or justice." The resultant barbarism becomes representative of Italy's official justice:

> Bravely did [the executioner] drum on this Cutwolfe's bones, not breaking them outright but, like a saddler knocking in of tacks, jarring on them quaveringly with his hammer a great while together. No joint about him but with a hatchet he had for the nonce he disjointed half, and then with boiling lead soldered up the wounds from bleeding. His tongue he pulled out, lest he should blaspheme in his torment. Venomous stinging worms he thrust into his ears to keep his head ravingly occupied. With cankers scruzed to pieces he rubbed his mouth and his gums. No limb of his but was lingeringly splintered in shivers. In this horror left they him on the wheel as in hell, where, yet living, he might behold his flesh legacied amongst the fowls of the air.[80]

There is perhaps little to add to this paragraph of grotesqueries, save that the people's vehement condemnation of Cutwolfe's perspective—his insistence that revenge is Italian, just, godly, and valorous—is revealed to be little more than empty hypocrisy by the grisly scene as the executioner deploys a most welcome torture and prolonged death to which all respond with enthusiastic approval. Although Cutwolfe's execrations and actions (i.e., causing Esdras to

---

78. Nashe, *The Unfortunate Traveller*, 369.
79. Ibid.
80. Ibid.

blaspheme and murdering him immediately thereafter) *ought* to retroactively function to legitimize the state punishment, the scene ultimately fails in that regard. Insofar as *The Unfortunate Traveller* shows state justice to be in vertiginous excess to the retribution enacted by Cutwolfe on Esdras, it urges readers to consider how spectacular vengeance masks the unimaginable extent of state violence. Or, put differently, state-sanctioned vengeance permits just enough distance from gratuitous violence to allow for a bit of pleasure in spectatorship. And this point returns us once more to Agamben, for that scopic pleasure derives in part from the spectators' relation to sovereignty. Here, Italian witnesses, who certainly do not regard themselves as precarious, function in alignment with sovereign power and are therefore able to disavow their vulnerability. As spectators issue imperatives to the executioner—the one who is specifically designated to carry out state justice—they, much like Alexander Iden, arrogate to themselves the sovereign privilege of determining which subjects live and die. Though the usurpation is in appearance only, it demonstrates their investment in the fantasy of existing as lesser sovereigns-by-proxy and of repudiating their collective vulnerability before authentic sovereignty.

For Jack Wilton, the spectacle is sufficiently disturbing to propel him back to his homeland. If, as the strange episode advances, an embrace of revenge is the hallmark of Italian identity, an authentic English identity, which is understood as antithetical to the Italian, would be opposed to the revenge depicted in this text. Wilton's own words appear to advance this conclusion: "One murder begetteth another; was never yet bloodshed barren from the beginning of the world to this day. Mortifiedly abjected and daunted was I with this truculent tragedy of Cutwolfe and Esdras. To such straight life did it thenceforward incite me that ere I went out of Bologna I married my courtesan, performed many alms-deeds, and hasted so fast out of the Sodom of Italy, that within forty days I arrived at the King of England's camp twixt Ardes and Guines in France."[81] If vengefulness is concomitant with Italian identity, Wilton's subsequent repudiation is an embrace of his Englishness. Whereas the Italian legal system and its witnesses engage in partisan violence, Wilton laments the tragic ends of Cutwolfe and Esdras in a detached fashion. In so doing, he confirms his English identity, as viewing the violence does not inspire him to engage in retributive violence on anyone's behalf. Insofar as he rectifies his unwieldy ways (i.e., marrying Diamante and performing penance for his misdeeds), a thoroughly rehabilitated Wilton escapes from Italy and the aimlessness of his wandering, now plodding back to English soil to enjoy the

---

81. Ibid., 369–70.

promises of the "straight life." And *The Unfortunate Traveller* seems all too eager to accommodate this orthodox interpretation.

But a skeptical eye might perceive a second interpretation wriggling below the surface, one that is indebted to but ironizes this initial reading. Indeed, Nashe's final trick is to embed a sly satire of nationalism and the fantasies it engenders in the reformation of Jack Wilton. To begin, the English camp "twixt Ardes and Guines in France" (i.e., the Pale of Calais) to which Wilton retreats no longer belongs to England by the time *The Unfortunate Traveller* is published in 1594. And insofar as the text grounds its national identity in tenuous earth—that is, land that belongs to France and has since 1558—Nashe calls into question a coherent sense of Englishness. Put simply, if the very borders of England are unstable or, at the least, subject to revision, how could one isolate something so abstract as English character?

The second indication of satire arises from the description of Cutwolfe's execution. While Nashe lingers on the depravity of Italian executions, it is scarcely a far cry from English capital punishment, which relied on the public hanging and mutilation of convicted persons as well as the strategic display of their rotting flesh. Consider, for instance, the 1570 execution of Thomas and Christopher Norton at Tyburn, who were found guilty of treason: "With that the Hangman executed his office, and beyng hanged a little while, and then cut downe, the Butcher opening him, and as he tooke out his Bowels he cried, and said Oh, Lorde, Lorde, have mercie on me, and so yelded up the Ghost: then being likewise quartered as the other was, and their Bowels burned, *as the manner is*: their Quarters were put into a Basket, provided for the purpose, and so carried to Newgate, where they were perboyled. And afterward their Heads set on London Brydge, and their Quarters set up on sundrie severall gates of the Citie of London."[82] Even as the passage is unconcerned with the matter of English identity, its curious aside used to describe the incineration of entrails—"as the manner is"—functions as a placeholder, even as shorthand, for the cultural practices of and expectations for English executions. Whatever manner of torture distinguishes English executioners from their Italian counterparts, both the fictionalized account of state justice in Italy and the historical sentences of early modern England are united in their capacity for incommensurately gruesome and spectacular violence against individual bodies. Indeed, their discomfiting proximity suggests one mode by which *The Unfortunate Traveller* draws attention to the fictive nature of national identities.

---

82. *The severall confessions of Thomas Norton, and Christopher Norton: two of the northern rebels: who suffred at Tiburne, and were drawen, hanged, and quartered, for treason, May 27, 1570* (London: William How[e], [1570]), A6v–A7r. Emphasis mine.

What the text then divulges is the construction of national fantasies—for England, Italy is a necessary "Sodom" and site of vengefulness such that England, by contrast, might inhabit the place of righteousness and justice. Thus, if we take those readings together, we see clearly the fantasy of England's identity and the mode by which this construction takes place. The first is a flattering, untroubled reading that aggrandizes England in contrast to Italy; this second reading ironizes the first, revealing the flimsiness on which England stakes its national identity. In terms of the chapter's focus on vengeance and vagrancy, the impoverished vagrant offers social cohesion to normative subjects within the domestic project of nationalism, while the affluent cosmopolitan vagrant and his eventual recoil from other cultures extends the fantasy of a secure English identity. One's embrace of and participation in civil vengeance against vagrant types—as opposed to the enactment of "uncivilized" vengeful spectacles—function as a litmus test for belonging, even for Englishness itself.

As *The Unfortunate Traveller* expands its definition of vagrancy to encapsulate travel abroad or, more specifically, cosmopolitanism, it symptomatizes the anxiety regarding England's identity, an identity that, in spite of the text's preoccupation with Englishness, fails to articulate its specific parameters. Neither Wilton nor his interlocutors explain Englishness, and the conspicuous absence is instead managed by the earl's aggressive caricatures of global competitors. If we take seriously the grim satire at the text's conclusion, England's identity is defined only by negation—not French, not Italian, not German, neither vengeful nor vagrant, and so forth. What *The Unfortunate Traveller* reveals is the constitutive emptiness upon which Englishness founds itself and its floundering efforts to articulate an identity as an emerging nation-state and empire.

Extending the focus on English identity, the final chapter explores the construction of national memory during the Interregnum. If, by aligning oneself with the sovereign and his aims, normative subjects disavow the material reality of their collective precariousness and jettison vagrants from the social body, how does the dynamic change when the sovereign is executed? Specifically, how does republicanism shift the dynamics of social cohesion, particularly as it relates to narratives of memory and history? And how might civil vengeance mutate in these strange new circumstances?

CHAPTER 4

Commemorating Revenge

Mourning, Memory, and Retributive Alternatives in the English Interregnum

> . . . Despising,
> For you, the city, thus I turn my back:
> There is a world elsewhere.
>
> —Shakespeare, *Coriolanus*

In chapter 3, I proposed that normative members of a social collective embrace a fantasy of victimhood to retroactively justify their violent actions, a narrative that reorients otherwise indefensible behavior as part of a revised causality sustained by civil vengeance. In so doing, members reaffirm their social bonds through communal antipathy toward designated scapegoats—a dynamic present in early modern England in relation to its peripatetic population. Vengeance also informs the precarious identity of the emergent nation-state insofar as one's stance on spectacular revenge serves as the litmus test for one's barbarism. Put simply, a repudiation of this type of revenge emerges as the mark of proper Englishness.

Chapter 4 moves forward several decades in history to focus on the English Interregnum and is perched between two arresting acts of revenge. The first is the trial and public execution of Charles I—perceived by some as fitting vengeance for his tyranny and gross misuse of power, while regarded by others as the sacrilegious murder of God's divine appointee on earth. From the spectacle of the sovereign body on a scaffold springs a second episode of choreographed revenge, which occurs on the twelve-year anniversary of the first: the disinterment of Oliver Cromwell, Henry Ireton, and John Bradshaw; the hanging of their corpses at Tyburn; and their eventual decapitation and the ignominious burial of their trunks in a pit. If civil vengeance facilitates cohesion within England and participates in its identity-making abroad, how does that phenomenon materialize between these episodes of spectacular revenge, episodes that hearken back to the blood-speckled stages of the most gruesome revenge tragedies? What are the diffuse effects of civil vengeance, and how do subjects grapple with them during this period?

Against the backdrop of this perverse twinning—that of the executed monarch with the symbolic retaliation against those who held power during the Interregnum—I extend the previous chapter's focus on national identity through an exploration of memory and history, individual and national. Specifically, the final chapter probes the relational contours of civil vengeance and national memory. In the wake of Charles's disposal, how might civil vengeance shape national memory? How are subjects inculcated, especially ones who are opposed to the new national narrative promoted by the Interregnum government, and what forms does the inculcation take? Finally, if we consider that the enforcement of national memory constitutes an example of civil vengeance, what are the opportunities for resistance? To organize my answers to these questions, I divide this final chapter into three sections. In the first, I look to parliamentary documents to establish how the new government conceives of its own recent history and disseminates that information—that is, how it enforces national memory—to skeptical subjects. In the second section, I examine a collection of royalist literary responses to explore how such writers refute the national narrative and, in their refutation, exact revenge for the king's death. Against the intractability of these opposing political stances and their competition to define the dominant ideological narrative, I read Margaret Cavendish's *Sociable Letters* to explore possibilities for resistance to civil vengeance in the third and final section. Insofar as civil vengeance has saturated the Interregnum's political discourse as I trace it, Cavendish offers us a rare glimpse of how individuals might sidestep or, at the very least, negotiate this intractability.

Given this chapter's focus on national memory, I begin with three accounts of Charles I's execution to examine how trauma shapes both the historical record and individual perceptions. Displaying remarkable self-consciousness concerning how future generations would remember the execution and how they would be remembered as the subjects who permitted it in the first place, the following accounts engage actively with history-making and questions of memory. Let us commence, then, with the morning of 30 January 1649 and the rupture it presaged for England and its inhabitants. In *A compleat history of the life and raigne of King Charles*, William Sanderson insists that news of the king's death prompted much physiological distress in his loyal subjects: "Women miscarried, men fell into melancholly, some with Consternations expired; men, women, and children, then, and yet unborn, suffering in him and for him.["1] As Sanderson recounts these spontaneous reactions of sympathy, he forges a connection between the "unnatural" regicide and its equally "unnatural" effects reverberating throughout the kingdom. That Charles's execution could provoke all this demonstrates the malignancy of a topsy-turvy country that murdered its king. But beyond this, Sanderson also introduces a temporal glitch in an attempt to articulate the event's enormity. In detailing the diverse reactions to the king's execution, much of his chronicle remains appropriately in the past tense, but his treatment of the future—in the form of the "yet unborn"—is less straightforward. The "yet unborn" are the previously miscarried fetuses, and they are, to put plainly the sad matter, never to be born. I read this not as mere euphemism but rather as a mode of maintaining the fetuses' potentiality and carrying it forward into the future such that they might suffer indefinitely, a point emphasized by the participle phrase in the final clause, along with and for the deceased king. Such are the means by which Sanderson resuscitates Charles I to extract sympathy from his readers and on behalf of the royalist cause, a sympathy that would then avenge the deceased king against the new government and its supporters. Yet this strange sentence also points to the ways in which the event's magnitude—or, more precisely, the means by which grieving subjects process it—halts time altogether. While past actions are transferred into the future through the participle phrase, England's future, insofar as it is secured through reproduction, is stopped in its tracks.

Time remains a central actor in Lord Thomas Fairfax's recollections of the execution, functioning strangely in an enigmatic sentence: "Oh let that day from time be blotted quite."[2] Even for the parliamentarian Fairfax, no great admirer of Charles I, the regicide's enormity ought to expunge the day itself from all record and every memory; his pitiful "oh" persists as a lamentation for that impossibility.[3] And while the politics of Dr. Thomas Fuller differed from those of Lord Fairfax, Fuller's biographer records his reactions in similar terms: "For what shall I write said he, of the *Worthies* of *England*, when this Horrid Act will bring such an infamy upon the whole nation as will ever cloud and darken all its former, and suppresse its future rising glories?"[4] Even as Fuller's biography exists as a record of the past, the consequences of

---

1. William Sanderson, *A compleat history of the life and raigne of King Charles from his cradle to his grave* (London, 1658), 1139.

2. Quoted in C. V. Wedgwood, *The Trial of Charles I* (London: Penguin, 1983), 195.

3. Fairfax served as commander in chief of the parliamentary army (the "New Model Army") during the Civil War. Despite participating in Pride's Purge, he blanched at the prospect of putting the king on trial and resigned his position.

4. John Fell, *The life of that reverend divine, and learned historian, Dr. Thomas Fuller* (London, 1661), D4r.

regicide are described in a claustrophobic future tense that is perpetually circumscribed by the event. And while Fairfax desires the day to be excised from the historical record, Fuller's remarks imagine its contaminating effects both backward in time—in which the present enacts a malevolent revision of England's past history—and forward into its now-limited future. Thus, the regicide becomes an atemporal blot that brings teleology to its knees and revises reputation abroad. It erupts as the singularly monstrous feature that defines Englishness.

I chart these examples to suggest how contemporaries engaged questions of time and history—that is, narrative—in order to make legible social fissures and to metabolize trauma.[5] Yet these emergent narratives are also vulnerable to political machinations and ideological manipulations, a matter to which much of this final chapter is devoted. For the moment, though, I want to establish how I understand the relation between historical narrative in the Interregnum and the phenomenon of civil vengeance as I have defined it thus far. To have defeated their political opposition, put the king on trial, carried out his execution, and constructed a government in their own image, republicans achieved unequivocal victory. But to interpret these events as victories first requires the composition and dissemination of a triumphal narrative, one that is capable of overriding the palpable horror expressed by each of the three accounts that I have just discussed. In promulgating their tale of victory, republicans oblige those most resistant to their historical interpretation to remember differently. Even as the enforcement of national memory strips agency from subjects, a maneuver that is at once coercive and unethical, the act alone would not seem to lend itself to associations with vengeance, civil or otherwise.

Yet there are at least two reasons why national memory may be characterized as civil vengeance. To begin, constitutive excess marks the phenomenon,

---

5. On the matter of narrative, numerous studies have attended to the literary implications of the mid-seventeenth-century political upheaval. For an examination of primarily canonical literature and its political strategies, see Thomas N. Corns, *Uncloistered Virtue: English Political Literature, 1640–1660* (Oxford: Oxford University Press, 1992). Studies that investigate less traditional texts and their effects include Joad Raymond's *The Invention of the Newspaper: English Newsbooks, 1641–1649* (Oxford: Oxford University Press, 1996), which traces the evolution of the English newsbook; and Sharon Achinstein's *Milton and the Revolutionary Reader* (Princeton, NJ: Princeton University Press, 1994), which argues that the period's proliferation of texts generated a new political reader. For an analysis of the ongoing polemicization of literature, see Paul Salzman, *Literature and Politics in the 1620s: "Whisper'd Counsells"* (Basingstoke, UK: Palgrave Macmillan, 2014); Nigel Smith, *Literature and Revolution in England, 1640–1660* (New Haven, CT: Yale University Press, 1997); and Steven Zwicker, *Lines of Authority: Politics and English Literary Culture, 1649–1689* (Ithaca, NY: Cornell University Press, 1993). David Norbrook charts England's distinctly republican legacy in literary culture in *Writing the English Republic: Poetry, Rhetoric and Politics, 1627–1660* (Cambridge: Cambridge University Press, 2000).

thanks in part to its rejection of episodic structure. While the event of spectacular revenge is contained within temporal boundaries—there is a clear demarcation of the episode's start and conclusion—civil vengeance features no such tidiness. That the demand to remember differently be heaped onto the indisputable military defeat of royalists, republicans reveal a perverse insistence on *more*. Ordinary victory proves insufficient. And because their victory is expansive, it is the capaciousness of the future, not the inadequacy of the present, that is required to hold its full potential. Thus, in compelling subjects to remember differently, these enforced memories extend generationally beyond individuals, and the distortions are transmitted into the future. In so doing, national memory—a flattering narrative in the service only of the nation-state, its leaders, and its beneficiaries—approximates most closely the unceasing quality of civil vengeance.[6] As when Queen Elizabeth admonished a knight at her coronation and extracted from him an admission of his inferiority,[7] national memory coerces subjects into agreement with the proffered narrative and elicits yet another disclosure of their failure. It is not enough to roundly trounce others; they must be made to admit, "Yes, yes, you've roundly trounced me."

Although national memory offers the semblance of agency—after all, what could be more private and beyond the purview of the law than one's memory?—its mandatory participation makes it a choiceless choice. Indeed, the disingenuous invitation of civic participation, an invitation that exacts punishment but remains illegible as such, returns us to the realm of civil vengeance as well. National memory appropriates something as personal and as subjective as private memory in order to force subjects to pay homage to another sort of narrative. And when one participates in national memory even (or especially) when one remembers the history differently, one is obliged to disavow the reality of the situation and "permit" one's memories to be overwritten by the national narrative. In many cases—of which the Interregnum period is only one example—remembering differently constitutes a material danger for resistant subjects, even as authorities conceal the level of that danger through their rhetorical insistence on choice and agency.

---

6. Although my final chapter restricts itself to the matter of national memory as civil vengeance during the English Interregnum, I support the exportation of this argument to other historical periods. That is, I would contend that the enforcement of national memory—regardless of the techniques or methods—constitutes civil vengeance insofar as the campaign of national memory necessarily accompanies and supplements the military triumphs that establish the nation-state in the first place.

7. I discuss this episode in greater detail in my introduction. For an account of the exchange, see Puttenham, *The arte of English poesie*, 3.24.50.

If, as I have been arguing, civil vengeance demands a surplus on top of its triumph, the republicans' successes make explicit that requirement. The execution of Charles I ushered in not only the dissolution of the monarchy but also the abolition of the House of Lords as well as the Church of England. Yet such victories necessitated a reorientation of reluctant segments of the English populace. Because martial superiority accomplished little in this regard, the attempted reorientation—that is, how republicans unleashed the full scope of their civil vengeance—was achieved through the institution of a new national memory. Whether or not the republican campaign was a success in that regard is not this chapter's consideration; rather, my aim here is to trace how the new authorities sought to inculcate national memory. But before I turn my attention to that argument, I wish to first explain briefly this chapter's use of national memory and how it arises from ongoing discussions of collective memory.

Its origins located in Maurice Halbwachs's pioneering work, collective memory is defined as "the social phenomenon or cultural dimension of what groups remember."[8] Astrid Erll observes that collective memory proceeds from an "operative metaphor" that takes the "concept of 'remembering' (a cognitive process which takes place in individual brains) [and] is metaphorically transferred to the level of culture."[9] For Laura Doan, the metaphoric transfer that gives rise to collective memory "confirms and consolidates, distills and simplifies," often through commemorative and other communal rituals.[10] By contrast, "personal recollections" constitute individual memory.[11] Despite its difference, individual memory need not be at odds with collective memory, for both categories mutually affect and structure each other. Because remembering, whether individual or collective, reconstructs the past, such work is "only possible because the individual mind has recourse to the group mind," as Marc Bloch insists, "which provides a framework for reconstructing the past."[12] If we accept Bloch's claim, then, collective memory might be revised as "simply everyday communication between individuals."[13]

8. Laura Doan, "Queer History / Queer Memory: The Case of Alan Turing," *GLQ: A Journal of Lesbian and Gay Studies* 23, no. 1 (2017): 113–36, quote from 113–14.

9. Astrid Erll, "Cultural Memory Studies: An Introduction," in *A Companion to Cultural Memory Studies*, ed. Astrid Erll and Ansgar Nünning (Berlin: De Gruyter, 2010), 1–18, quote from 4.

10. Doan, "Queer History / Queer Memory," 118.

11. Ibid., 113–14.

12. Marc Bloch, "Memoire collective, tradition et coutume: A propos d'un livre recent," in *The Collective Memory Reader*, ed. Jeffrey K. Olick, Vered Vinitzky-Seroussi, and Daniel Levy (New York: Oxford University Press, 2011), 150–55, quote from 151.

13. Ibid., 153. For an excellent discussion of custom, its relation to memory, and social stratification, see Andy Wood, *The Memory of the People: Custom and Popular Senses of the Past in Early Modern England* (Cambridge: Cambridge University Press, 2013).

National history is a form of collective memory, remaining indebted to the recollections of individual witnesses.[14] For this reason, I understand national history as related to national memory, so I often use the terms interchangeably throughout the chapter. And yet the whiff of institutional privilege about national history masks a more complicated construction. Derrida gestures toward this work when he observes how the process of history generates excess as well as the interpretative work necessitated by that excess. He writes: "'One must' means *one must* filter, sift, criticize, one must sort out several different possibilities that inhabit the same injunction . . . If the readability of a legacy were given, natural, transparent, univocal, if it did not call for and at the same time defy interpretation, we would never have anything to inherit from it."[15] To do the task of national history demands that state authorities consolidate, simplify, or simply forget other competing narratives. Ernest Renan details the relation between the formation of the nation-state and memory, attesting to the singular role of this deliberate amnesia: "Forgetting, I would even go so far as to say historical error, is a crucial factor in the creation of a nation."[16] Narratives of national history sustain nation-states, and in the republic and later in the protectorate, we may discern the development of the new government's narrative and the modes by which authorities inculcated subjects. This was achieved, I will argue, through literary responses and, in particular, through the republican institution of national days of mourning and thanksgiving.

To make the case that the government's efforts to craft a national narrative and enforce its memory constitute civil vengeance against its citizens, this section first examines the suppression of royalist tracts and the production of alternative texts. From there, I proceed to an analysis of parliamentary acts that designate specific holidays, which, as I will show, function to manipulate affective and memorial relations to the recent past. Even as some degree of tolerance characterized the Commonwealth—Andrew Lacey calls it "not particularly draconian"[17]—a declaration of royalist sympathies carried with it serious consequences.[18] Yet in spite of penalty and punishment, royalist

14. Erll, "Cultural Memory Studies," 7.

15. Jacques Derrida, *Specters of Marx: The State of the Debt, the Work of Mourning, and the New International*, trans. Peggy Kamuf (New York: Routledge, 1994), 16.

16. Ernest Renan, "What Is a Nation?," in Olick, Vinitzky-Seroussi, and Levy, *The Collective Memory Reader*, 80–33, quote from 80.

17. Andrew Lacey, *The Cult of King Charles the Martyr* (Suffolk, UK: Boydell Press, 2003), 51.

18. There were discernible limits to the republic's tolerance. Consider, for instance, the general suppression of Quakers as well as the highly publicized case and punishment of Quaker leader James Naylor, who reenacted Christ's arrival in Jerusalem.

publications proliferated during the period, and to combat incendiary materials that contradicted the republic's national narrative, authorities sought to confiscate copies. Among these contraband texts, which include elegies, broadside ballads, sermons, and satirical plays, *Eikon Basilike*—the purported memoir and prayers of the recently deceased king—is best known. To suppress subsequent publications, republican authorities targeted involved printers who operated within their borders.[19] Yet the confiscation and suppression of print—and even the temporary imprisonment and fining of involved printers—were time-intensive activities difficult to implement, especially in the absence of enforcement bodies.[20]

To combat more effectively this literary liability, the Council of State recruited specific writers and even formerly royalist printers to support their propaganda machine.[21] For instance, in response to the political and affective success of *Eikon Basilike*, the government put forth *Eikonoklastes*, in which John Milton, in his capacity as secretary for foreign tongues, refutes the claims of the deceased king point by point.[22] Though *Eikonoklastes* lacks the literary finesse with which Milton is typically associated, it represents a formidable refutation of the Christological narrative proffered by royalists, who generally regarded Charles's execution as a sacrilegious echo of the crucifixion.[23] By eschewing emotional appeals altogether and, in this manner, diverging from the approach of most royalist authors, Milton limits the terms of the debate to the repercussions of the king's political decisions. Indeed, by comparing

19. Regarding specific attempts to disrupt London printers and summon them before the Council of State, see Lacey, *The Cult of King Charles*, 86–88.

20. Even prior to the establishment of the republic, censorship apparatuses had crumbled during the Civil War. The disintegration of censorship and the temporary end of licensing, part of which was due to the 1641 abolition of the Star Chamber, left Charles vulnerable during the later years of his reign thanks, in particular, to the publication of deeply conflicting interpretations of his rule. Joad Raymond summarizes his unique position: "[He] was the first ruler of England, Wales, Scotland, or Ireland to be represented by a popular press beyond his control" ("Popular Representations of Charles I," in *The Royal Image: Representations of Charles I*, ed. Thomas N. Corns [Cambridge: Cambridge University Press, 1999], 47–73, quote from 47).

21. William Dugard was one such an example who, following his arrest for printing *Eikon* and his imprisonment in Newgate, recanted his royalism. For that, he was rewarded with an appointment as printer for the Council of State. See Lacey, *The Cult of King Charles*, 86–87.

22. Technically, *Eikon Alethine*, not *Eikonoklastes*, was the first republican response to *Eikon Basilike*. For an analysis of the similarities between the two texts, see Laura Blair McKnight, "Crucifixion or Apocalypse? Refiguring the *Eikon Basilike*," in *Religion, Literature, and Politics in Post-Reformation England, 1540–1688*, ed. Donna B. Hamilton and Richard Strier (Cambridge: Cambridge University Press, 1996), 138–60, esp. 149–50.

23. The royalist insistence on the parallels between Charles I and Christ was not only an opportunistic narrative, though. On the day that Charles I was executed, the Book of Common Prayer had appointed the trial and crucifixion of Christ from Matthew's Gospel as its second lesson. See Helen W. Randall, "The Rise and Fall of a Martyrology: Sermons on Charles I," *Huntington Library Quarterly* 10 (1947): 135–67, esp. 137.

Eikon's rhetorical claims to historical fact—that is, comparing printed words to documented deeds—he leverages his most effective criticisms of Charles and the royalist cause. Locating the primary battleground of this publicity campaign in personal memory, Milton shifts the conversation to place a premium on the perceptions, interpretations, and recollections of his readers.[24] When he explains that his goal is "only remembering them the truth of what they themselves know to be here [in *Eikon Basilike*] misaffirmed," he demonstrates an awareness of the technique and its intended consequence.[25] Thus, Milton understands himself not as an ideologue but as a conduit through which his readers might free themselves from the constraints of the deceased king's words, and his readership, then, collaborates with him—and, by extension, with the new government—in a collective resistance to what they perceive to be historical revision.

Even as the restrictions on print materials and the eventual deployment of print for political ends hardly constituted violent or paranoid suppression for the time, it was precisely the government's general policy of tolerance that ushered in the disingenuousness that I associate with civil vengeance. For this reason, I interpret the self-styled displays of magnanimity as a method by which authorities more effectively and discreetly construct a new national memory as well as affectively reorient the Commonwealth's members. Early in its tenure, the new government recognized the political benefits of instituting compulsory days of fasting and prayer through which inculcation most often occurred. Lois Potter contends that these days were the "chief means" in the government's attempts to "achieve a sense of communal unity."[26] Moreover, the institution of such events distinguished the republic from its monarchical predecessors. Elizabeth I, for example, rejected the first request for a public fast in 1580, whereas Charles I begrudgingly granted a 1628 petition of fasting but made clear that "he hoped it would not become a precedent."[27] Against this landscape of general reluctance and feet-dragging, Parliament appointed mandatory days of fasting each month after December 1641; later, it would reserve the second Tuesday of each month as a day of thanksgiving.[28]

---

24. "To avoid alienating readers," Jim Daems and Holly Faith Nelson write, "Milton frequently appeals to [his readers'] memory and cognition" (Introduction to *Eikon Basilike*, ed. Jim Daems and Holly Faith Nelson [Peterborough, ON: Broadview Press, 2006], 13–39, quote from 32).

25. John Milton, "Selections from *Eikonoklastes*," in Daems and Nelson, *Eikon Basilike*, 217–83, quote from 222.

26. Lois Potter, *Secret Rites and Secret Writing: Royalist Literature, 1641–1660* (Cambridge: Cambridge University Press, 1989), 139.

27. Ibid.

28. Ibid.

The specific declarations and appointments to which we now turn our attention are in excess of this established schedule.

Releasing an act that declared a solemn day set aside for "humiliation, fasting, and prayer" in February 1650, Parliament established its rationale thusly:

> The Lord who Ruleth over the Nations, who disposeth and ordereth all things . . . in rescuing Us out of the destroying hands of Tyranny, Popery, and Superstition: Which experience of the Lords wonderful Goodness and Mercy towards this Nation, might have wrought an answerable return of Duty and Obedience; and the sense of the want hereof ought to fill us with shame, astonishment and confusion of face, especially when (in stead thereof) we finde in the midst of it, such crying Sins, hideous Blasphemies, and unheard of Abominations (and that by some under pretence of Liberty, and greater measure of Light) as after all our wondrous Deliverances, do manifest themselves to the exceeding dishonor of God, and reproach of our Christian Profession: To the end therefore that this Nation in general, and every one in particular may have an opportunity to know and acknowledge their Sins in the sight of God, and be truly humbled for them.[29]

Those sympathetic to the plight of exiled Stuarts shared Alexander Leslie's assessment that the king's execution was "a parricide so heinous, so horrible," that its parallel may be located only in the "murther of Christ."[30] Yet here Parliament rehabilitates that unpleasantry into God's heroic rescue efforts from an overwhelming Catholic conspiracy of "Tyranny, Popery, and Superstition," while royalists are recast as sinners who act on the "pretence of Liberty." Only after upending the values of their detractors (e.g., monarchical rule, adherence to God's divine order, and holy resistance to an illegitimate government) may the government then denounce its subjects for their errant ingratitude for the many blessings and "wondrous Deliverances" visited on them and the nation as a whole. To do so, Parliament enumerates the sins of the populace, moving from "crying" ones—a biblical allusion to the first murder—to a reliance on supplementary logic whereby the abominations occurring in England are "unheard of" and wholly inconceivable. And though royalists have insisted that republicans are guilty of such abominations, Parliament turns the accusation against English subjects as a whole. Figurative language reinforces the point as the cited sins shift from that which can be discerned in an aural reg-

---

29. *An Act appointing Thursday the last day of February, 1649. for a solemn day of humiliation, fasting and prayer and declaring the grounds thereof* (London: Edward Husband and John Field, 1650).

30. Robert Wilcher, *The Writing of Royalism, 1628–1660* (Cambridge: Cambridge University Press, 2001), 293.

ister (i.e., "crying") to that which escapes it (i.e., "unheard") but nevertheless blights the republic. Only after subjects have comprehended the extent of their sins—or, more exactly, comprehended the extent to which they cannot comprehend their near-infinite culpability—may they be "truly humbled" before God. Though perhaps desirable from a religious perspective, this humility signals subjects' malleability before the new government. Thus, the aim here is the deliberate cultivation of subjects who are not only subdued but also acquiescent to both the terms and history of their conquerors.

But, to the government's credit, this is no empty exercise in abjection, as Parliament specifies ambitious outcomes for the day of solemnity. Among those listed are the following: "That all Differences among Brethren might be reconciled in love; That the Designs, Combinations and Conspiracies of all wicked men (whether within or without us) to imbroil this Nation in a New War, may be discovered and prevented; and that Whilest ungodly men do make the Arm of Flesh their Confidence, We may testifie (from an abundant experience of the Lords Goodness) That our Strength is onely in the Living God."[31] In particular, I want to meditate on the emergent tension between the "wicked" or "ungodly" men and the forceful "We" that concludes the passage. Such antagonistic positioning enables its authors to espouse a desire to reconcile "in love" a divided nation, a wish that is revealed as disingenuous by subsequent clauses that recite plots to plunge an already precarious nation into further war. Against these purported intrigues, Parliament supplies the monstrous "We" to consolidate a membership that not only is contingent on one's acceptance of the new government but also yokes that acceptance to an alignment with God. And it is through this divine alignment that the republican government frames its success as a foregone conclusion, a historical inevitability that will dissolve all rivals. Put simply, that dissolution occurs because they place their opposition in an untenable position: Who could willingly inhabit the stance of rebel against God?

Yet in spite of Parliament's attempts at censure, the day failed to absolve England's populace. Mere months later, in a tone more insistent and edged with frustration, authorities declared another day of fasting and mourning: "Although this Nation hath enjoyed many Blessings, and great Deliverances from the hands of God; yet have the People thereof multiplied their Sins, as God hath multiplyed his Blessings upon them, especially the Sins of Unthankfulness and Unfruitfulness . . . [Such sins] may most justly provoke the Lord to multiply his Judgements upon This Nation. The Parliament taking the same into serious consideration, as also the pernicious Designs of the Enemies of

---

31. *An Act appointing Thursday the last day of February, 1649.*

this Commonwealth, to engage the same in a New and Bloody War."[32] As the authors draw a correlation between the plentiful blessings heaped on England and the escalating sins of its people, they point to the relationship as a susceptibility to future divine judgment and punishment. As such, the immorality of the English people becomes a matter of national security insofar as it courts collective chastisement. Gone is the divided nation remarked on in the prior declaration: "the People" are finally reconciled here, if only in their united capacity for gross ingratitude.

Concurrent with these campaigns of abstention is the establishment of days of thanksgiving. Whatever their favorable or affirmative associations, days of thanksgiving also existed as opportunities to rebuke resistant subjects and coerce them into some semblance of gratitude before government authorities. In the 1649 Act for a Day of Publique Thanksgiving, Parliament declares: "The great and wonderful Providences, wherein the Lord hath eminently gone forth in mercy towards this Nation, have been such, that however many do shut their eyes, or murmure against them, or at least refuse to joyn in Publique Acknowledgements, and Thanksgiving to Almighty God for the same; Nevertheless, the Lord hath been pleased to publish to all the world, That it is the work of his own hand."[33] The authors commence their proclamation by foregrounding the presence of those who, like the intransigent Bartleby, would prefer not to accept as providential the recent events that catapulted Cromwell to power. Yet, from Parliament's perspective, detractors appear to pose no significant threat precisely because they engage in impotent modes of refusal—shutting one's eyes, murmuring disapproval, or refusing to join in public displays—even as these acts are recoded as indifference to God. Inherent in their characterization of wary subjects is a strain of anti-Semitism that charges Jews with a pathological blindness to Christ's divinity.[34] In so doing, the text upends associations between Charles I and Christ advocated by royalists and instead defines royalists as the new Jews who are unwilling to accept Cromwell's leadership in English governance and military.

But for whom are these days of thanksgiving designed? And why? Insofar as Parliament conflates political alliances with religious ones and casts its de-

---

32. *An act appointing Thursday the thirteenth of June 1650. to be kept as a day of solemn fasting and humiliation and declaring the reasons and grounds thereof* (London: Edward Husband and John Field, 1650).

33. *An Act for a day of publique thanksgiving to be observed throughout England and Wales, on Thursday on the first of November, 1649* (London: John Field, 1649).

34. This presumed deficiency was a prominent trope in medieval Christian art and architecture and was signaled through the figures of Ecclesia and Synagoga. To associate the figure of Synagoga with spiritual ignorance, she was often depicted as blindfolded, averting her face or even turning her back. See Heinz Schreckenberg, *The Jews in Christian Art: An Illustrated History* (New York: Continuum, 1996), 16–18.

tractors as heretical unbelievers, the act deploys shame to coerce their participation, which is urged further thanks to the mandatory nature of the day and
its accompanying penalty if ignored. Yet the approach does not prompt a genuine transformation in resisters; that is, the tedious institution and compulsory celebration of these holidays cannot possibly convince the doubtful. As
for those already supportive of the republican government or, at the very least,
amenable to it, the enforcement of thanksgiving undermines the natural font
of gratitude presumed to spring forth from devout citizens. Indeed, the very
fact that Parliament views it necessary to create such days implicates their supporters, casting them in a most unflattering light and, by extension, inadvertently framing the new government as uniquely vulnerable to the affective
orientations of its members.

Even as authorities demonstrate a keen investment in managing narratives
of the past, the future is not beyond their purview—here, the rhetorical acrobatics required to construct national memory and to overwrite private memory are especially discernible when it comes to the question of futurity. Citing
specific victories achieved by Cromwell and his army against royalist and con-
federate forces in Ireland, Parliament concludes its list with a peculiar clause:
"and some other additional Victories which God hath cast in since."[35] Though
this act of national thanksgiving is designed as a record of and vehicle for the
dissemination of prior conquests, by including "other additional Victories"—
victories that cannot be cited by name because they have not yet occurred—
the holiday is rendered sufficiently pliable to celebrate the army's victories
achieved after the time of writing but prior to the circulation of the act.
Stranger still is the fact that the text situates these unnamed, yet-to-have-
occurred victories in the present perfect tense, a tense that positions triumph
as a foregone conclusion for the parliamentary army. By eschewing the more
appropriate subjunctive mood and instead deploying the present perfect, Parliament usurps tomorrow by casting it as already determined, thereby disavow-
ing the contingency and radical unknowability of possible futures.

This temporal manipulation, which serves the construction of national
memory, casts the future as past insofar as what is to come is already decided.
Not surprisingly, the effect of this manipulation on the historical past is
one of revision as well. Designating the thirtieth of January—that is, the
anniversary of Charles I's death—as yet another instance of compulsory
thanksgiving, Parliament supplants the individual and necessarily private
commemorations for the deceased king. By toppling acts of memorialization,
acts that tacitly question the government's foundations, authorities erode the

---

35. These so-called victories in Ireland include the notorious Massacre of Drogheda.

already restricted resistance of its opponents. Much like the irreverent joke that arrives too soon, the enforced thanksgiving that is appointed on the two-year anniversary of Charles I's execution rewrites what many regard as traumatic or even sacrilegious into a narrative of divine triumph. The declaration's authors query: "Who is there but must acknowledge, to the Glory and Praise of the Divine Majesty, That *it hath not been by Might, nor by Power, but by the Spirit of the Lord*, that *Englands* Safety and Deliverances have been obtained? So that the People of God throughout this Nation have abundant cause not onely of Admiration, but of Exaltation in the Lord their God."[36] Aided by the flourish of their rhetorical question, the writers compel their readers into agreement and dissolve the possibility of a contrary position, much less an alternative to the terms they propose.

But there is still more, for the institution of thanksgiving constitutes an excruciating turn of the proverbial screw. The cessation of resistance and begrudging submission to its authority emerge as insufficient for the republic: all subjects are obliged to display publicly their gratitude for the republican government and its martial triumphs. And the creation of thanksgiving holidays marshals the affective energies of a populace, making use of their outward displays as the "proof" of the subject's righteousness and, by extension, that of the new government. Therefore, Parliament's declaration of thanksgiving functions not only to stamp out resistance but also to coerce English subjects into displaying its affective opposite, and it is this opposition (i.e., substituting gratitude for resistance) that is then taken as the tautological (and retroactive) justification for the execution of Charles I. Put simply, the mandatory holiday demands the outward embrace of the king's murder and of his murderers, and in the specific designation of 30 January, government authorities make explicit their affective-political maneuvering.

Because the purpose of this book is to both gesture toward and define the diffuse phenomena of civil vengeance, I find myself pausing with this document—a vivid example of the dynamics I have been discussing. As Parliament conflates one's religious orientation with one's political sympathies, it presents its audience with a double bind to effectively silence detractors: for to contradict the triumphal political narrative is to exhibit contempt for God. Even as the flimsiness of the formulation makes visible the manipulation of its authors, the act's language restricts the permissible terms with which one can grapple. The consequence of these narrow parameters is designed to coerce

---

36. *An act for setting apart Thursday the thirtieth day of January, 1650. for a day of publique thanksgiving: together with a declaration of the grounds and reasons thereof* (London: Edward Husband and John Field, [1651]), 1270.

its auditors into an outward display of agreement, if not an inward one as well, or risk inhabiting a position untenable for its early modern audience—manifest thanklessness for or indifference to God's bountiful mercies. To contradict Parliament's request for thanksgiving is to venture into the wilderness and persist in deliberate opposition to God.

As the religious rhetoric of authorities placed royalists and others who harbored sympathies for the deceased king in an indefensible position, the violence of enforced national memory qua civil vengeance was laid bare. And while the new government aimed to stake its claim to legitimacy in memory and narrative, an insistence on remembering differently presented as one technique for negotiating the quandary. That is, individual memory emerged as one way to resist the hegemonic violence of a national historical narrative.[37] Such an elevation of individual memory, as Pierre Nora observes, has "come to resemble the revenge of the underdog or injured party, the outcast, the history of those denied the right to History."[38] Though individual memory might reinvent itself as revenge, it also contains insufficiencies. Memory alone is fragile, and people are vulnerable and subject to erasure. Even as the Interregnum was a relatively brief period of time, and, as such, resistant memories did not die out, memory must be documented and circulated if it is to be considered a viable mode of resistance and revenge. In the following section, I ask how royalist commemorative texts engage with and combat the republican national narrative along the lines of memory and vengeance. What are the specific mechanisms by which authors contest and supplant national memory as well as disseminate alternatives? And if the enforcement of a new national memory indeed constitutes civil vengeance, could we isolate a viable antidote to the phenomenon through counternarrative—that is, narrative that challenges the national story?

Although the split between national narrative and individual memory had been occurring for some time in early modern England, that rupture was perhaps most palpable at the execution of Charles I. Attuned to the troubling

---

37. Warning against the conflation of textual production with positive audience reception, Joad Raymond reminds us that consumption also changes these texts and their reception in the royalist imaginary ("Popular Representations of Charles I," 48). Consider, for example, Laura Lunger Knoppers's insightful assessment of newsbook accounts of Cromwell's protectoral ceremony, which uniformly insist that the occasion was celebrated by all. She notes that other accounts—which include both intercepted missives and diplomatic letters written in cipher—record waning public affection and outright derision (*Constructing Cromwell: Ceremony, Portrait, and Print, 1645–1661* [Cambridge: Cambridge University Press, 2000], 70–72).

38. Pierre Nora, "Reasons for the Current Upsurge in Memory," in Olick, Vinitzky-Seroussi, and Levy, *The Collective Memory Reader*, 437–41, quote from 440.

optics of the spectacle, army troops dispersed gathered crowds after the king expired, an act that, as Lois Potter remarks, effectively banned public mourning.[39] In the face of prohibition, many held the anniversary as a private day of fasting, reflection, and prayer, while others engaged in outward signs of mourning through ordinary acts.[40] For example, some vowed to never again cut their beards, thereby imbuing relatively minor acts with personal meaning and political resistance.[41] Others wore mourning jewelry and, in particular, rings, which often made use of lockets to conceal portraits of the deceased king. Yet on the morning of 30 January, soldiers were unable to stop the many witnesses who rushed to the scaffold to sop up the king's blood with bits of cloth. Of the moment of execution and shortly thereafter, John Nalson recounts: "After a very short pause, his Majesty stretching forth his Hands, the *Executioner* severed his head from his Body: Which being held up and shewed to the People, was with his Body put into a Coffin covered with Velvet, and carried into his Lodging. His Blood was taken up by divers Persons for different ends: By some as trophies of their Villainy, by others as Reliques of a Martyr; and in some hath had the same effect by the Blessing of God, which was often found in his Sacred Touch when living."[42] Whether gruesome trophy, curious artifact, or holy relic, the polysemous blood of Charles continued to exert power well after his death, and published accounts amplified the miraculous qualities of its afterlife. An especially popular pamphlet, *A Miracle of Miracles*, documented the extraordinary recovery of a young woman from Deptford who had been cured of the King's Evil, or scrofula, thanks to her contact with Charles's dried blood.[43] Likewise John Browne's *Adenochoiradelogia* extolled the successful healing of those who relied on and circulated the dried blood of the royal martyr preserved in handkerchiefs.[44] As such, Charles I is the only post-Reformation British ruler to be credited with healing his subjects after his death.[45] But these accounts also conflict with the

---

39. Lois Potter, "The Royal Martyr in the Restoration: National Grief and National Sin," in Korns, *The Royal Image*, 240–62, esp. 241.

40. It is worth remembering that only Ireland and Scotland engaged in military struggle for the restoration of Charles II. As for England and the rest of Europe, these events provoked, according to C. V. Wedgwood, "expressions of anger, indignation and horror followed by feeble action, apathetic acquiescence or shamefaced diplomatic approaches to the murderers" (*A Coffin for King Charles: The Trial and Execution of Charles I* [London: Palgrave Macmillan, 1964], 250).

41. Lacey, *The Cult of King Charles*, 49.

42. J[ohn] Nalson, *A True copy of the journal of the High Court of Justice for the trial of K. Charles I* (London: H. C., 1684), 118.

43. *A Miracle of Miracles: Wrought by the Blood of King Charles the First* (London, 1649).

44. John Browne, *Adenochoiradelogia, or An anatomick-chirurgical treatise of glandules and strumaes or, Kings-evil-swellings* (London: Tho[mas] Newcomb, 1684), 131–37.

45. Lacey, *The Cult of King Charles*, 62.

historical reality of Charles's documented aversion to touching his subjects, especially during the early years of his reign.[46] Yet, in spite of the discrepancy, these miraculous reports attest to and reassert the divinity of the executed king, existing collectively as a powerful rebuke of the nation's current government. As Andrew Lacey puts the matter, "Every healing claimed for the dead king in the 1650s was an affront to the existence of the Republic."[47] And perhaps less dramatically, such accounts also sustained those with Stuart sympathies—a gentle reminder of God's literal hand at work amid the chaos and as a palpable reward for the faithful.

If acts of private commemoration and encounters with Charles's sacred remains might be deemed quiet resistance, the publication of *Eikon Basilike* constituted an unambiguous attack. John Gauden, who is largely credited with editing *Eikon* from papers left by Charles, famously proclaimed of its release: "When [Eikon] came out, just upon the King's death, good God! What shame, rage, and despite filled his murderers! What comfort his friends! How many enemies did it convert! . . . In a word, it was an army and did vanquish more than any sword could."[48] What accounted for *Eikon*'s considerable impact on Charles's legacy? Kevin Sharpe argues that the text "raised the king above the political fray, enshrined his memory, and so deprived the fruits of victory to his conquerors."[49] To write against the republic's historical narrative, *Eikon* embeds itself into existing Protestant narratives, among them the genre of spiritual autobiography.[50] While *Eikon* deployed the trope of "suffering kingship" that aligned Charles with Christ, it also situated him within a greater legacy of Protestant martyrs.[51] In terms of its formal structure, *Eikon* features prayers and meditations, which stylistically resemble psalms, that conclude each chapter, and by mapping the narrative of Charles's divine suffering onto scriptural precedent, *Eikon* yields a remarkably consistent portrait of the sovereign-martyr. Yet the death of Charles was critical to the consolidation of

46. When it was most politically advantageous to position himself as the divine and legitimate ruler against parliamentarians' attacks, Charles extended his sacred touch to cure those afflicted with the King's Evil (Raymond, "Popular Representations of Charles I," 53).

47. Lacey, *The Cult of King Charles*, 61.

48. Richard Helgerson, "Milton Reads the King's Book: Print, Performance, and the Making of a Bourgeois Idol," *Criticism* 29, no. 1 (1987): 1–25, quote from 1.

49. Kevin Sharpe, "'An Image Doting Rabble': The Failure of Republican Culture in Seventeenth-Century England," in *Refiguring Revolutions: Aesthetics and Politics from the English Revolution to the Romantic Revolution*, ed. Kevin Sharpe and Steven N. Zwicker (Berkeley: University of California Press, 1998), 25–56, quote from 33.

50. Daems and Nelson, Introduction to *Eikon Basilike*, 24.

51. The stylistic similarities to Protestant scripture and Foxe's *Book of Martyrs* work to situate Charles within a larger family of those who died for the Protestant cause. See Lacey, *The Cult of King Charles*, 7, 82.

his image, for only then could his supporters "elaborate the image of the pa-tient, Anglican martyr safe in the knowledge that he was not going to frus-trate their efforts by any precipitate actions of his own."[52] And while Puritans equated earthly success with virtue, Charles's death enabled his supporters to contradict that narrative. For them, his defeat and death were amassed as evi-dence of his authority not in the transient material realm but in heaven.

Yet for all its religiosity, one cannot overlook *Eikon*'s central objective: its thinly veiled project of vengeance. In measured tones, J. P. Kenyon calls it a "mixture of pietistic moralising and shrewd historical revisionism," while Linda Woodbridge declares it the "best-selling blockbuster of vengeful self-pity."[53] As a whole, *Eikon* embraces and exploits the principles of civil vengeance through its use of religious rhetoric.[54] Although Charles insists that "[his] blood," like that of Abel, "will cry aloud for vengeance to heaven," he admon-ishes his readers to refrain from retribution on his behalf.[55] In a nod to the inevitability of divine vengeance and its sacred timing, Charles commands his son: "Let then no passion betray You to any study of revenge upon those, whose own sin and folly will sufficiently punish them in due time."[56] Else-where, his vengeful magnanimity furthers the royalist agenda by emphasiz-ing his proximity to Christ, a connection that underscores his divine kingship as the rightful form of government and the gravity of having executed the king. Imploring God, Charles prays: *"O let not My blood be upon them and their Children, whom the fraud and faction of some, not the malice of all, have excited to crucify Me."*[57] Through the tacit threat of generational retribution—held in reserve for the unrepentant—as well as the insistence that only "some" are guilty of this crime, Charles's words in *Eikon* function as a deft text of recruit-ment for royalist resistance.

The consolidated image of Charles achieved by *Eikon Basilike* is later dis-seminated through a profusion of royalist commemorative texts that range

---

52. Ibid., 50–51.

53. J. P. Kenyon, *Stuart England*, 2nd ed. (London: Penguin, 1985), 178; Woodbridge, *English Revenge Drama*, 198.

54. The primary preoccupation of *Eikon*, as Jim Daems and Holly Faith Nelson observe, is not an admission of the sins of the speaker/writer but rather a "sustained condemnation of his political enemies" (Introduction to *Eikon Basilike*, 24).

55. Charles I, "Selections from *Eikon Basilike*," in Daems and Nelson, *Eikon Basilike*, 47–216, quote from 193.

56. Ibid., 190.

57. Ibid., 183. Recurrent throughout the text is Charles's expression of vengeful forgiveness, an element of civil vengeance that I discussed in chapter 2. In another moment, he writes: "I can both forgive them, and pray for them, that God would not impute My blood to them further than to con-vince them, what need they have of Christ's blood to wash their souls from the guilt of shedding mine" (ibid., 199).

from elegy to broadsheet.[58] For the remainder of this section, I will examine a handful of texts that include the poems of Henry King and John Quarles as well as the work of royalists writing and publishing under the cover of anonymity who aim to counter the new national memory. While *Eikon* engages in a rhetoric of vengeful pacificism, subsequent texts evince a greater investment in spectacular moments of comeuppance as a means by which to combat the government's narrative. Like Charles's words in *Eikon*, these texts regularly insist that divine judgment looms, admonishing readers to remain unswayed by the successes of a temporary administration. In particular, their warnings hinge on a construction of the future that permits royalist supporters to account for the apparent delay in heavenly retribution. *A Coffin for King Charles*, a broadside ballad, offers an example of how one might negotiate the ideological conflict by cultivating a fundamental suspicion of appearances:

> But theres a *thunderer* above,
> who though he winke *a while*,
> Is not *with* your *black deeds* in love:
> he *hates* your *damned guile*.
> And though a *time* you *pearce* upon
> The top of *fortunes wheele*,
> You shortly unto *Acheron*,
> (*drunke* with your crimes) shall *reele*.[59]

By invoking the imagery of the wheel, the author associates republican triumphs not with cosmic endorsement but rather with the vagaries of fortune. Furthermore, the "winke *a while*" waiting period emerges as an especially dangerous form of retributive guile, designed to lull offenders into complacency before damning them forever. Such examples refuse the dominant political narrative that insists on God's participation in unseating Charles in favor of establishing the Commonwealth and Protectorate; instead, these royalist narratives claim God for their political purposes and maintain that the delay in divine retribution will prove all the more deadly for their opponents.

Other texts, though insisting on the temporary nature of republican dominance, claim that opportunities for repentance remain. In *King Charles, His*

---

58. On the use of royalist political satire in Interregnum plays, see Woodbridge, *English Revenge Drama*, 189–222.

59. *A Coffin for King Charles a crowne for Cromwell: a pit for the people* (London, 1649). This was written for and sung to the tune of "Fain I Would if I Could," and I thank the UCSB English Broadside Ballad Archive (EBBA) for making available media recordings of these works: https://ebba.english.ucsb.edu.

Glory, ballad singers promise to purge Whitehall and Parliament and fetch Charles II to govern England.[60] Relying on an equally simplistic formulation—that fortune's wheel will turn once more—the lines maintain that sincere repentance is the only means to evade retribution:

> When Dame Fortune castesth a frown,
> These upstart Gallants fall headlong down,
> I could wish they would view their own state,
> And Repent before tis to late,
> For fear lest a Gibbet will be their last fate
> *or whipping about the Town.*[61]

In this and in other texts, the emphasis on repentance serves to invigorate the royalist agenda and recruit potential members. Curiously, though, repentance in this ballad is intended only for those directly involved in the current government and thereby tacitly absolves the populace of any responsibility, even as it urges them to political action on behalf of the exiled Stuarts.

Elsewhere, authors divulge far more accusation, as in *A Flattering Elegie*, which was published in the same year as Charles's death. Here, its anonymous author confronts the new authorities, laying bare their hypocrisies in the enforcement of days of thanksgiving and prayer and prophesying their downfall:

> And as sure as [God's] Word and he are true,
> So sure damnation is the Rebels due . . .
> Their feigned Fasts and seeming penitence
> Were mockeries of Gods high omnipotence:
> Daies of Thanksgiving were in use no further,
> But to praise God for their committing murther;
> Or when they had done mischiefe to the King . . .
> Some good those wicked Imps of Hell have done,
> We may choose our Religion all, or none.[62]

---

60. For a comprehensive study of how the printing industry promoted English ballads, see Natascha Würzbach, *The Rise of the English Street Ballad, 1550–1650*, trans. Gayna Walls (Cambridge: Cambridge University Press, 1990).

61. *King Charles his glory, and rebels shame* (London, 1660).

62. *A Flattering elegie upon the death of King Charles the cleane contrary way: with a parallel something significant* (London, 1649), A2r.

The ironic culmination of the republic's deployment of religious pieties is the evacuation of meaning from Christianity and the "freedom" to embrace any number of heretical religions or even atheism. For their perverse machinations, the king's antagonists are credited with malice, not ignorance or poor judgment:

> You knew the King was innocent and right,
> You knew your cursed hearts were full of spight:
> You knew your malice 'gainst his life conspir'd,
> You knew false witnesses suborn'd and hir'd.[63]

Even as the poem's context signals that its direct addressees are the conspirators, the anaphoric insistence on "you" as well as the term's grammatical broadness invites the reader to remain under the collective umbrella of guilt. But despite the poem's inclusiveness around the question of responsibility for Charles's demise and in stark contrast to other royalist texts, repentance is not its preoccupation. In fact, the possibility is raised only in the poem's final lines: "As you accurs'd have liv'd, accursed dye, / Or else repent, or damn perpetually."[64] Here, the author levels the logic of talionic law at readers such that repentance, which would include a renunciation of one's republican politics, becomes the only way to circumvent the inevitability of unceasing vengeance.

Issuing dire predictions, the poem specifies how this accursed life might proceed in the wake of regicide:

> For this black deed, I'le tell what will ensue,
> Three Kingdomes spoyle, damnation unto you:
> All Christendome will hold you most abhorr'd
> For murdering of your gracious Soveraigne Lord:
> In any Countrey where this crime is knowne,
> An English man dares not his Country owne.[65]

Although the dissolution of monarchical government did much to destabilize England, Scotland, and Ireland, the emphasis here is on the consequences to the nation's reputation in the global world. That is, regicide taints national identity, Englishness itself, and in the crime's aftermath, subjects are

---

63. Ibid., A4r.
64. Ibid., A4v.
65. Ibid.

discouraged from claiming England as their home. But does the disinclination derive from shame? Guilt? Or a fear of retribution while abroad?[66] By extending the consequences of the execution to include the evacuation of meaning from both Christianity and Englishness, the author signals its commensurately awful nature.

Whereas *A Flattering Elegie* implies broad, though largely unspecified, consequences for Englishmen everywhere, Henry King, bishop of Chichester, promises more spectacular acts of retribution for guilty parties in *A Deepe Groan*. In this text as in others at which we have glimpsed, prophecy functions to undermine the premise on which the republican national memory rests. Cautioning his readers that present happiness does not correspond to or indicate moral victory, King maintains that the delay in vengeance, much like the temporal delays employed by Italianate avengers on the early modern stage, corresponds to frightful futures:

> And though his sleepie Arme suspend the scourge,
> Nor doth loud Bloud in winged Vengeance urge,
> Though the soft houres a while in pleasures flie,
> And conquering Treason sing her Lullabie.
> The guilt at length in fury he'l inroule
> With barbed Arrows on the trayt'rous Soule.
> Time may be when the *John-à-Leyden* King
> His Quarters to this Tombe an Offring bring . . .
> Yet if just Providence reprieve the Fate,
> The Judgment will be deeper, though't be late.[67]

Though royalist texts almost uniformly insist that God is luring the republican government and their sympathizers into a false sense of security, King turns to Continental history in order to predict future events and issue a transparent threat to Cromwell and his associates. His mention of "John-à-Leyden" is a reference to the opportunistic Anabaptist leader John of Leiden, who reigned as king of Munster for one mere year. After he was tortured and executed, Leiden's remains were on display for fifty years; such are the gruesome rituals of both historical upheaval and early modern revenge tragedy. And while it is only from our present vantage point that we can recognize King's

---

66. Such fears were well founded. On the Continent, royalist exiles murdered those who had participated in the execution of Charles I. For specific examples, see Wedgwood, *A Coffin for King Charles*, 249–50.

67. Henry King, *A deepe groane, fetch'd at the funerall of that incomparable and glorious monarch, Charles the First, King of Great Britaine, France and Ireland* (London, 1649), A2r–A2v.

prescience—for Cromwell's disinterred corpse would indeed be violated, hanged, gawked at, dismembered, and left in an ignoble pit—his words persist as a kind of future echo, a temporal hiccup.

If King's historical interpretations permit him to embed maledictions for Cromwell and his government and thereby remember differently, John Quarles's "A Curse Against the Enemies of Peace" in *Regale Lectum Miseriae* mobilizes the logic of execration to explicitly disrupt the republic's past history and future narratives. To do so, he relies on the future as the repository for the seemingly boundless retribution envisioned for republicans, and this formulation necessitates generations onto whom he may project his revenge on behalf of the deceased king. Quarles writes: "May *heav'n* whose frowning *countenance* doth show / An *angry* resolution, overthrow / You, and your *prick-ear'd Progeny*, and make / Your *children suffer* for their *parents* sake."[68] The curses that follow—which include plagues, famine, and disease—are some of the most explicitly vengeful in the royalist literary cult, corresponding to the republicans' presumed criminality. Yet the temporal logic of malediction is such that one can only recognize its power retrospectively: insofar as the curse links both quotidian and spectacular moments of misfortune, it evolves into the retributive narrative that organizes these otherwise unrelated events. And if we understand cursing as inextricably connected to early modern theater, as Björn Quiring has persuasively argued, then these documents bear the imprint of early modern theater and its apoplectic onstage avengers.[69]

The connection to theater and the traditional genre of revenge tragedy only strengthens as Quarles's execrations reach a fever pitch. Conflating what was once anticipatory vengeance with his contemporary moment, he writes:

> May your souls burn, till *heav'n* shall think it good
> To quench them in your *generations* blood,
> That all the world may hear you *hisse*, and *cry*
> *Who lov'd no Peace, in Peace shall never dye.*[70]

Envisioning a hell on earth in which the souls of the damned are extinguished in the blood of their progeny, Quarles effects a dizzying temporal shift. Though

---

68. John Quarles, "A Curse Against the Enemies of Peace," in *Regale lectum miseriae, or A kingly bed of misery* (London, 1649), E2r.

69. Elsewhere Björn Quiring writes, "The ritual of execration might be seen as a dark precursor of theatre itself" (*Shakespeare's Curse: The Aporias of Ritual Exclusion in Early Modern Royal Drama*, trans. Michael Winkler and Björn Quiring [New York: Routledge, 2014], 14).

70. Quarles, "A Curse Against the Enemies of Peace," E2v.

he begins in the subjunctive present as he addresses the traitors (i.e., "May your souls burn"), the vengeance on behalf of Charles I is only completed when the generations issuing forth from these traitors have died as well. Much like the conclusion to *The Spanish Tragedy*, which extends acts of spectacular vengeance into the perpetual anguish of the afterlife, the poem aims toward unceasing revenge. Finally, Quarles's fantasy demands that the true nature of the conspirators be revealed, for the "hisse" that we hear is not only of liquid encountering burning objects, but also aligns the traitors with the "hiss" of that devilish serpent. This contradicts—and powerfully so—the godliness to which republicans lay claim in their historical memory and inflated expectations for future success.

At the risk of oversimplifying the political upheaval of the mid-seventeenth century in England, we might assert that royalists and republicans occupy antagonistic positions, their very identities rooted in the mutual refusal of the other. While I have aligned the republic's construction of national memory with civil vengeance, royalist tracts most often relied on the promise of spectacular and episodic eruptions of divine revenge, that is, traditional vengeance. Yet we ought to be cautious of too hastily extending the structural antagonism of the two groups to the techniques on which they rely, for though these techniques function differently, they do so in complementary registers. Even as this study broadens existing definitions of revenge and, to that end, distinguishes the phenomenon of civil vengeance from spectacular or "traditional" revenge, their differences do not render them opposites. Indeed, it may be more productive to regard them as counterparts that do not cancel but rather amplify each other. To return to the two acts of spectacular vengeance that bookend the Interregnum and with which this final chapter begins—that is, the 1649 execution of Charles I and the 1661 symbolic torture and hanging of the Commonwealth's major leaders—we can visualize how these highly theatrical demonstrations of retribution instantiate new regimes. Once an authority secures unequivocal triumph, civil vengeance functions to augment its power in more insidiously ordinary ways.

While republicans and royalists sought to invalidate each other, their tactics had an unexpected effect. For instance, when Charles II made his triumphant entry into London, the fevered destruction of Cromwellian effigies celebrated his return. Reading this cultural response, Laura Knoppers reminds us that though these acts were unequivocally royalist, especially in their endeavors to annihilate, quite literally, republican memory, the destructive acts also "did the opposite: displaying, reminding, and remembering in the very process of erasing."[71] That is, attempts to contest, contradict, and expunge also strengthen the opposition's stance. If we subscribe to Knoppers's assessment, we might also consider how royal sympathizers, who sought to topple the Interregnum government's claim to godly success through the creation and dissemination of contradictory narratives, simultaneously reinscribed the very accounts to which they were so strenuously opposed. The cumulative effect, then, of this opposition and inadvertent reification of the other side is the construction of a revenge machine from which it is difficult to advance one's position, much less extricate oneself. In fact, a primary limitation of the royalist literary resistance is its protracted engagement with the very terms established by the temporarily dominant narrative and historical memory of the republic. This is, at its core, the grammatical logic of negative utterances: insofar as they contradict an assertion already in existence, negative utterances always presuppose a positive utterance.[72] The negative utterance cannot occur without also conjuring the ghost of its obverse.[73] Thus, neither the royalist nor republican narrative may exist independently but instead arise out of and are sustained by ongoing antagonism; this is how I account for their mutual intractability.

As vengeance saturates public and political discourse, an intervention is needed to disrupt this formidable impasse. What remains forestalled in royalist commemorative verse and elegy—that is, a viable disruption of the Interregnum government's civil vengeance enacted through the consolidation of national memory—is pursued more effectively in Margaret Cavendish's *Sociable Letters*. That she is an avowed royalist makes her work an apt subject for a chapter that examines literary resistance to republican narratives. Yet in spite of her documented support of the Stuarts, Cavendish leaves aside intractable politics, though not politics altogether, to center world-making and the pursuit of alternatives in her published work. Rather than debating with critics of monarchical government or insisting on the illegitimacy of the Lord Protector—and thereby contributing to the entrenchment of the political divide—she models how imagination might disrupt the revenge machine, which is produced by the ideological competition between royalists and republicans. She gives some indication of the technique when she writes famously: "Though I cannot be *Henry* the Fifth, or *Charles* the Second, yet I endeavour to be *Margaret* the First: and though I have neither Power, Time, nor Occasion, to be a great Conqueror, like *Alexander*, or *Cesar*, yet, rather than

---

71. Knoppers, *Constructing Cromwell*, 173.

72. Talmy Givón, *On Understanding Grammar* (New York: Academic Press, 1979), 139.

73. Susan Fitzmaurice, *The Familiar Letter in Early Modern English: A Pragmatic Approach* (Philadelphia: John Benjamins, 2002), 87–128, esp. 179.

not be Mistress of a World, since Fortune and the Fates would give me none, I have made One of my own."[74] In her citation of world leaders, past and present, she anchors her discourse to traditional history, even as that narrative soon becomes little more than a jumping-off point for her self-created world and self-coronation. This is a game that pays dividends for Cavendish when she engages the historical realities of her external world but positions herself beyond their strictures. Through imagination and possibility, she demonstrates a mode of coping with and even thriving despite interim times; however, her approach is neither blithe dismissal nor willful denial but rather a disinterest in duality.[75] This focus on world-making constitutes not so much a resistance of civil vengeance, which would suggest ongoing engagement with antagonists, but a refusal of its imperatives to, in the specific case for this chapter, remember differently.

Yet how does *Sociable Letters* and its alternatives enrich our understanding of civil vengeance? In a book devoted to uncovering the permeation of civil vengeance in early modern literature and culture, I believe that some exploration of available strategies to manage the social phenomenon and its diffuse effects is both responsible and valuable. Because civil vengeance boasts an extensive reach and, in its capacities for mutation, a chameleonlike character, it would seem as if capitulation is inevitable. Even so, Cavendish charts a path that eludes its grasp in *Sociable Letters*, and I map her repeated challenges to conceptions of linear time and the narrow subjectivity it organizes. That is, she leaves claims to national history and memory to the political factions invested in them, marking instead another kind of time and creating other modes of memorialization. To foreground this section's focus on an alternative to civil vengeance, I employ a framework composed of the work of Giorgio Agamben and José Esteban Muñoz on potentiality. And to demonstrate how Cavendish signals these alternatives on the level of the sentence, I attend to what Jack Halberstam calls a "grammar of possibility," which "expresses a basic desire to live life otherwise."[76]

---

74. Margaret Cavendish, *The Blazing World and Other Writings*, ed. Kate Lilley (London: Penguin, 1994), 124.

75. Cavendish's mode of creating and inhabiting an alternative reality resembles what Katherine Eggert calls "disknowledge," which describes not a state of ignorance but rather "the conscious and deliberate setting aside of one compelling mode of understanding the world—one discipline, one theory—in favor of another." See *Disknowledge: Literature, Alchemy, and the End of Humanism in Renaissance England* (Philadelphia: University of Pennsylvania Press, 2015), 3. For Eggert's excellent discussion of Cavendish and *The Blazing World*, see 230–42.

76. As such, my chapter exists in conversation with the work of Muñoz and Halberstam on queer utopias and failures, ongoing debates regarding teleology, history, considerations of negative affects, and their modes of transmission. Jack Halberstam, *The Queer Art of Failure* (Durham, NC: Duke University Press, 2011), 2. See also Halberstam, *In a Queer Time and Place: Transgender Bodies* (New York:

To locate a world elsewhere, José Esteban Muñoz suggests queerness—that is, a "structured mode of desiring"—as a means to transcend the present with its myriad limitations and diurnal disappointments. The potential inherent in queerness is not achievable or inhabitable per se but is only approached asymptotically in the future. He writes: "We must dream and enact new and better pleasures, other ways of being in the world, and ultimately new worlds. Queerness is a longing that propels us onward, beyond romances of the negative and toiling in the present. Queerness is that thing that lets us feel that this world is not enough, that indeed something is missing."[77] In its utopic atmosphere, queerness opens up a liminal space between existence and nonexistence, a space aligned with Giorgio Agamben's concept of "potentiality."[78] "Unlike a possibility, a thing that simply might happen," Muñoz explains, "a potentiality is a certain mode of nonbeing that is eminent [*sic*], a thing that is present but not actually existing in the present tense."[79] As a consequence, queerness ushers in potentialities that enable vulnerable subjects to navigate, cope with, or temporarily ignore negative affects, internal and external.

From this liminal space springs the subjunctive mood. Its grammatical magic—expressed in, for example, the counterfactual conditional—carves out fictional spaces set aside from reality that nevertheless vie for our attention. Counterfactuals, these "conditional trajectories structured by a speculative 'what if,'" upend declarative statements, prizing potentiality over reality.[80] The rhetorical and imaginative effects capture our attention and shift it elsewhere, even if that elsewhere is not circumscribed by material reality. In particular, Cavendish's *Sociable Letters* insistently reveals the queerness of the subjunctive insofar as its usage challenges linear time, orthodox understandings of history,

New York University Press, 2005); and José Esteban Muñoz, *Cruising Utopia: The Then and There of Queer Futurity* (New York: New York University Press, 2009). For discussions of history and teleology in early modern scholarship, see the work of Carla Freccero, Jonathan Goldberg, Jonathan Gil Harris, Madhavi Menon, Valerie Rohy, Kathryn Schwarz, and Valerie Traub. Regarding affects and their modes of transmission, see Sara Ahmed, *The Promise of Happiness* (Durham, NC: Duke University Press, 2010); Brennan, *The Transmission of Affect*; and Ngai, *Ugly Feelings*.

77. Muñoz, *Cruising Utopia*, 1.

78. Giorgio Agamben, *Potentialities: Collected Essays in Philosophy*, ed. and trans. Daniel Heller-Roazen (Stanford, CA: Stanford University Press, 1999).

79. Muñoz, *Cruising Utopia*, 9. Though I make use of queer theory to uncover potential futures, there are other modes of arrival. In her excellent study of literary futures, J. K. Barret models one such path as she pursues "approaches to the future that ask us to imagine nondeterministic ends and boundless potential . . . while also decoupling open-endedness from modernity." If scholars wish to examine the "variety of futures to be found in these imaginative texts," Barret rightly advises, "agency must be restored to literature, not given away to history" (*Untold Futures: Time and Literary Culture in Renaissance England* [Ithaca, NY: Cornell University Press, 2016], 8–9, 10).

80. Kathryn Schwarz, "Death and Theory: Or, the Problem of Counterfactual Sex," in *Sex before Sex: Figuring the Act in Early Modern England*, ed. James M. Bromley and Will Stockton (Minneapolis: University of Minnesota Press, 2013), 53–88, quote from 59.

subjectivity, and even relational possibilities. Whatever reprieve these formulations may extend to the interlocutors who rely on them, such pleasures are admittedly temporary. Yet in these imaginative encounters, however brief, Cavendish's letters crack open what has been largely settled as a matter of factual history, leaving traces of what could have been or what still might be. Therefore, in tracing a queer grammar that undercuts, revises, and even turns one's back on normative syntax and subjectivity, I read these imaginative encounters as temporary refuges from and alternatives to the world her contemporaries inhabited, a world saturated in civil vengeance.

Scholarship on Cavendish is as wide-ranging as the genres she employs and the topics on which she writes. Given the lengths she goes to distinguish herself from other writers, much has been written on the recovery and defense of Cavendish's stylistic idiosyncrasies.[81] Feminist scholars have examined her texts in relation to the domestic sphere and reproductive labor, while others have used them to illuminate women's seventeenth-century reading and writing practices.[82] Insofar as Cavendish's work routinely thwarts heteronormative expectations, queer readings abound as well.[83] Still others attend to her engagement with scientific discourse and well-documented interest in the Royal Society.[84] And given Cavendish's innovative, frequently contradictory narrative voice, often scholars bring considerations of subjectivity to bear on her writing. Because her work often features an "autobiographical imperative,"

---

81. See, for instance, Sylvia Bowerbank, "'The Spider's Delight: Margaret Cavendish and the 'Female' Imagination," *English Literary Renaissance* 14, no. 3 (1984): 392–408. Lara Dodds examines the critical tradition of metamorphosing Cavendish's perceived aesthetic defects into virtues and instead proposes the embrace of this so-called bad writing as the vehicle of her literary achievement ("Bawds and Housewives: Margaret Cavendish and the Work of 'Bad Writing,'" *Early Modern Studies Journal* 6 [2014]: 29–65).

82. See, for example Lara Dodds, "Reading and Writing in *Sociable Letters*; or, How Margaret Cavendish Read Her Plutarch," in *The Literary Invention of Margaret Cavendish* (Pittsburgh: Duquesne University Press, 2013), 23–56; Rosemary Kegl, "'The World I Have Made': Margaret Cavendish, Feminism, and the *Blazing-World*," in *Feminist Readings of Early Modern Culture: Emerging Subjects*, ed. Valerie Traub, M. Lindsay Kaplan, and Dympna Callaghan (Cambridge: Cambridge University Press, 1996), 119–41; and Megan J. Fung, "Art, Authority, and Domesticity in Margaret Cavendish's *Poems and Fancies*," *Early Modern Women: An Introduction* 10, no. 1 (2015): 27–47.

83. Judith Haber, *Desire and Dramatic Form in Early Modern England* (Cambridge: Cambridge University Press, 2009), 117–30; Katherine Kellett, "Performance, Performativity, and Identity in Margaret Cavendish's *The Convent of Pleasure*," *Studies in English Literature* 48, no. 2 (2008): 419–42; Heather Kerr, "Trembling Hyphen / Shaking Hinge: Margaret Cavendish and Queer Literary Subjectivity," in *Women Writing, 1550–1750*, ed. Jo Wallwork and Paul Salzman (Bundoora, AU: Meridian, 2001), 215–36; and Rachel Warburton, "'[A] Woman Hath No . . . Room to Desire Children for Her Own Sake': Margaret Cavendish Reads Lee Edelman," *Literature Interpretation Theory* 27, no. 3 (2016): 234–51.

84. See, for instance, Sujata Iyengar, "Royalist, Romanticist, Racialist: Rank, Gender, and Race in the Science Fiction of Margaret Cavendish," *English Literary History* 69, no. 3 (2002): 649–72; and Eve Keller, "Producing Petty Gods: Margaret Cavendish's Critique of Experimental Science," *English Literary History* 64, no. 2 (1997): 447–71.

as Elspeth Graham observes, scholarship frequently extends to Cavendish the writer as well as to issues of authorship and collaboration.[85]

Though her investment in creating new worlds, specifically the engendering of worlds within oneself, is present throughout her oeuvre, how does this investment culminate in an alternative to civil vengeance and the intractability present in the political discourse in *Sociable Letters*?[86] She makes room for herself and her world, which is to say that she creates the world in her own vision and does so, I will argue, through impersonation, equivocation, and the subjunctive mood. In a prefatory letter addressing "Professors of Learning and Art," she writes, "If any of your Noble Profession should Humble themselves so Low as to Read my Works, or part of them, I pray Consider my Sex and Breeding, and they will fully Excuse those Faults which must Unavoidably be found in my Works."[87] Here, Cavendish appears to embrace gender essentialism and its insistence on feminine inadequacy—a stance that she contradicts in preceding pages and repudiates strenuously throughout much of her published writings—as part of her deployment of the *humilitas topos*, or the rhetorical convention of modesty.[88]

Yet, as she continues the prefatory address, her sly humor rears its head: "For certainly, were I Emperess of the World, I would Advance those that have most Learning and Wit, by which I believe the Earth would rather be an Heaven, since both Men and Government would be as Celestial."[89] The sentence begins in the subjunctive, a mood that dominates many of the letters to follow, and if we trace its logic, she would necessarily advance those illustrious professors to whom she writes. However, in advancing "those [who] have

---

85. Harris, *Untimely Matter in the Time of Shakespeare*, 148–68; Elspeth Graham, "Intersubjectivity, Intertextuality, and Form in the Self-Writings of Margaret Cavendish," in *Genre and Women's Life Writing in Early Modern England*, ed. Michelle M. Dowd and Julie A. Eckerle (Burlington, VT: Ashgate, 2007), 131–50, quote from 131.

86. *The Blazing World*, a utopian text that depicts a fantastic world accessible only through the North Pole, exists as perhaps the most obvious expression of this world-making; see Geraldine Wagner, "Romancing Multiplicity: Female Subjectivity and the Body Divisible in Margaret Cavendish's *Blazing World*," *Early Modern Literary Studies* 9, no. 1 (2003): 1–59. As the (fictional) Empress instructs the (real-life) Duchess to engage in the creation of personal sovereignty in *The Blazing World*, she explains, "By creating a world within yourself, you may enjoy all both in whole and in parts, without control or opposition, and may make what world you please, and alter it when you please, and enjoy as much pleasure and delight as a world can afford you" (Cavendish, *The Blazing World*, 186).

87. Margaret Cavendish, Duchess of Newcastle, *CCXI Sociable Letters* (London: William Wilson, 1664), b2r.

88. An encomium that follows this prefatory letter—"Upon her Excellency the Authoress"—would seem to complicate Cavendish's performance of self-deprecation. Regarding the rhetoric of modesty as a "doubled discourse," Patricia Pender contends that this does not curb but rather asserts the authorial agency of women writers (*Early Modern Women's Writing and the Rhetoric of Modesty* [New York: Palgrave Macmillan, 2012], 148).

89. Cavendish, *CCXI Sociable Letters*, b2r.

most Learning and Wit" and not tying the statement to her addressees, Cavendish leaves absent, or rather open, the question of gender. That is, she invites any, regardless of "Sex and Breeding," to be elevated. Moreover, she inverts the traditional rhetoric of modesty with which she commences her letter by metamorphosing herself from humble supplicant to superlative "Emperess of the World" who, rather than the "Professors of Learning and Art," makes promotion decisions. Through this savvy exploitation of the *humilitas topos* and the surface embrace of male superiority, Cavendish thumbs her nose at a patriarchal system that would, and indeed did, diminish her standing and literary endeavors. In her use of the subjunctive mood, she embodies political power and literary patronage, shrugging off the posture of cringing petitioner that would seem to trail her persona in the letter's early paragraphs. Finally, the subjunctive enables her to extend a tacit critique of her esteemed addressees: in her articulation of a world otherwise, she suggests that the most learned and witty are not, in point of fact, advanced and, furthermore, that neither men nor the government is celestial. Thanks to her deployment of this grammar of possibility in the preface, she sets the stage to draw her reader's attention to a world otherwise.

The world-making she broaches in her preface is more systematically explored in the letters themselves, where she discusses, for example, exclusionary governmental policies. She refashions a negative experience—here, the barring of women from the political sphere—into nearly anarchic freedom, accomplishing the feat through evasion, inconsistency, and downright contradiction. This is Cavendish at her most maddening but also at her most powerful. To her imaginary interlocutor, she muses: "And as for the matter of Governments, we Women understand them not, yet if we did, we are excluded from intermedling therewith, and almost from being subject thereto; we are not tied, nor bound to State or Crown; we are free, not Sworn to Allegiance, nor do we take the Oath of Supremacy; we are not made Citizens of the Commonwealth, we hold no Offices, nor bear we any Authority therein; we are accounted neither Useful in Peace, nor Serviceable in War; and if we be not Citizens in the Commonwealth, I know no reason we should be Subjects to the Commonwealth: And the truth is, we are no Subjects, unless it be to our Husbands, and not alwayes to them, for sometimes we usurp their Authority."[90] Through her use of the first-person plural subject, Cavendish establishes a

---

90. Margaret Cavendish, *Sociable Letters*, ed. James Fitzmaurice (Peterborough, ON: Broadview Press, 2004), 61. In light of Cavendish's false assertions concerning the role of women in government, see Nadine Akkerman's fascinating examination of female espionage, which supported Charles I during his imprisonment from 1646 to his execution (*Invisible Agents: Women and Espionage in Seventeenth-Century Britain* [Oxford: Oxford University Press, 2018], 27–63).

universal truth: women do not comprehend governance—an ironic "truth" that many of her letters manifestly contradict, even as her "we" invites and makes visible a community of women, citizens of another sort of commonwealth. Swerving from self-deprecation to the conditional ("yet if we did"), she argues that the exclusion results in a different identity, one not "bound to State or Crown." To distinguish the subjectivity predicated on alterity from the construction of normative (i.e., masculine) citizens, she cites how they are sworn to allegiance and forced to take the oath of supremacy and, as a consequence, are restricted by others. For Cavendish, men's inclusion and participation in governance do not result in greater amounts of power, for she privileges existence on the periphery as noncitizens. Even as religious and political authorities admonish women to subjugate themselves before their husbands, that orientation is qualified heavily such that she may declare by the letter's conclusion that women "govern as it were by an insensible power, so as men perceive not how they are Led, Guided, and Rul'd by the Feminine Sex."[91]

Yet it is too facile to assert that Cavendish's glib tone enables her to carve out spaces of agency, power, and play for women; although this is perhaps still true, we might be better served by regarding her as a theorist of history and temporality. In the same missive, she confronts the material realities of the civil war as well as the concomitant disturbances in governance. Steeped in the subjunctive, she writes: "But howsoever, Madam, the disturbance in this Countrey hath made no breach of Friendship betwixt us, for though there hath been a Civil War in the Kingdom, and a general War amongst the Men, yet there hath been none amongst the Women, they have not fought pitch'd battels; and if they had, there hath been no particular quarrel betwixt her and me, *for her Ladiship is the same in my affection, as if the Kingdom had been in a calm Peace.*"[92] Cavendish identifies the normative historical reality—"there hath been a Civil War in the Kingdom"—then posits another claim—"yet there hath been none amongst the Women"—that would seem to contradict the first statement. How could this be so? By its very nature, civil war upends not only political structures but also familial alliances—a sad fact to which she devotes another letter, writing, "For in Civil War, Brothers against Brothers, Fathers against Sons, and Sons against Fathers, become Enemies, and Spill each others Blood, Triumphing on their Graves."[93] Yet whatever the savagery of war enacts on the family unit, it remains restricted to male relationships.

91. Cavendish, *Sociable Letters*, 61.

92. Ibid., 61. Emphasis mine. For a contradictory stance regarding women's involvement in the war, see Letter 9 (p. 53).

93. Ibid., 174.

By contrast, civil war does not effect the collapse of the relationship between Cavendish and her female interlocutor, the intimacy among female
friends, or even that which flourishes between writer and generous reader, and
these impervious relationships serve as guarantors of a peaceful kingdom. Or,
more precisely: their uninterrupted affection, despite the realities of civil wars,
gives the semblance of a country in "calm Peace," a country that never was—
at least not according to the dominant narrative. Thus, their presence makes
readers aware of other possibilities for marking time. By making these seemingly illogical claims, Cavendish crafts a partial revision of traditional history,
what Walter Benjamin calls the "document of civilization" that is always simultaneously a "document of barbarism."[94] For Benjamin, the victorious annihilate the past and the artifacts that do not suit their triumphal narrative of
progression; that narrative is what we regard as our history. And while Cavendish does not contradict the historical record per se, she proposes another kind
of history, one that does not dissolve the barbarous document but rather co-
exists alongside it.

Lest one suspect that such a feat is due to women's removal from war and
its material consequences, Cavendish reminds her readers elsewhere in *Sociable Letters* that "in the Ruines of War [women] suffer Equally with Men."[95]
Thanks to the erosion of governance and impartial enforcement bodies, "all
the Evil Passions and Debauch'd Appetites are let Loose," and Cavendish's letters demonstrate more than a passing acquaintance with these macabre realities.[96] She recalls, "For I did observe, that in this last War the Urns of the Dead
were Digged up, their Dust Dispersed, and their Bones Thrown about, and I
suppose that in all Civil or Home-wars such Inhuman Acts are Committed."[97]
Although many regard this moment as a reference to the desecration of her
family tombs in Colchester by parliamentary soldiers,[98] Cavendish remains
uncharacteristically reserved on the matter, writing, "I have Suffered so much
in [the Civil War] . . . that I may desire to Forget it."[99] And while she gives no

---

94. Walter Benjamin, "Theses on the Philosophy of History," in *Illuminations: Essays and Reflections*, ed. Hannah Arendt, trans. Harry Zohn (New York: Schocken Books, 1969), 253–64, quote from
256.

95. Cavendish, *Sociable Letters*, 140.

96. Ibid., 175.

97. Ibid., 174.

98. Cavendish returns to the matter of grave desecration in subsequent letters (*Sociable Letters*,
252–54). For an examination of what occurred to the Lucas family tomb, see Frances E. Dolan, "Scattered Remains and Paper Bodies: Margaret Cavendish and the Siege of Colchester," *Postmedieval* 4,
no. 4 (2013): 452–64.

99. Cavendish, *Sociable Letters*, 175.

indication that she has forgotten unpleasant events, in spite of her espoused desire to do so, this does not hinder her from pursuing other possibilities.

Here I wish to situate the specifics of this section's argument within the broader chapter and offer some clarification. Whereas republicans and royalists engage in an intractable ideological battle to lay claim to national memory, which I link to civil vengeance, Cavendish instantiates another history and gestures beyond civil vengeance. In so doing, she detaches from and renders moot the competing claims of her contemporaries to historical narrative and national memory. And in her proposal of alternative histories, those predicated on "affection" rather than military triumph, she also offers another mode of marking time. That is, if we understand linear time as that which is taken up with wars among men—what Elizabeth Freeman *pace* Benjamin describes as "spatialized featureless calendrical time across which the history of nations supposedly marches forward"—the feminine affection that remains the "same" could hardly be considered historical progression in the traditional sense.[100] Here in this sameness, there are no causal relationships to be postulated from absent ruptures, events, and epochs. When we shift our optic to view time as composed of unchanging female affection, Cavendish's proposal gives us a glimpse of a temporality that is not preoccupied with or punctured by the insubstantiality of masculine affection. And it is precisely this "women's time"—which heralds what Freeman introduces as "queer temporalities"—that is occluded by the traditional linear time that commemorates victorious (and decidedly male) exploits, adventures, and wars. "Visible in the forms of interruption," Freeman explains, queer temporalities "are points of resistance to this temporal order that, in turn, propose other possibilities for living in relation to indeterminately past, present, and future others."[101] Through her usage of the subjunctive mood—"as if the Kingdom had been in a calm Peace"—Cavendish brings other possibilities to the fore and makes us aware of what could have been or what may yet be.

Queer temporalities, such as the alternative mode of marking time present in *Sociable Letters*, consequently revise individuated and discrete subjects into stranger, more permeable beings. Meditating on death and the duration of memory elsewhere, Cavendish admits to her companion: "There is nothing I Dread more than Death, I do not mean the Strokes of Death, nor the Pains, but the Oblivion in Death . . . for I could willingly part with my Present Life, to have it Redoubled in after Memory, and would willingly Die in my Self, so

---

100. Elizabeth Freeman, *Time Binds: Queer Temporalities, Queer Histories* (Durham, NC: Duke University Press, 2010), xxii.

101. Ibid.

I might Live in my Friends; Such a Life have I with you, and you with me, our Persons being at a Distance, we live to each other no otherwise than if we were Dead."[102] Insofar as Cavendish envisions a method by which her present self is multiplied by her friends in the future, she traces an alternative to traditional lineage and therefore to linear time itself. Given that her focus throughout *Sociable Letters* has remained on the relations between women, it is not for nothing that female friendships and affinities emerge as the vehicles whereby this "Redoubl[ing]" occurs.[103] And even as she insists on a fairly orthodox understanding of historical time—that is, she understands herself as author to be writing in her present yet anticipates, indeed depends upon, a future in which she could be multiplied—there is something strange regarding the syntactical positioning of the events. When she writes that her aim is "to have it Redoubled in after Memory," the most immediate interpretation is that her friend's memories will maintain, even multiply, her legacy. This, surely, is how Cavendish skirts the "Oblivion in Death." Yet the phrase "after Memory" specifies a temporal orientation, though one that fails to make much logical sense. What would follow or persist *after* memory?

One method of approaching the question is to consider how Cavendish's implicit charge resembles the infernal injunction—"remember me"—of King Hamlet's ghost and its echoes present in the royalist literature that commemorates the beloved Charles I. Spectacular revenge, whether it manifests itself as fantasy or action, is one way to fulfill that imperative to memorialize, an option pursued by Hamlet and by royalists. For Hamlet, the adherence to the dictum of his dead father courts madness and culminates in oblivion; for royalists, it generates an intractable relationship from those whose views and actions they detest. By contrast, Cavendish's mode of memorialization accumulates more memories as it generates an ever-expanding network composed of connections throughout time. This, too, is a way to "remember me" and, as a dying Hamlet implores of Horatio, "to tell my story."

If Cavendish locates alternatives to patrilineal legacy and historical time, the relation to her interlocutor expands further these possibilities. In the final sentence of the above passage, she moves from the subjunctive mood (i.e., "So I might live") and posits a mutually shared life—"Such a Life have I with you, and you with me." In so doing, she conflates the anticipated, potential future

---

102. Cavendish, *Sociable Letters*, 142. On the consequences of the Reformation's erasure of purgatory and alternative modes of relationality between the living and the dead as envisioned by women writers, see Elizabeth Hodgson, *Grief and Women Writers in the English Renaissance* (Cambridge: Cambridge University Press, 2015).

103. For another model of queer reproduction, see Val Rohy's concept of the meme ("On Homosexual Reproduction," *Differences* 23, no. 1 [2012]: 101–30).

with the immediate present. And even as these letters are written to a specific, though imaginary, addressee, that insistent "you" interpolates the reader who encounters her words and, with neither consent nor intention, keeps alive her memory.[104] Through the peculiar temporality of Cavendish's letters, she transmutes the precariousness of an unknown and unknowable future into a present intimacy with veritable strangers *right now*. Of her yearning for these eccentric unions, she writes: "And as I desire to Live in every Age, and in every Brain, so I desire to Live in every Heart."[105] Here, she makes available a mode of promiscuous contact that permits a coherent, fully articulated "I" to flourish in future ages, brains, and hearts through the vibrancy of her ideas. And through her invocation of the heart, she charts out possibilities of contact predicated on both intellect *and* affect.

As we have already seen, it is through affection—and specifically feminine affection—that Cavendish proposes an alternative kinship in spite of spatial and temporal distance. She reimagines potential networks or communities of belonging, communities that originally arise out of women's exclusion from governance and boast tenacity such that these collectives are untouched by war or conflict. Finally, her proposed alternative to linear time and patrilineal inheritance—that is, her embrace of a future ever more capacious—widens perpetually the possibilities for belonging. Such are the ways that Cavendish's *Sociable Letters* creates anew. In her institution of affective communities, she redefines history, proffers alternative temporalities, and locates points of contiguity. Most radically, perhaps, she conceives of subjectivity—instantiated through the vehicle of literature and literary writing—as an amalgam of discrete individuals.

Yet even such energizing, encompassing collectives also admit a degree of vulnerability. Importuning her friend to flee the city in the face of the latest plague outbreak, Cavendish writes, "For if you Die, all those Friends you Leave, or Think of, or Remember, partly Die with you, nay, some perchance for Ever, if they were Personally Dead before, and onely Live in your Memory."[106] In linking legacy to precarious bodies, she emphasizes the wide-ranging consequences of a subject's death on the collective. Indeed, I do not think that Cavendish is merely trading in metaphor, because the claim arises as a logical extension of prior statements. While her belief in memorial reproduction extends the promise of infinite life insofar as beloved friends and even readers

---

104. In the opening lines of "Upon her Excellency," Cavendish admits as much when she writes: "This lady only to her self she Writes / And all her Letters to her self Indites; / For in her self so many Creatures be / Like many Commonwealths" (*Sociable Letters*, 44).

105. Ibid., 142.

106. Ibid., 143.

keep one alive after biological death, it is this same belief that heightens the perilousness of death: so much may be lost in one individual. Her investment in an interconnected web—all that occurs necessarily reverberates beyond a single person—has implications for subjectivity as well. Jonathan Gil Harris discusses her permeability and its effect on subjects, observing that Cavendish "does not just subdivide internally [as in the case of her interlocutor in *Sociable Letters*] but also finds traces of the other in herself and vice versa."[107] Yet as she locates "traces" of alterity within and without, this neither dilutes her identity nor takes away from the premium she places on individuated agency.

How, then, do Cavendish's reimagined communities and sprawling connections return us to the impasse with which we first began this final section? How might we locate an alternative to the oppressive institution of national memory, and how could *Sociable Letters* model one mode by which to circumvent civil vengeance? In Cavendish's radically reimagined subject and her connection to infinitely inclusive networks, she flouts the inculcation of linear time, memory, and traditional (i.e., separate and hierarchically organized) subjectivity. Her insistence on and valorization of interdependence introduce a multitude of variables such that causal relationships, which organize the illusion of progressive teleology, are confused. And she upsets linear history as well insofar as it depends on teleology. Given that affection, for Cavendish, bridges temporal gaps and enables kinship to flourish with those centuries into the future, it is also these promiscuous connections that open up the collective to vulnerability. What occurs on the level of the individual reverberates beyond time to and through affective networks—for worse and for better. Yet such interdependent networks remain far more resilient in the face of biological death or the extermination of individual memory. These networks that afford mobility and connection to polytemporal subjects inhibit the very possibility of a coherent, much less uniform, national memory.[108] In this way, Cavendish's imaginative reconstructions of subjectivity and the networks that tie them together persist as a far more generative alternative than the royalist resistance to the inculcated national memory of English subjects in the republic.

In Cavendish's pursuit of possibility, signaled through subjunctive moods and counterfactual constructions, she engenders affectively sustained queer networks and embraces, as in the epigraph from *Coriolanus* with which this

---

107. Cavendish conceives of matter, Jonathan Gil Harris concludes, "as irreducibly plural" (*Untimely Matter in the Time of Shakespeare*, 159).

108. Tracing his usage of "polytemporal" through Bruno Latour and Michel Serres, Harris adapts the term to mean both polychronic and multitemporal—the essence of untimely matter itself. Ibid., 3–4.

chapter commences, "a world elsewhere."[109] When confronted with the detestable reality of exile from a country that he has too long defended, Coriolanus pronounces his enraged rejoinder: "I banish you." Much like royalists grappling with, to their minds, the indecency of a republican government, Coriolanus preserves the terms of his sentence but inverts the terms to cast them onto his antagonists. But through a litany of maledictions, oddly enough, Coriolanus shifts beyond the intractability of his initial position such that, when he insists that "there is a world elsewhere," he combines the vast optimism of the subjunctive with the present tense. No longer might there be a world elsewhere, or if one imagines otherwise, there could be one: *there is, in this very moment, another world*. As he turns his back on increasingly polarized positions, his is the pivot pursued by Cavendish.

Of course, Coriolanus's pursuit of a world elsewhere returns him to the Volscian capital of Antium—and thus he succumbs to the binary logic that demands a world composed only of Romans and Volsces. Yet at the time when the speech is made, neither the audience nor Coriolanus knows where he will venture—in this moment, he only repudiates the insufficient terms extended by authorities and insists on pursuing something else. Still, if we dilate this space with its loathsome uncertainty and limitless promise, we find ourselves resting in the temporary oasis of potentiality, the place where something that has yet to be might come into being, the space in which we see that something else has been there all along. And it is in this pause that individuals might locate a temporary respite from the logic and effects of civil vengeance.

109. William Shakespeare, *Coriolanus*, in Greenblatt et al., *The Norton Shakespeare*, 2802–80, which is based on the 1623 First Folio. The cited lines are from 3.3.124–39.

Afterword
What Remains of Civil Vengeance?

Revenge seduces. As theatrical vengeance pursues its trajectory of debauched violence and mayhem, it shuttles back and forth from the plaintive to the bathetic and from the disgusting to the discomfitingly comical. To audience members and readers alike, it extends the vicarious pleasures of inhabiting a universe in which our enemies, political and personal, finally receive their unbearable due. Such are the ways that revenge plays clamor for our attention, and we oblige, happily. But in our collective affinity for the drama that provides our retributive fix, we construct a feedback loop that reinforces a predictable definition, and this loop becomes canon. Familiar plays confirm our belief that revenge is spectacular, lethal, and relentless in its antisociality; armed with this definition, we only recognize occurrences with these qualities as vengeance. Yet once we exit the theaters, retreat from the libraries, or depart from our classrooms, something else persists— not merely the residual pleasure of spectacle or of vicarious revenge, but an insistent murmur beneath it all: the quiet retribution inhabiting early modern English culture.

To make visible a more comprehensive spectrum of retaliation that encompasses quotidian acts of revenge, acts that facilitate sociality and enhance the existing power of civil institutions, I coined the phrase "civil vengeance." Incorporating a range of heterogeneous artifacts—religious sermons, conducts books intended for children, and even parliamentary acts of thanksgiving— I assembled them alongside well-trod dramatic texts in surprising configurations. But even as my study aimed to diversify revenge literature, this is no anti-revenge tragedy polemic. After all, these are inescapably pleasurable plays to teach, study, watch, and read. I have included traditional revenge tragedies not only due to personal preference but also to demonstrate how the phenomenon of civil vengeance is present here too, if only we had the means to recognize it. The twofold result, then, is an illumination of the myriad examples of civil vengeance that permeate the early modern world and the development of a revised optic through which to interpret the revenge tragedy genre.

Progressing chronologically through early modern English culture, this study remains anchored to the historical context in which revenge literature flourished. In support of the Tudor prohibition on private vengeance, which emerged as a way by which monarchs consolidated their power, conduct literature trained its young readers in the principles of social mobility and civil vengeance. Religious texts signaled their support for the prohibition as well as an affinity for civil vengeance, often incentivizing orthodox behavior by emphasizing its unpleasant effects on one's enemies. Yet, as we have seen, civil vengeance does not simply act on the level of the individual but also structures social bodies. Because the phenomenon assisted the English to unify in outrage against the parasitic figure of the vagrant, it supported the formation of the social body and strengthened the relational bonds between its members. In so doing, civil vengeance informed English identity, domestically and abroad, and also manifested itself in the consolidation and enforcement of national memory during the Interregnum.

Yet in making visible ordinary forms of retribution against the overwhelming focus on spectacular revenge, I am not replicating a binary structure that would situate them as antagonists. Even as there are vast differences between the two, even as episodes of spectacular revenge may occlude or distract from civil vengeance, they are not necessarily at odds. As I proposed in my final chapter, the two modes may—and frequently do—work in tandem. When an act of spectacular revenge signals a regime change in, say, the 1649 execution of Charles I, it exists as a form of political theater designed to extract a set of specific responses from the populace. Though spectacular revenge may surely enrage, as it certainly did in this case, it also frightens and coerces subjects into outward resignation. Civil vengeance is then employed to preserve the new government's authority and to expand its power in, for example, the consolidation and enforcement of a new national memory. Even as spectacular revenge makes possible political upheaval and regime changes, civil institutions exist in an uneasy relationship to it, perhaps ill at ease with their temporary association with theatrical maneuvers. But as we must surely recognize by now, spectacular vengeance is not simply the purview of early modern playwrights; contemporary nations deploy it routinely and then make opaque the tactic.

To think through the triangulation of civil institutions, civil vengeance, and spectacular revenge in an early modern register, let us turn to Thomas Middleton's *The Revenger's Tragedy*. There, Vindice unleashes his ingenious brand of vengeful mayhem to purge the dukedom of its vicious immorality such that he achieves his objectives of avenging father, lover, sister, and self by the play's conclusion. After establishing the revered Antonio as the new duke, Vindice cannot resist soliciting acclaim for his witty machinations. He observes to Antonio, who had suffered the untimely loss of his wife under the previous administration, "The rape of your good lady has been quited / with death on death" (5.3.108–9).[1] Here, "quited" functions in two ways—as that which has been paid back and as that which has been concluded—such that, together, they construct the quid pro quo exchange demanded by spectacular revenge in which retaliation substitutes for and concludes the original act of injustice. Signaling his agreement with Vindice's assessment and his appreciation for the mysterious workings of divine vengeance, Antonio exclaims, "Just is the law above!" (5.3.109). While private wrongs prompted Vindice's pursuit of wild justice, the spectacular revenge he enacted simultaneously functions in service to the law and other civil institutions. That Antonio—now exemplar of law as Duke—voices his approval of the recent events emphasizes further the symbiotic relationship between civil institutions and spectacular revenge. Yet Antonio's response proves insufficient, and Vindice, much like Hieronimo when he presumes too much familiarity with his social superiors, whispers: "We may be bold to speak it now. / 'Twas somewhat witty carried, though we say it. / 'Twas we two murdered him" (5.3.115–17). What confronts this disclosure is not gratitude, as Vindice mistakenly assumes, but extreme denunciation and swift punishment, for he and his brother, Hippolito, are seized by government officials for imminent execution.

How are we to make sense of Antonio's abrupt shift? And what might it reveal about the relationship between civil vengeance and spectacular revenge? Most immediately, his condemnation stems from a perception of his vulnerability and his repeated anxieties around age. "Such an old man as he," Antonio chides Vindice, "you that would murder him would murder me" (5.3.124–25).[2] Beyond the confines of self-interest, the death sentence he pronounces also adheres to a tradition present in early modern politics

---

1. All references are to Thomas Middleton, *The Revenger's Tragedy*, in *English Renaissance Drama*, ed. David Bevington et al. (New York: W. W. Norton, 2002), 1297–369.

2. Antonio refashions the indignity of his wife's death into a testament not only to her chastity but also to his virility despite his age. See 1.4.74–78.

and plays in which actors who supported a regime change are exported so as not to tarnish the new leader with unsavory associations. Although *The Revenger's Tragedy* shows how state hypocrisy and personal vanity mingle in the exchange, the play also illuminates the law's disingenuous relationship to spectacular revenge. When anonymous hands mete out godly justice, Antonio marvels at the results and reaps enormous benefit; but when anonymity metamorphoses into corporeal agents—or, more precisely, when fortunate acts of spectacular revenge may be traced back to the state and are orchestrated with its preservation in mind—he withdraws his support in a performance of horror. And this is, as the lines make clear, an unconvincing performance, for Antonio's objections derive not from quibbles about ethics or concerns about the state's stability in the midst of vigilantism but rather from anxious self-interest. That is, he collapses the gravity of sovereign speech into that of a self-preoccupied subject. Much like Alexander Iden as he murders the upstart Jack Cade, Antonio's decision to execute the avengers combines preservation of self with that of the state—a blurring that masks violence as civil necessity. In this way, *The Revenger's Tragedy* puts on display the hypocrisy of the state's distance from spectacular revenge.

Ever quick to adapt to his new circumstances, Vindice chastises his brother and coconspirator for his resistance to their death sentence: "Thou has no conscience. Are we not revenged? / Is there one enemy left alive amongst those? / 'Tis time to die when we are ourselves our foes" (5.3.128–30). Although Vindice's cheeky lines skewer the generic convention of beleaguered avengers who come to embody evil in their pursuit of justice and who are then purged by the play's conclusion, the passage presents something more regarding the intersection of civil vengeance and spectacular revenge. When he raises the specter of time, he remarks on the play's pressing need for expediency as it nears its conclusion. But because Vindice's mention of time is extended by the homophonous play on "our/hour," this aural connection returns us to the social body. From his retribution a collective has emerged such that there is no "enemy left alive," and while that collective might have sympathized originally with their plight or even appreciated the gains secured by their revenge, he and his brother now find themselves in opposition to that social body. Never one to overstay his welcome, Vindice speaks from an impasse—he inhabits both the position of an agent of civil society and social alien to it such that his amorphous "our" may refer not only to his brother and himself but also to the collective at large.

If we understand Vindice to represent spectacular revenge, we might then read his cheerful acceptance not as an acknowledgment of his transgression but of his coincidence with civil vengeance. That is, the spectacular revenge executed by Vindice and his brother propels Antonio's rise to power. Vindice's real sense that he has exhausted his trajectory and annihilated all his enemies is an admission that he has passed over the threshold from spectacular revenge to civil vengeance. And it is through their sentencing that Vindice further supports Antonio by urging him to prove his newfound sovereignty in two distinct ways: his command over spectacular revenge and his adjudication over matters of life and death. Played out to its logical extreme in *The Revenger's Tragedy*, spectacular revenge intersects with civil vengeance and is brought under the control of civil institutions, whose sovereign agenda it has served. Yet once spectacular revenge, with its conspicuously punk incivility, may be traced back to civil institutions, once it can be connected to and understood as an extension of their institutions, it must be disappeared, for civility demands disavowals and lies. If tragedy affixes itself to avengers, we might locate its origins in the state's reliance on their acts and its violent repudiation of spectacular revenge performed by anyone but itself or its silent agents. In the end, this deliberate erasure constitutes the last twist of civil vengeance, one final "there" for revenge's endless tragedy.

BIBLIOGRAPHY

Primary Sources

An Act appointing Thursday the last day of February, 1649. for a solemn day of humiliation, fasting and prayer and declaring the grounds thereof. London: Edward Husband and John Field, [1650].

An act appointing Thursday the thirteenth of June 1650. to be kept as a day of solemn fasting and humiliation and declaring the reasons and grounds thereof. London: Edward Husband and John Field, 1650.

An Act for a day of publique thanksgiving to be observed throughout England and Wales, on Thursday on the first of November, 1649. London: John Field, 1649.

An act for setting apart Thursday the thirtieth day of January, 1650. for a day of publique thanksgiving: together with a declaration of the grounds and reasons thereof. London: Edward Husband and John Field, [1651].

Ascham, Roger. *The Scholemaster or Plaine and Perfite Way of Teachyng Children.* London: John Daye, 1570.

Bacon, Francis. *An Account of the Life and Times of Francis Bacon.* Edited by James Spedding. London: Trübner, 1878.

———. *The charge of Sir Francis Bacon.* London: George Eld, 1614.

———. "Of Revenge." In *Essays,* edited by John Pitcher, 72–73. London: Penguin, 1986.

Beard, Thomas, and Thomas Taylor. *The theatre of Gods judgements wherein is represented the admirable justice of God against all notorious sinners.* London: S. I. and M. H., 1642.

Bright, Timothie. *A treatise of melancholie.* London: Thomas Vautrollier, 1586.

Browne, John. *Adenochoiradelogia, or An anatomick-chirurgical treatise of glandules and strumaes or, Kings-evil-swellings.* London, Tho[mas] Newcomb, 1684.

Bulwer, John. *Chirologia, or the Naturall Language of the Hand.* London: Tho[mas] Harper, 1644.

Burton, Robert. *The anatomy of melancholy.* London: John Lichfield and James Short, 1621.

Castiglione, Baldassare. *The Courtier.* Translated by Thomas Hoby. London: Wyllyam Seres, 1561.

Cavendish, Margaret. *The Blazing World and Other Writings.* Edited by Kate Lilley. London: Penguin, 1994.

———. *CCXI Sociable Letters.* London: William Wilson, 1664.

———. *Sociable Letters.* Edited by James Fitzmaurice. Peterborough, ON: Broadview Press, 2004.

Charles I. "Selections from *Eikon Basilike*." In *Eikon Basilike*, edited by Jim Daems and Holly Faith Nelson, 47–216. Peterborough, ON: Broadview Press, 2006.

Chassanion, Jean de, and Thomas Beard. *The theatre of Gods judgements: or, a collection of histories out of sacred, ecclesiasticall, and prophane authours concerning the admirable judgements of God upon the transgressours of his commandements*. London: Adam Islip, 1597.

A Coffin for King Charles a crowne for Cromwell: a pit for the people. London, 1649.

Crooke, Helkiah. *Microcosmographia, or, a Description of the Body of Man*. London: William Jaggard, 1615.

Dekker, Thomas. *News from Graves-end: Sent to Nobody*. London: T[homas] C[reede], 1604.

Donne, John. *Deaths Duell, or A Consolation to the Soule, against the Dying Life, and Living Death of the Body*. London: B. Alsop and T. Fawcet, 1633.

——. *Deaths Duell, or a Consolation to the Soule, against the Dying Life, and Living Death of the Body*. London: Thomas Harper, 1632.

——. *The Sermons of John Donne*. Edited by Evelyn M. Simpson and George R. Potter. 10 vols. Berkeley: University of California Press, 1954.

Downame, George. *Lectures on the XV. Psalme read in the cathedrall church of S. Paule*. London: Adam Islip, 1604.

Erasmus, Desiderius. *The Civilitie of Childehode*. Translated by Thomas Paynell. London: John Tisdale, 1560.

——. *De Civilitate Morum Puerilium*. Translated by Robert Whytyngton. London, 1532.

——. *A godly boke wherein is contained certayne fruitefull, godlye, and necessarye rules, to bee exercised and put in practice by all Christian souldiers lynynge in the campe of this worlde*. London: Wyllyam Seres, 1561.

Fell, John. *The life of that reverend divine, and learned historian, Dr. Thomas Fuller*. London, 1661.

Fenner, William. *Treatise of the Affections, or, The Soules Pulse Wherby a Christian May Know Whether He Be Living or Dying*. London: R. H., 1642.

Fiston, William. *The Schoole of Good Manners*. London: J. Danter, 1595.

A Flattering elegie upon the death of King Charles the cleane contrary way: with a parallel something significant. London, 1649.

Guazzo, Stefano. *The civile conversation*. Translated by George Pettie. London: Richard Watkins, 1581.

Hawkins, Francis. *Youths Behaviour, or Decency in conversation amongst men*. London: W. Wilson, 1646.

Hieron, Samuel. *Three Sermons ful of Necessarie Advertisements, and Gracious Comforts, for All Those Whose Care Is to Worke Out Their Owne Salvation with Feare and Trembling*. London: B. Alsop, 1616.

Hill, Adam. *The crie of England A sermon preached at Paules Crosse in September 1593*. London: Ed. Allde, 1595.

Hyperius, Andreas. *The Practis of Preaching, Otherwise Called the Pathway to the Pulpet conteyning an Excellent Method How to Frame Divine Sermons, and to Interpret the Holy Scriptures according to the Capacitie of the Vulgar People*. Translated by John Ludham. London: Thomas East, 1577.

——. *The regiment of the povertie*. Translated by Henry Tripp. London: F. Coldock and H. Bynneman, 1572.

——. *The true tryall and examination of a mans owne selfe wherein every faithfull Christian.* . . . Translated by Tho[mas] Newton. London: John Windet, 1587.

King Charles his glory, and rebels shame. London, 1660.

King, Henry. *A deepe groane, fetch'd at the funerall of that incomparable and glorious monarch, Charles the First, King of Great Britaine, France and Ireland.* London, 1649.

Kyd, Thomas. *The Spanish tragedie.* London: W. W[hite], 1602.

——. "The Spanish Tragedy." In *English Renaissance Drama*, edited by David Bevington et al., 8–73. New York: W. W. Norton, 2002.

Lodge, Thomas. *A Treatise of the Plague.* London: Thomas Creede and Valentine Simmes, 1603.

Manning, James. *Complexions Castle.* London: John Legat, 1604.

Marston, John. *Antonio's Revenge.* In *Tragedies and comedies collected into one volume.* London: A. M[atthewes], 1633.

——. *Antonio's Revenge: The second part of Antonio and Mellida.* Edited by G. K. Hunter. London: Edward Arnold, 1966.

Mayne, Jasper. "On Dr. Donnes Death." In *Poems*, by John Donne. London: M[iles] F[lesher], 1633.

Middleton, Thomas. *The Revenger's Tragedy.* In *English Renaissance Drama*, edited by David Bevington et al., 1297–1369. New York: W. W. Norton, 2002.

Milton, John. "Selections from *Eikonoklastes*." In *Eikon Basilike*, edited by Jim Daems and Holly Faith Nelson, 217–83. Peterborough, ON: Broadview Press, 2006.

A Miracle of Miracles: Wrought by the Blood of King Charles the First. London, 1649.

Nalson, J[ohn]. *A True copy of the journal of the High Court of Justice for the trial of K. Charles I.* London: H. C., 1684.

Nashe, Thomas. *The Unfortunate Traveller, or The Life of Jack Wilton.* In *The Unfortunate Traveller and Other Works*, edited by J. B. Steane, 251–370. London: Penguin Books, 1985.

Perkins, William. *The Arte of Prophecying: Or, A Treatise concerning the Sacred and Onely True Manner and Methode of Preaching.* London: Felix Kyngston, 1607.

——. *A garden of spirituall flowers.* London: W. White, 1610.

——. *A godly and learned exposition of Christs Sermon in the Mount.* Cambridge: Thomas Brooke and Cantrell Legge, 1608.

——. *A Treatise of the vocations, or, Callings of Men.* London: John Legat, 1603.

Puttenham, George. *The arte of English poesie.* London: Richard Field, 1589.

Quarles, John. *Regale lectum miseriae, or A kingly bed of misery.* London, 1649.

Quintilian. *Institutes of Oratory: Or, Education of an Orator.* Translated by John Selby Watson. London: George Bell and Sons, 1891.

Sanderson, William. *A compleat history of the life and raigne of King Charles from his cradle to his grave.* London, 1658.

Seager, Francis. *The Schoole of Vertue.* London: Wyllyam Seres, 1557.

The severall confessions, of Thomas Norton, and Christopher Norton: two of the northern rebels: who suffred at Tiburne, and were drawen, hanged, and quartered, for treason. London: William How[e], 1570.

Shakespeare, William. *Coriolanus.* In *The Norton Shakespeare*, edited by Stephen Greenblatt et al., 2802–80. New York: W. W. Norton, 1997.

——. *Hamlet.* In *The Norton Shakespeare*, edited by Stephen Greenblatt et al., 1683–2108. New York: W. W. Norton, 1997.

——. *Henry VI, Part II*. In *The Norton Shakespeare*, edited by Stephen Greenblatt et al., 203–90. New York: W. W. Norton, 1997.

Stuart Royal Proclamations. Vol. 1, *Royal Proclamations of King James I, 1603–1625*. Edited by James F. Larkin and Paul L. Hughes. Oxford: Oxford University Press, 1973.

Tudor Royal Proclamations. Vol. 3, *The Late Tudors (1588–1603)*. Edited by Paul L. Hughes and James F. Larkin. New Haven, CT: Yale University Press, 1969.

Tyndale, William. "Prologue to the Book of Numbers." In *The Pentateuch*. Antwerp: Johan Hoochstraten, 1530.

Walton, Izaak. *The Life of John Donne, Dr. in Divinity, and Late Dean of Saint Pauls Church London*. London: J. G., 1658.

Willan, Edward. *Six Sermons*. London: Printed for R. Royston, 1651.

Wright, Thomas. *The passions of the minde in generall*. London: Valentine Simmes and Adam Islip, 1604.

Secondary Sources

Achinstein, Sharon. *Milton and the Revolutionary Reader*. Princeton, NJ: Princeton University Press, 1994.

Agamben, Giorgio. *Homo Sacer: Sovereign Power and Bare Life*. Translated by Daniel Heller-Roazen. Stanford, CA: Stanford University Press, 1998.

——. *Potentialities: Collected Essays in Philosophy*. Edited and translated by Daniel Heller-Roazen. Stanford, CA: Stanford University Press, 1999.

Ahmed, Sara. "Happy Objects." In *The Affect Theory Reader*, edited by Melissa Gregg and Gregory J. Seigworth, 29–51. Durham, NC: Duke University Press, 2010.

——. *Living a Feminist Life*. Durham, NC: Duke University Press, 2017.

——. *The Promise of Happiness*. Durham, NC: Duke University Press, 2010.

Akkerman, Nadine. *Invisible Agents: Women and Espionage in Seventeenth-Century Britain*. Oxford: Oxford University Press, 2018.

Albala, Ken. *Eating Right in the Renaissance*. Berkeley: University of California Press, 2002.

Allman, Eileen. *Jacobean Revenge Tragedy and the Politics of Virtue*. Newark: University of Delaware Press, 1999.

Anderson, Benedict. *Imagined Communities: Reflections on the Origin and Spread of Nationalism*. Rev. ed. London: Verso, 2006.

Anderson, Judith H. "Body of Death: The Pauline Inheritance in Donne's Sermons, Spenser's Maleger, and Milton's Sin and Death." In *Rhetorics of Bodily Disease and Health in Medieval and Early Modern England*, edited by Jennifer C. Vaught, 171–92. Farnham, UK: Ashgate, 2010.

Arab, Ronda, Michelle M. Dowd, and Adam Zucker, eds. *Historical Affects and the Early Modern Theater*. New York: Routledge, 2015.

Archer, Ian. *The Pursuit of Stability*. Cambridge: Cambridge University Press, 1991.

Armstrong, Kate. "Sermons in Performance." In *The Oxford Handbook of the Early Modern Sermon*, edited by Peter McCullough, Hugh Adlington, and Emma Rhatigan, 120–36. Oxford: Oxford University Press, 2011.

Aydelotte, Frank. *Elizabethan Rogues and Vagabonds*. Oxford: Clarendon Press, 1913.

Bailey, Amanda, and Mario DiGangi, eds. *Affect Theory and Early Modern Texts*. New York: Palgrave Macmillan, 2017.

Balibar, Étienne. *Violence and Civility: On the Limits of Political Philosophy*. Translated by G. M. Goshgarian. New York: Columbia University Press, 2015.

Barber, C. L. *Creating Elizabethan Tragedy: The Theater of Marlowe and Kyd*. Chicago: University of Chicago Press, 1988.

Barret, J. K. *Untold Futures: Time and Literary Culture in Renaissance England*. Ithaca, NY: Cornell University Press, 2016.

Bartolovich, Crystal. "Utopian Cosmopolitanism." *Shakespeare Studies* 35 (2007): 47–57.

Beecher, Donald, Travis DeCook, Andrew Wallace, and Grant Williams, eds. *Taking Exception to the Law: Materializing Injustice in Early Modern Literature*. Toronto: University of Toronto Press, 2015.

Beier, A. L. *Masterless Men: The Vagrancy Problem in England 1560–1640*. London: Methuen, 1985.

Belsey, Catherine. *The Subject of Tragedy*. London: Methuen, 1985.

Benjamin, Walter. "Theses on the Philosophy of History." In *Illuminations: Essays and Reflections*, edited by Hannah Arendt and translated by Harry Zohn. New York: Schocken Books, 1969.

Berlant, Lauren. "Thinking about Feeling Historical." *Emotion, Space and Society* 1 (2008): 4–9.

Bevan, Jonquil. "*Hebdomada Mortium*: The Structure of Donne's Last Sermon." *Review of English Studies* 45, no. 178 (1994): 185–203.

Bierlaire, Franz. "Erasmus in School: The *De Civilitate Morum Puerilium*." In *Essays on the Works of Erasmus*, edited by Richard DeMolen, 239–51. New Haven, CT: Yale University Press, 1978.

Bloch, Marc. "Memoire collective, tradition et coutume: A propos d'un livre recent." In *The Collective Memory Reader*, edited by Jeffrey K. Olick, Vered Vinitzky-Seroussi, and Daniel Levy, 150–55. Oxford: Oxford University Press, 2011.

Bowerbank, Sylvia. "The Spider's Delight: Margaret Cavendish and the 'Female' Imagination." *English Literary Renaissance* 14, no. 3 (1984): 392–408.

Bowers, Fredson Thayer. *Elizabethan Revenge Tragedy, 1587–1642*. Princeton, NJ: Princeton University Press, 1940.

——. *Elizabethan Revenge Tragedy, 1587–1642*. 2nd ed. Gloucester, MA: Peter Smith, 1959.

Braden, Gordon. *Renaissance Tragedy and the Senecan Tradition: Anger's Privilege*. New Haven, CT: Yale University Press, 1985.

Bray, Alan. "Homosexuality and the Signs of Male Friendship in Elizabethan England." In *Queering the Renaissance*, edited by Jonathan Goldberg, 40–61. Durham, NC: Duke University Press, 1994.

Brennan, Teresa. *The Transmission of Affect*. Ithaca, NY: Cornell University Press, 2004.

Brooks, Christopher. "Apprenticeship, Social Mobility and the Middling Sort, 1550–1800." In *The Middling Sort of People: Culture, Society, and Politics in England, 1550–1800*, edited by Jonathan Barry and Christopher Brooks, 52–79. New York: St. Martin's Press, 1994.

Broude, Ronald. "Revenge and Revenge Tragedy in Renaissance England." *Renaissance Quarterly* 28, no. 1 (1975): 38–58.

Bryson, Anna. *From Courtesy to Civility: Changing Codes of Conduct in Early Modern England*. Oxford: Oxford University Press, 1998.

Caldwell, Ellen C. "Jack Cade and Shakespeare's *Henry VI, Part II*." *Studies in Philology* 92, no. 1 (1995): 18–79.

Camp, Cynthia Turner. "The Temporal Excesses of Dead Flesh." *Postmedieval* 4, no. 4 (2013): 416–26.

Campana, Joseph. "The State of England's Camp: Courtesans, Curses, and the Violence of Style in *The Unfortunate Traveller*." *Prose Studies* 29, no. 3 (2007): 347–58.

Carey, John. *John Donne: Life, Mind, and Art*. Oxford: Oxford University Press, 1981.

Carroll, William C. *Fat King, Lean Beggar: Representations of Poverty in the Age of Shakespeare*. Ithaca, NY: Cornell University Press, 1996.

Cartelli, Thomas. "Jack Cade in the Garden: Class Consciousness and Class Conflict in *2 Henry VI*." In *Enclosure Acts: Sexuality, Property, and Culture in Early Modern England*, edited by Richard Burt and John Michael Archer, 48–67. Ithaca, NY: Cornell University Press, 1994.

Cefalu, Paul. *Revisionist Shakespeare: Transitional Ideologies in Texts and Contexts*. New York: Palgrave Macmillan, 2004.

Clement, Jennifer. *Reading Humility in Early Modern England*. Burlington, VT: Ashgate, 2015.

Cohen, Walter. *Drama of a Nation: Public Theater in Renaissance England and Spain*. Ithaca, NY: Cornell University Press, 1985.

Corns, Thomas N. *Uncloistered Virtue: English Political Literature, 1640–1660*. Oxford: Oxford University Press, 1992.

Correll, Barbara. *The End of Conduct: "Grobianus" and the Renaissance Text of the Subject*. Ithaca, NY: Cornell University Press, 1996.

Cressy, David. *Birth, Marriage, and Death: Ritual, Religion, and the Life-Cycle in Tudor and Stuart England*. Oxford: Oxford University Press, 1997.

Crosbie, Christopher. "*Oeconomia* and the Vegetative Soul: Rethinking Revenge in *The Spanish Tragedy*." *English Literary Renaissance* 38, no. 1 (2008): 3–33.

——. *Revenge Tragedy and Classical Philosophy on the Early Modern Stage*. Edinburgh: Edinburgh University Press, 2018.

Cummings, Brian. "Animal Passions and Human Sciences: Shame, Blushing, and Nakedness in Early Modern Europe and the New World." In *At the Borders of the Human: Beasts, Bodies, and Natural Philosophy in the Early Modern Period*, edited by Erica Fudge, Susan Wiseman, and Ruth Gilbert, 26–50. London: Palgrave Macmillan, 1999.

Daems, Jim, and Holly Faith Nelson. Introduction to *Eikon Basilike*, edited by Jim Daems and Holly Faith Nelson, 13–39. Peterborough, ON: Broadview Press, 2006.

Derrida, Jacques. *Specters of Marx: The State of the Debt, the Work of Mourning, and the New International*. Translated by Peggy Kamuf. New York: Routledge, 1994.

Dillinger, Johannes. "Organized Arson as a Political Crime: The Construction of a 'Terrorist' Menace in the Early Modern Period." *Crime, History, and Societies* 10, no. 2 (2006): 101–21.

——. "Terrorists and Witches: Popular Ideas of Evil in the Early Modern Period." *History of European Ideas* 30, no. 2 (2004): 167–82.

Dimberg, Ulf, Monika Thunberg, and Sara Grunedal. "Facial Reactions to Emotional Stimuli: Automatically Controlled Emotional Responses." *Cognition and Emotion* 16, no. 4 (2002): 449–71.

Dinshaw, Carolyn. *How Soon Is Now? Medieval Texts, Amateur Readers, and the Queerness of Time.* Durham, NC: Duke University Press, 2012.

Doan, Laura. "Queer History / Queer Memory: The Case of Alan Turing." *GLQ: A Journal of Lesbian and Gay Studies* 23, no. 1 (2017): 113–36.

Dodds, Lara. "Bawds and Housewives: Margaret Cavendish and the Work of 'Bad Writing.'" *Early Modern Studies Journal* 6 (2014): 29–65.

——. *The Literary Invention of Margaret Cavendish.* Pittsburgh: Duquesne University Press, 2013.

Dolan, Frances E. "Ashes and 'The Archive': The London Fire of 1666, Partisanship, and Proof." *Journal of Medieval and Early Modern Studies* 31, no. 2 (2006): 383–86.

——. "Scattered Remains and Paper Bodies: Margaret Cavendish and the Siege of Colchester." *Postmedieval* 4, no. 4 (2013): 452–64.

Dugan, Holly. *The Ephemeral History of Perfume: Scent and Sense in Early Modern England.* Baltimore: Johns Hopkins University Press, 2011.

Dunn, Kevin. "'Action, Passion, Motion': The Gestural Politics of Counsel in *The Spanish Tragedy.*" *Renaissance Drama* 31 (2002): 27–60.

Dunne, Derek. *Shakespeare, Revenge Tragedy, and Early Modern Law: Vindictive Justice.* London: Palgrave Macmillan, 2016.

Eggert, Katherine. *Disknowledge: Literature, Alchemy, and the End of Humanism in Renaissance England.* Philadelphia: University of Pennsylvania Press, 2015.

Eklund, Hillary. *Literature and Moral Economy in the Early Modern Atlantic.* Burlington, VT: Ashgate, 2015.

——. "Revolting Diets: Jack Cade's 'Sallet' and the Politics of Hunger in *2 Henry VI.*" *Shakespeare Studies* 42 (2014): 51–62.

Elias, Norbert. *The Civilizing Process: Sociogenetic and Psychogenetic Investigations.* London: Blackwell, 2000.

Eliot, T. S. "Lancelot Andrewes." In *Selected Essays: New Edition*, 289–300. New York: Harcourt, Brace, 1950.

Engert, Veronika, Franzika Plessow, Robert Miller, Clemens Kirschbaum, and Tania Singer. "Cortisol Increase in Empathic Stress Is Modulated by Emotional Closeness and Observation Modality." *Psychoneuroendocrinology* 45 (2014): 192–201.

Enterline, Lynn. *Shakespeare's Schoolroom: Rhetoric, Discipline, Emotion.* Philadelphia: University of Pennsylvania Press, 2011.

Erll, Astrid. "Cultural Memory Studies: An Introduction." In *A Companion to Cultural Memory Studies*, edited by Erll Astrid and Ansgar Nünning, 1–18. Berlin: De Gruyter, 2010.

Erne, Lukas. *Beyond "The Spanish Tragedy": A Study of the Works of Thomas Kyd.* Manchester, UK: Manchester University Press, 2001.

Eschenbaum, Natalie K., and Barbara Correll, eds. Introduction to *Disgust in Early Modern English Literature*, 1–20. New York: Routledge, 2016.

Farmer, Alan B. "Cosmopolitanism and Foreign Bodies in Early Modern England." *Shakespeare Studies* 35 (2007): 58–65.

Findlay, Alison. *A Feminist Perspective on Renaissance Drama.* Oxford: Blackwell, 1999.

Fish, Stanley. "Masculine Persuasive Force: Donne and Verbal Power." In *Soliciting Interpretation: Literary Theory and Seventeenth-Century English Poetry*, edited by Elizabeth D. Harvey and Katharine Eisaman Maus, 223–52. Chicago: University of Chicago Press, 1990.

Fitter, Chris. "'Your Captain Is Brave and Vows Reformation': Jack Cade, the Hacket Rising, and Shakespeare's Vision of Popular Rebellion." *Shakespeare Studies* 32 (2004): 173–219.

Fitzmaurice, Susan. *The Familiar Letter in Early Modern English: A Pragmatic Approach.* Philadelphia: John Benjamins Publishing, 2002.

Frank, Adam. "Some Avenues for Feeling." *Criticism* 46, no. 3 (2004): 511–24.

Freeman, Arthur. *Thomas Kyd: Facts and Problems.* Oxford: Clarendon Press, 1967.

Freeman, Elizabeth. *Time Binds: Queer Temporalities, Queer Histories.* Durham, NC: Duke University Press, 2010.

Freud, Sigmund. *Beyond the Pleasure Principle.* Translated and edited by James Strachey. New York: W. W. Norton, 1989.

Fumerton, Patricia. *Unsettled: The Culture of Mobility and the Working Poor in Early Modern England.* Chicago: University of Chicago Press, 2006.

Fung, Megan J. "Art, Authority, and Domesticity in Margaret Cavendish's *Poems and Fancies*." *Early Modern Women: An Introduction* 10, no. 1 (2015): 27–47.

Gardner, Helen. "Dean Donne's Monument in St. Paul's." In *Evidence in Literary Scholarship: Essays in Memory of James Marshall Osborn*, edited by René Welleck and Alvaro Ribeiro, 29–44. Oxford: Clarendon Press, 1979.

Gibbs, Anna. "After Affect: Sympathy, Synchrony, and Mimetic Communication." In *The Affect Theory Reader*, edited by Melissa Gregg and Gregory J. Seigworth, 186–205. Durham, NC: Duke University Press, 2010.

Givón, Talmy. *On Understanding Grammar.* New York: Academic Press, 1979.

Graham, Elspeth. "Intersubjectivity, Intertextuality, and Form in the Self-Writings of Margaret Cavendish." In *Genre and Women's Life Writing in Early Modern England*, edited by Michelle M. Dowd and Julie A. Eckerle, 131–50. Burlington, VT: Ashgate, 2007.

Greenblatt, Stephen. "Murdering Peasants: Status, Genre, and the Representation of Rebellion." In *Representing the English Renaissance*, edited by Stephen Greenblatt, 1–29. Berkeley: University of California Press, 1988.

———. *Tyrant: Shakespeare on Politics.* New York: W. W. Norton, 2018.

Greteman, Blaine. "'All This Seed Pearl': John Donne and Bodily Presence." *College Literature* 37, no. 3 (2010): 26–42.

Griffin, Andrew. "Thomas Heywood and London Exceptionalism." *Studies in Philology* 110, no. 1 (2013): 85–114.

Grosser, Bernard I., Louis Monti-Bloch, Clive Jennigs-White, and David L. Berliner. "Behavioral and Electrophysiological Effects of Androstadienone, a Human Pheromone." *Psychoneuroendocrinology* 25, no. 3 (2000): 289–99.

Haber, Judith. *Desire and Dramatic Form in Early Modern England*. Cambridge: Cambridge University Press, 2009.

Halberstam, Jack. *In a Queer Time and Place: Transgender Bodies*. New York: New York University Press, 2005.

——. *The Queer Art of Failure*. Durham, NC: Duke University Press, 2011.

Hallett, Charles A., and Elaine S. Hallett. *The Revenger's Madness: A Study of Revenge Tragedy Motifs*. Lincoln: University of Nebraska Press, 1981.

Hampton-Reeves, Stuart. "Kent's Best Man: Radical Chorographic Consciousness and the Identity Politics of Local History in Shakespeare's *2 Henry VI*." *Journal of Early Modern Cultural Studies* 14, no. 1 (2014): 63–87.

Hardt, Michael. "Foreword: What Affects Are Good For." In *The Affective Turn: Theorizing the Social*, edited by Patricia Ticineto Clough and Jean Halley, ix–xiii. Durham, NC: Duke University Press, 2007.

Harris, Jonathan Gil. "The Time of Shakespeare's Jewry." *Shakespeare Studies* 35 (2007): 39–46.

——. *Untimely Matter in the Time of Shakespeare*. Philadelphia: University of Pennsylvania Press, 2009.

Hatfield, Elaine, Richard L. Rapson, and Yen-Chi L. Le. "Emotional Contagion and Empathy." In *The Social Neuroscience of Empathy*, edited by Jean Decety and William Ickes, 19–30. Cambridge, MA: MIT Press, 2009.

Healy, Margaret. *Fictions of Disease in Early Modern England: Bodies, Plagues and Politics*. New York: Palgrave Macmillan, 2001.

Helgerson, Richard. "Milton Reads the King's Book: Print, Performance, and the Making of a Bourgeois Idol." *Criticism* 29, no. 1 (1987): 1–25.

Hindle, Steve. *On the Parish? The Micro-Politics of Poor Relief in Rural England, c. 1550–1750*. New York: Clarendon Press, 2004.

Hobgood, Allison P. *Passionate Playgoing in Early Modern England*. Cambridge: Cambridge University Press, 2015.

Hodgson, Elizabeth. *Grief and Women Writers in the English Renaissance*. Cambridge: Cambridge University Press, 2015.

Huebert, Ronald. *Privacy in the Age of Shakespeare: Evolving Relationships in a Changing Environment*. Toronto: University of Toronto Press, 2016.

Hunt, Arnold. *The Art of Hearing: English Preachers and Their Audiences, 1590–1640*. Cambridge: Cambridge University Press, 2010.

Ibbett, Katherine. *Compassion's Edge: Fellow-Feeling and Its Limits in Early Modern France*. Philadelphia: University of Pennsylvania Press, 2017.

Irish, Bradley J. *Emotion in the Tudor Court: Literature, History, and Early Modern Feeling*. Evanston, IL: Northwestern University Press, 2018.

Iyengar, Sujata. "Royalist, Romanticist, Racialist: Rank, Gender, and Race in the Science Fiction of Margaret Cavendish." *English Literary History* 69, no. 3 (2002): 649–72.

James, Susan. *Passions and Action: The Emotions in Seventeenth-Century Philosophy*. Oxford: Oxford University Press, 2000.

Johnson, Kimberly. "The Persistence of the Flesh in *Deaths Duell*." In *Shakespeare Up Close: Reading Early Modern Texts*, edited by Russ McDonald, Nicholas D. Nace, and Travis D. Williams, 64–69. London: Bloomsbury, 2012.

Jones, Ann Rosalind. "Nets and Bridles: Early Modern Conduct Books and Sixteenth-Century Women's Lyrics." In *The Ideology of Conduct: Essays on Literature and the History of Sexuality*, edited by Nancy Armstrong and Leonard Tennenhouse, 39–72. New York: Methuen, 1987.

Jordan, June. *Civil Wars: Observations from the Front Lines of America*. New York: Touchstone, 1995.

Kastan, David Scott. *A Will to Believe: Shakespeare and Religion*. Oxford: Oxford University Press, 2014.

Kegl, Rosemary. "'The World I Have Made': Margaret Cavendish, Feminism, and the *Blazing-World*." In *Feminist Readings of Early Modern Culture: Emerging Subjects*, edited by Valerie Traub, M. Lindsay Kaplan, and Dympna Callaghan, 119–41. Cambridge: Cambridge University Press, 1996.

Keller, Eve. "Producing Petty Gods: Margaret Cavendish's Critique of Experimental Science." *English Literary History* 64, no. 2 (1997): 447–71.

Keller, James R. "The Science of Salvation: Spiritual Alchemy in Donne's Final Sermon." *Sixteenth Century Journal* 23, no. 3 (1992): 486–93.

Kellett, Katherine. "Performance, Performativity, and Identity in Margaret Cavendish's *The Convent of Pleasure*." *Studies in English Literature* 48, no. 2 (2008): 419–42.

Kelso, Ruth. "Sixteenth Century Definitions of the Gentleman in England." *Journal of English and Germanic Philology* 24, no. 3 (1925): 370–82.

Kenyon, J. P. *Stuart England*. 2nd ed. London: Penguin, 1985.

Kerr, Heather. "Trembling Hyphen / Shaking Hinge: Margaret Cavendish and Queer Literary Subjectivity." In *Women Writing, 1550–1750*, edited by Jo Wallwork and Paul Salzman, 215–36. Bundoora, AU: Meridian, 2001.

Kerrigan, John. *Revenge Tragedy: Aeschylus to Armageddon*. Oxford: Clarendon Press, 1996.

Keyishian, Harry. *The Shapes of Revenge: Victimization, Vengeance, and Vindictiveness in Shakespeare*. Atlantic Highlands, NJ: Humanities Press International, 1995.

King, Emily. "Dirty Jokes: Disgust, Desire, and the Pornographic Narrative in Thomas Nashe's *The Unfortunate Traveller*." In *Disgust in Early Modern English Literature*, edited by Natalie K. Eschenbaum and Barbara Correll, 23–37. New York: Routledge, 2016.

Kinney, Arthur. "Afterword: (Re)presenting the Early Modern Rogue." In *Rogues and Early Modern English Culture*, edited by Craig Donne and Steve Mentz, 361–81. Ann Arbor: University of Michigan Press, 2004.

Knapp, Jeffrey. *Shakespeare's Tribe: Church, Nation, and Theater in Renaissance England*. Chicago: University of Chicago Press, 2002.

Knoppers, Laura Lunger. *Constructing Cromwell: Ceremony, Portrait, and Print, 1645–1661*. Cambridge: Cambridge University Press, 2000.

Korsmeyer, Carolyn. *Savoring Disgust: The Foul and the Fair in Aesthetics*. Oxford: Oxford University Press, 2011.

Lacan, Jacques. "The Mirror Stage as Formative of the Function of the I as Revealed in Psychoanalytic Experience." In *The Norton Anthology of Criticism and Theory*, edited by Vincent B. Leitch et al., 1285–90. New York: W. W. Norton, 2001.

Lacey, Andrew. *The Cult of King Charles the Martyr*. Suffolk, UK: Boydell Press, 2003.

Lamb, Julian. *Rules of Use: Language and Instruction in Early Modern England*. London: Bloomsbury, 2014.

Lockey, Brian C. "Catholics and Cosmpolitans Writing the Nation: The Pope's Scholars and the 1579 Student Rebellion at the English Roman College." In *Representing Imperial Rivalry in the Early Modern Mediterranean*, edited by Barbara Fuchs and Emily Weissbourd, 233–54. Toronto: University of Toronto Press, 2015.

Longstaffe, Stephen. "'A Short Report and Not Otherwise': Jack Cade in *2 Henry VI*." In *Shakespeare and Carnival: After Bakhtin*, edited by Ronald Knowles, 13–35. New York: St. Martin's Press, 1998.

Lupton, Julia Reinhard. *Citizen-Saints: Shakespeare and Political Theology*. Chicago: University of Chicago Press, 2005.

Lynch, Beth. *John Bunyan and the Language of Conviction: Studies in Renaissance Literature*. Cambridge: D. S. Brewer, 2004.

Manning, Roger. *Village Revolts: Social Protest and Popular Disturbances in England, 1509–1640*. Oxford: Oxford University Press, 1988.

Martin, Jessica. *Walton's Lives: Conformist Commemorations and the Rise of Biography*. Oxford: Oxford University Press, 2011.

Maus, Katharine Eisaman. Introduction to *Four Revenge Tragedies: "The Spanish Tragedy"; "The Revenger's Tragedy"; "The Revenge of Bussy d'Ambois"; and "The Atheist's Tragedy,"* edited by Katharine Eisaman Maus, ix–xxxi. Oxford: Oxford University Press, 2008.

———. *Inwardness and Theater in the English Renaissance*. Chicago: University of Chicago Press, 1995.

McCullough, Peter. "Preaching and Context: John Donne's Sermon in the Funerals of Sir William Cokayne." In *The Oxford Handbook of the Early Modern Sermon*, edited by Peter McCullough, Hugh Adlington, and Emma Rhatigan, 213–70. Oxford: Oxford University Press, 2011.

———. *Sermons at Court: Politics and Religion in Elizabethan and Jacobean Preaching*. Cambridge: Cambridge University Press, 1998.

McDuffie, Felecia Wright. *To Our Bodies Then We Turn: Body as Word and Sacrament in the Works of John Donne*. New York: Continuum, 2005.

McGinn, Colin. *The Meaning of Disgust*. Oxford: Oxford University Press, 2011.

McKnight, Laura Blair. "Crucifixion or Apocalypse? Refiguring the *Eikon Basilike*." In *Religion, Literature, and Politics in Post-Reformation England, 1540–1688*, edited by Donna B. Hamilton and Richard Strier, 138–60. Cambridge: Cambridge University Press, 1996.

McMahon, Chris. *Family and the State of Early Modern Revenge Drama*. London: Routledge, 2011.

McNeill, Fiona. *Poor Women in Shakespeare*. Cambridge: Cambridge University Press, 2007.

Meek, Richard, and Erin Sullivan. Introduction to *The Renaissance of Emotion: Understanding Affect in Shakespeare and His Contemporaries*, edited by Richard

Meek and Erin Sullivan, 1–24. Manchester, UK: Manchester University Press, 2015.

Mikics, David. *The Limits of Moralizing: Pathos in Subjectivity in Spenser and Milton.* Lewisburg, PA: Bucknell University Press, 1994.

Miller, William Ian. *The Anatomy of Disgust.* Cambridge, MA: Harvard University Press, 1997.

——. *Eye for an Eye.* Cambridge: Cambridge University Press, 2006.

Morrissey, Mary. *Politics and the Paul's Cross Sermons, 1558–1642.* Oxford: Oxford University Press, 2011.

Mullaney, Steven. *The Reformation of Emotions in the Age of Shakespeare.* Chicago: University of Chicago Press, 2015.

Muñoz, José Esteban. *Cruising Utopia: The Then and There of Queer Futurity.* New York: New York University Press, 2009.

Neill, Michael. "English Revenge Tragedy." In *A Companion to Tragedy,* edited by Rebecca Bushnell, 328–50. Malden, MA: Blackwell, 2005.

——. *Issues of Death: Mortality and Identity in English Renaissance Tragedy.* Oxford: Oxford University Press, 1997.

Ngai, Sianne. *Ugly Feelings.* Cambridge, MA: Harvard University Press, 2005.

Nora, Pierre. "Reasons for the Current Upsurge in Memory." In *The Collective Memory Reader,* edited by Jeffrey K. Olick, Vered Vinitzky-Seroussi, and Daniel Levy, 437–41. Oxford: Oxford University Press, 2011.

Norbrook, David. *Writing the English Republic: Poetry, Rhetoric and Politics, 1627–1660.* Cambridge: Cambridge University Press, 2000.

Oliver, Lisi. *The Body Legal in Barbarian Law.* Toronto: University of Toronto Press, 2011.

Orlin, Lena Cowen. *Private Matters and Public Culture in Post-Reformation England.* Ithaca, NY: Cornell University Press, 1994.

Paster, Gail Kern. *The Body Embarrassed: Drama and the Disciplines of Shame in Early Modern England.* Ithaca, NY: Cornell University Press, 1993.

Paster, Gail Kern, Katherine Rowe, and Mary Floyd-Wilson. Introduction to *Reading the Early Modern Passions: Essays in the Cultural History of Emotion,* edited by Gail Kern Paster, Katherine Rowe, and Mary Floyd-Wilson, 1–20. Philadelphia: University of Pennsylvania Press, 2004.

Pender, Patricia. *Early Modern Women's Writing and the Rhetoric of Modesty.* New York: Palgrave Macmillan, 2012.

Pippin, Anne Burnett. *Revenge in Attic and Later Tragedy.* Berkeley: University of California Press, 1998.

Pollard, Tanya. "Tragedy and Revenge." In *Cambridge Companion to English Renaissance Tragedy,* edited by Emma Smith and Garrett A. Sullivan Jr, 58–72. Cambridge: Cambridge University Press, 2010.

Pories, Kathleen. "The Intersection of Poor Laws and Literature in the Sixteenth Century: Fictional and Factual Categories." In *Framing Elizabethan Fictions: Contemporary Approaches to Early Modern Narrative Prose,* edited by Constance C. Relihan, 17–40. Kent, OH: Kent State University Press, 1996.

Potter, Lois. "The Royal Martyr in the Restoration: National Grief and National Sin." In *The Royal Image: Representation of Charles I,* edited by Thomas N. Corns, 240–62. Cambridge: Cambridge University Press, 1999.

——. *Secret Rites and Secret Writing: Royalist Literature, 1641–1660*. Cambridge: Cambridge University Press, 1989.

Prosser, Eleanor. *Hamlet and Revenge*. 2nd ed. Stanford, CA: Stanford University Press, 1971.

Pugliatti, Paola. *Beggary and Theatre in Early Modern England*. Farnham, UK: Ashgate, 2003.

Quiring, Björn. *Shakespeare's Curse: The Aporias of Ritual Exclusion in Early Modern Royal Drama*. Translated by Michael Winkler and Björn Quiring. New York: Routledge, 2014.

Randall, Helen W. "The Rise and Fall of a Martyrology: Sermons on Charles I." *Huntington Library Quarterly* 10 (1947): 136–67.

Raymond, Joad. *The Invention of the Newspaper: English Newsbooks, 1641–1649*. Oxford: Oxford University Press, 1996.

——. "Popular Representations of Charles I." In *The Royal Image: Representations of Charles I*, edited by Thomas N. Corns, 47–73. Cambridge: Cambridge University Press, 1999.

Renan, Ernest. "What Is a Nation?" In *The Collective Memory Reader*, edited by Jeffrey K. Olick, Vered Vinitzky-Seroussi, and Daniel Levy, 80–83. Oxford: Oxford University Press, 2011.

Rhatigan, Emma. "Preaching Venues: Architecture and Auditories." In *The Oxford Handbook of the Early Modern Sermon*, edited by Peter McCullough, Hugh Adlington, and Emma Rhatigan, 87–119. Oxford: Oxford University Press, 2011.

Rigney, James. "Sermons into Print." In *The Oxford Handbook of the Early Modern Sermon*, edited by Peter McCullough, Hugh Adlington, and Emma Rhatigan, 198–212. Oxford: Oxford University Press, 2011.

Rist, Thomas. *Revenge Tragedy and the Drama of Commemoration in Reforming England*. Farnham, UK: Ashgate, 2008.

Roberts, Donald Ramsay. "The Death Wish of John Donne." *PMLA* 62, no. 4 (1947): 958–76.

Roberts, Penny. "Arson, Conspiracy and Rumour in Early Modern Europe." *Continuity and Change* 12, no. 1 (1997): 9–29.

Robinson, Benedict. "Disgust c. 1600." *English Literary History* 81, no. 2 (2014): 553–83.

Rohy, Val. "On Homosexual Reproduction." *Differences* 23, no. 1 (2012): 101–30.

Salzman, Paul. *Literature and Politics in the 1620s: "Whisper'd Counsells."* Basingstoke, UK: Palgrave Macmillan, 2014.

Schreckenberg, Heinz. *The Jews in Christian Art: An Illustrated History*. New York: Continuum, 1996.

Schwarz, Kathryn. "Death and Theory: Or, the Problem of Counterfactual Sex." In *Sex before Sex: Figuring the Act in Early Modern England*, edited by James M. Bromley and Will Stockton, 53–88. Minneapolis: University of Minnesota Press, 2013.

Shami, Jeanne. "The Sermon." In *The Oxford Handbook of John Donne*, edited by Jeanne Shami, Dennis Flynn, and M. Thomas Hester, 318–37. Oxford: Oxford University Press, 2011.

Sharpe, Kevin. "'An Image Doting Rabble': The Failure of Republican Culture in Seventeenth-Century England." In *Refiguring Revolutions: Aesthetics and Politics from the English Revolution to the Romantic Revolution*, edited by Kevin Sharpe and Steven N. Zwicker, 25–56. Berkeley: University of California Press, 1998.

Sheerin, Brian. "Patronage and Perverse Bestowal in *The Spanish Tragedy* and *Antonio's Revenge*." *English Literary Renaissance* 41, no. 2 (2011): 247–79.

Sherman, Anita Gilman. "Donne's Sermons as Re-enactments of the Word: A Response to Margret Fetzer." *Connotations* 19, no. 1–3 (2009/2010): 14–20.

Shuger, Debora K. *Sacred Rhetoric: The Christian Grand Style in the English Renaissance*. Princeton, NJ: Princeton University Press, 1988.

Siemon, James. "Sporting Kyd." *English Literary Renaissance* 24, no. 3 (1994): 553–82.

Simkin, Stevie. Introduction to *Revenge Tragedy: A New Casebook*, edited by Stevie Simkin, 1–23. London: Palgrave Macmillan, 2001.

Simpson, Evelyn M. *A Study of the Prose Works of John Donne*. 2nd ed. Oxford: Clarendon Press, 1948.

Slack, Paul. *Poverty and Policy in Tudor and Stuart England*. London: Longman, 1988.

Smith, Bruce R. *The Acoustic World of Early Modern England*. Chicago: University of Chicago Press, 1999.

——. *Phenomenal Shakespeare*. Malden, MA: Wiley-Blackwell, 2010.

Smith, Nigel. *Literature and Revolution in England, 1640–1660*. New Haven, CT: Yale University Press, 1997.

Stavreva, Kirilka. *Words Like Daggers: Violent Female Speech in Early Modern England*. Lincoln: University of Nebraska Press, 2015.

Stein, Arnold. "Handling Death: John Donne in Public Meditation." *English Literary History* 48, no. 3 (1981): 496–515.

Stern, Kathleen, and Martha K. McClintock. "Regulation of Ovulation by Human Pheromones." *Nature* 392, no. 6672 (12 March 1998): 177–79.

Stone, Lawrence. "Social Mobility in England, 1500–1700." *Past and Present* 33 (1966): 16–55.

Targoff, Ramie. *John Donne, Body and Soul*. Chicago: University of Chicago Press, 2008.

Tassi, Marguerite A. *Women and Revenge in Shakespeare: Gender, Genre, and Ethics*. Selinsgrove, PA: Susquehanna University Press, 2012.

Thorndike, A. H. "The Relations of *Hamlet* to the Contemporary Revenge Play." *PMLA* 17 (1902): 125–220.

"Virtual Paul's Cross Project: A Digital Re-creation of John Donne's Gunpowder Day Sermon." North Carolina State University, November 5, 2013. http://vpcp.chass.ncsu.edu.

Wagner, Geraldine. "Romancing Multiplicity: Female Subjectivity and the Body Divisible in Margaret Cavendish's *Blazing World*." *Early Modern Literary Studies* 9, no. 1 (2003): 1–59.

Warburton, Rachel. "'[A] Woman Hath No . . . Room to Desire Children for Her Own Sake': Margaret Cavendish Reads Lee Edelman." *Literary Interpretation Theory* 27, no. 3 (2016): 234–51.

Ward, Allyna E. *Women and Tudor Tragedy: Feminizing Counsel and Representing Gender*. Teaneck, NJ: Fairleigh Dickinson University Press, 2013.

Wedgwood, C. V. *A Coffin for King Charles: The Trial and Execution of Charles I.* London: Palgrave Macmillan, 1964.

———. *The Trial of Charles I.* London: Penguin, 1983.

Weil, Judith. "Visible Hecubas." In *The Female Tragic Hero in English Renaissance Drama.* Edited by Naomi Conn Liebler, 51–69. New York: Palgrave Macmillan, 2002.

Weil, Simone. "The *Iliad*, or, The Poem of Force." Translated by Mary McCarthy. *Chicago Review* 18, no. 2 (1965): 5–30.

Whigham, Frank. *Ambition and Privilege: The Social Tropes of Elizabethan Courtesy Theory.* Berkeley: University of California Press, 1984.

Wilcher, Robert. *The Writing of Royalism, 1628–1660.* Cambridge: Cambridge University Press, 2001.

Wilson, Richard. *Will Power: Essays on Shakespearean Authority.* Detroit: Wayne State University Press, 1993.

Winston, Jessica. "Seneca and Early Elizabethan England." *Renaissance Quarterly* 59, no. 1 (2006): 29–59.

Wissinger, Elizabeth. "Always on Display: Affective Production in the Modeling Industry." In *The Affective Turn: Theorizing the Social*, edited by Patricia Ticineto Clough and Jean Halley, 231–60. Durham, NC: Duke University Press, 2007.

Wood, Andy. *The Memory of the People: Custom and Popular Senses of the Past in Early Modern England.* Cambridge: Cambridge University Press, 2013.

Woodbridge, Linda. *English Revenge Drama: Money, Resistance, Equality.* Cambridge: Cambridge University Press, 2010.

———. *Vagrancy, Homelessness, and English Renaissance Literature.* Champaign: University of Illinois Press, 2001.

Wrightson, Keith. "'Sorts of People' in Tudor and Stuart England." In *The Middling Sort of People: Culture, Society, and Politics in England, 1550–1800*, edited by Jonathan Barry and Christopher Brooks, 28–51. New York: St. Martin's Press, 1994.

Würzbach, Natascha. *The Rise of the English Street Ballad, 1550–1650.* Translated by Gayna Walls. Cambridge: Cambridge University Press, 1990.

Zwicker, Steven. *Lines of Authority: Politics and English Literary Culture, 1649–1689.* Ithaca, NY: Cornell University Press, 1993.

INDEX

CPSIA information can be obtained
at www.ICGtesting.com
Printed in the USA
BVHW032348300719
554727BV00003B/9/P